Harcourt Brace Guide to Peer Tutoring

Toni-Lee Capossela

Stonehill College

HARCOURT BRACE COLLEGE PUBLISHERS

Fort Worth   Philadelphia   San Diego   New York   Orlando   Austin   San Antonio
Toronto   Montreal   London   Sydney   Tokyo

ISBN: 0-15-508159-4

Address for orders:
Harcourt Brace College Publishers
6277 Sea Harbor Drive
Orlando, Florida 32887-6777
1-800-782-4479

Address for editorial correspondence:
Harcourt Brace College Publishers
301 Commerce Street, Suite 3700
Fort Worth, Texas 76102

Web site address:
http://www.harbrace.com/english

PRINTED IN THE UNITED STATES OF AMERICA
7890123456 023 987654321

This is what we can *all* do to nourish and strengthen one another: listen to one another very hard, ask hard questions, too, send one another away to work again, and laugh in all the right places.

—Nancy Mairs, *Voice Lessons*

To the Student

I hope this book will be both good company and a useful source as you prepare to become a writing consultant. Everything in it is intended to help you along your way, and there is no busy-work—just solid theory and useful practice.

The book's twelve chapters explore important consulting issues in the order in which they normally arise during a session. The rest of the book presents readings by writing teachers, consultants in training, and writing center veterans. The two parts are linked by assignments at the end of each chapter, which suggest reading, writing, discussion, and role-playing activities.

At the end of the first chapter are simple directions for keeping a journal. Because consulting is something you learn by doing, it's important to keep a detailed record of your experiences as you observe, practice, and begin consulting. You will slowly evolve your own consulting style, and the more you think about what has happened and what works for you, the more confident you will feel as time goes on and your experience mounts.

The readings present important theories about writing, along with the research and evidence supporting them. Essays by writing center consultants recount personal experiences that test—and sometimes contradict—these theories as well as the strategies described in the chapters of the book. The theories will give you a framework on which to hang your consulting practice, and they may also help you understand your own writing processes more thoroughly. Because most of these articles were written by and for writing teachers, you will be dealing with unfamiliar vocabulary, modes of organization, forms of evidence, and assumptions about background information. These are the same factors you will grapple with when reading a draft about an unfamiliar topic, so think of the readings as a low-risk rehearsal for this kind of session. Class discussion provides an opportunity to critique the rehearsal. Some useful questions to consider in class discussion are the following:

- What kinds of difficulties did you have with the reading?
- How did you deal with them?
- Can you evaluate the reading even if you don't understand it completely? What kinds of evaluation can you make?

- What did you learn about this kind of writing by reading this article or essay?
- What did you learn from your experience with this reading that you can use in a consulting session?

The end-of-chapter assignments have also been designed with a number of goals in mind. They invite you to think critically about the concepts you are reading about, to consider whether your experience confirms them and whether they give new meaning to your experience. They also require you to use writing formats other than the traditional academic essay. Because these formats are comparatively new to you, you will have to deliberate carefully about aspects of writing—tone, context, format, vocabulary, organization— you barely think about when you write in a familiar format. This is another kind of rehearsal for reading about an unfamiliar topic in a consulting session.

Acknowledgments

- Thanks to Stonehill's peer consultants, past and present, whose enthusiasm, intelligence, and commitment have made the writing center a success. You have contributed in countless ways to my understanding of collaborative learning, and your ideas appear here in ways I can no longer separate from my own.
- Thanks to my colleagues at Stonehill, who shared their writing assignments and explained the writing requirements of their discipline. In particular, thanks to David Almeida, Stonehill's learning disabilities specialist, who provided useful background information for chapter 11.
- Thanks to staff, both faculty and students, at writing centers across the country, who shared their favorite sources, explained their ideas, constructively critiqued mine, and graciously permitted me to quote or reprint their work.
- Thanks to my son Christopher, pre-publication reviewer of chapter 12 and my mentor in all matters electronic.
- Thanks to editors in acquisitions and development at Harcourt Brace College Publishers, Michael Rosenberg and Michell Phifer.

TABLE OF CONTENTS

Readings 115

Acknowledgments 250

Chapter 1

What a Peer Consultant Is and Isn't

For excellence, the presence of others is always required.
   —Hannah Arendt

When I became a writing center director and began recruiting peer consultants, I thought I knew what I was looking for—good writers with outgoing personalities. I soon discovered I was wrong on both counts.

Not all strong writers are good at helping others with their writing—some are impatient, and others are unable to explain a process that is second nature to them.[1] On the other hand, merely competent writers often make excellent consultants: in addition to reading critically and asking useful questions, they can sympathize with peers who find writing difficult.

Some extroverts are dandy in the writing center, but others are overwhelming. An insecure or self-contained writer can benefit in many ways from a less outgoing consultant, whose conversational style leaves enough room for the writer to lapse into silence, think, and come up with his own ideas. So if you're trying to decide whether you've got what it takes to be a writing consultant, don't measure yourself against a stereotype.

Consultants Wear Many Hats

Just as peer consulting is flexible enough to accommodate many personality types, it is elastic enough to embrace a wide variety of roles. At different times a consultant may function as a reader, a respondent, a questioner, a critic, a listener, a friend, a colleague, a collaborator, or a guide. In exploring their varied roles, consultants have come up with intriguing metaphors for what they do. Here are a few:

- I act as a wall, offering resistance against easy solutions.
- I act as a mirror, reflecting an accurate image of a draft.
- I act as a sounding board, against which a writer can test ideas and hear how they bounce back.
- I act as a coach, encouraging, giving advice, and cheering from the sidelines.

Two Roles to Avoid

Consultants, then, work hard to master a wide repertoire of roles. However, there are two roles experienced consultants work hard to avoid:

> *A peer consultant isn't a surrogate teacher.* Learning from peers is a natural and life-long process. Its effectiveness depends on a horizontal dynamic quite different from the hierarchical student-teacher relationship. At first "playing teacher" may feel like fun, but in the long run, assuming the teacher's mantle is an uncomfortable strain. At best, you will be only a mediocre surrogate teacher, but by building on your peer status, you can become an excellent consultant.

> *A peer consultant isn't the author this time around.* As an aspiring consultant, you are probably already a successful writer. While reading someone else's work, you may get lots of ideas about the improvements you would make if the draft were yours. But appropriating the writer's role is a big mistake.
>
> For one thing, if you get carried away, the paper WILL become yours—and as your contributions become tangled with the writer's, plagiarism will become harder and harder to avoid. Second, even if you control your enthusiasm, you may misinterpret or warp the author's ideas in the process of re-shaping them. Third, although the paper may be improved by your efforts, the author won't be. She won't have learned anything, and the next paper she writes will have the same problems as the one you've "fixed." Stephen North of State University of New York at Albany explains that the job of his and other writing centers "is to produce better writers, not better writing" (438).
>
> Of course, it doesn't have to be an either/or situation: it's possible to make better writers AND better writing, but not if the writing is made better by another hand. Writers improve when they use the questions of a thoughtful reader to shape their work, then eventually begin to ask themselves the same questions. Your writing skills are most helpful in a consulting situation when you use them to frame probing, open-ended questions.

What's in a Name?

At some time in the history of every writing center, staff members must decide how to refer to themselves. Although "tutor" has a lot going for it—it's familiar to faculty and students, and it has a handy corollary for describing the person it is done to ("tutee")—it also involves some negative baggage you and your colleagues may decide you'd rather not lug around. At my writing center, students have settled on the title "writing consultant," even though "consultee" is a clunky corollary.

"You go to a tutor when you're in trouble," one student noted, "but you go to a consultant when you really care about what you're doing and want to make it as good as you can." Another student put it this way: "A tutor knows more than you do, so you feel you should shut up and listen, but when you hire a consultant, the final decision is still up to you."

Just so: coming to the writing center is often a sign of savvy rather than of desperation.[2] A successful writer invariably seeks out the reactions of thoughtful readers while his draft is taking shape, because he needs two things he can't give himself:

Distance

The more involved a writer is in her subject—the more passionate her commitment to the idea—the harder it is to see it as others do. Reading her work, she sees the perfect text in her head, not the evolving draft on the page or the screen. She doesn't notice the gaps in logic, the unsupported generalizations, the undefined term, the disorienting shift in direction. To recognize flaws like these, she needs critical distance.

If circumstances permit, a writer can achieve distance by putting the work aside for awhile. After letting some time pass, he can then view his work with a reader's critical eye rather than a writer's loving eye. Poet Archibald MacLeish once said he always put his poems in a drawer for awhile to ripen, like apples: "I learned early and by sad experience never to publish a green poem"(45). Writers who set their own deadlines can afford to put their work aside, but semesters and due dates don't leave much time for ripening. For college writers, it is probably more practical to achieve distance by handing their writing to someone else and then stepping away from it.

Expert Feedback

Finding sources of feedback is essential for a writer. All kinds of feedback help, the more the better. Readers bring their own perspectives and specialties to the task, and each should address only the issues she feels qualified to comment on. For instance, a writer preparing a philosophy paper might have it read by a classmate, to check comprehension of the material; his professor, to verify that it meets the assignment guidelines; and his roommate the English major, to catch undetected surface errors. Using several readers keeps the writer in control, since he must decide which suggestions to adopt, especially when two readers give contradictory advice.

Why Peer Consulting Works

Peer consulting builds on a natural tendency to learn from one's age-mates. In addition, what we know about the writing process helps explain why peers make especially effective writing consultants. Three essential characteristics of writing contribute to the success of peer consulting.

1. Writing is a process as well as a product.

Good writers are good, not because they sit down and write effortlessly, turning out beautiful sentences without sweat. They are good because they believe that eventually, after lots of work and time and discarded drafts, they will come up with something worth a reader's attention. As a process, writing grows, changes, and evolves over time.

Teachers can't always incorporate the earlier stages of writing into a syllabus, but consultants are available throughout the writing process. Writers often find it helpful to talk to a consultant before they begin writing; an early session might consist of analyzing the assignment or exploring alternative ways of getting started.[3] Working with a consultant during these early stages also guarantees that writing occurs over a period of time, rather than being jammed into one frustrating marathon session the night before the due date.

2. Writing is social.

You may think you have to be alone to write, and this may be physically true. But your writing is saturated with the presence of others: your society, your culture, your readers. Writing is not complete until it has reached, physically and intellectually, the reader or readers for whom it was intended. As Ezra Pound puts it, when you write, "You not only get a thing off your own chest, but you get it into someone else's." A peer consultant is a visible reminder that writing is social—although it's possible, during the act of writing, to forget about your audience, you can hardly forget her when she is sitting next to you. Several readings in this book explore the link between talking and writing, and point out that talking about ideas is a good way to begin writing about them. As a peer consultant, you are a perfect partner in this kind of conversation. For one thing, you talk the same language as student writers—you ARE a student writer. You are also less likely than a teacher to confuse a writer with grammatical terminology or technical jargon. You have the potential to become what Nancy Sommers describes as the ideal reader: "a critical and productive collaborator—a collaborator who has yet to love [the writer's] work."

3. Writing is self-taught.

Writers learn by doing, not by listening to lectures about how to do it. In this way writing is like learning to ride a bike: although it helps to have someone hold the handlebars for the first few times, the best way to get good is to do it every day.

Writers may come to a consultant hoping to lighten their workload. But when things go right, they actually work harder with a consultant's help, because they get more ideas for improvement than they would have come up with on their own. Although they don't receive the shortcut they may have been seeking, their load *is* lightened as they spend less time worrying and more time making real improvements. By prompting writers to put more time and effort into their work, consultants help writers teach themselves more.

What's in It for You?

You will probably enjoy helping the writers you work with, but there are several selfish reasons to become a peer consultant. For one thing, it looks good on your resume. Employers and graduate school admissions officers want applicants with the strengths that consulting draws on: reliability, intelligence, initiative, imagination, critical thinking, and social skills.

Consulting will also make you a better writer. Talking with other writers will introduce you to new composing strategies, and even if your writing process has never failed you, it's reassuring to have options. But more importantly, as you learn how to ask the kinds of questions that help writers do their best work, you'll begin asking yourself the same questions.

ASSIGNMENTS

1. Starting a journal. Purchase a notebook that's convenient to carry around and write in. Make a dated entry in your journal every time you do anything connected to consulting. This includes—but needn't be limited to—class sessions, going to the writing center, observing, role-playing, reading and thinking about what you've read, and writing of any kind. Be alert for connections between consulting and other aspects of your life. For instance, you may notice that you're learning from peers in other classes or outside the classroom.

   Although your teacher may ask to see it periodically, your journal is primarily for you. Unless you feel like it, there's no need to produce essays with a thesis, introduction, and conclusion. Consider the journal a workspace, not a polished text—a place for doing the mental work it takes to become a confident consultant, whether it's exploring ideas, raising questions, telling stories, describing problems, considering solutions, or making connections. End-of-chapter assignments include suggestions for journal entries, but the best entries are the ones you create yourself.

2. Because your success as a consultant is rooted in your writing experience, the beginning of your training program is a good time to reflect upon that experience. Using any format you like, compose a sketch of yourself as a writer. Include anything you consider important, but address the following points:
   - What are your strengths as a writer?
   - What do you find most difficult about writing? How do you deal with this difficulty?

- What single piece of advice about writing has helped you most?
- What process do you go through when you write?
- What qualities do you think will make you an effective consultant?
- What aspects of grammar, punctuation, or mechanics do you have trouble with?

3. Read John Trimbur's "'Peer Tutoring': A Contradiction in Terms?" then do one of the following things.

   A. As you read, mark places in the margin that call attention to themselves. For instance, a passage may surprise you, puzzle you, raise a question, use language in an unusual way, remind you of something you've experienced or read, make you agree or disagree, or evoke an emotional response. When you're finished reading, go back and pick the two or three marked passages that interest you most, and explore them in journal entries. Identify each passage by page number and a brief label, so you can find it easily during class discussion. This method of active reading, developed by Ann E. Berthoff, is called a dialogic notebook, because it sets up a dialogue between you and the text.

   B. How concerned are you about the contradiction Trimbur explores? Write an essay explaining your feelings about this contradiction. In what ways are you like the peer consultants Trimbur has trained and supervised? In what ways do your feelings differ from theirs? Has Trimbur identified a significant problem or is he making a mountain out of a molehill? Is "peer consultant" a contradiction in terms too?

   C. Write about another kind of "cognitive dissonance": a situation that puts you in two apparently contradictory roles at once. How did you resolve the contradiction? Does this example contain any ideas for resolving the conflict Trimbur sees between the term "peer" and the term "tutor"?

4. Read Jennifer Maloney's "Progression." Maloney's essay appeared in an anthology for students who, like you, were beginning to train as peer consultants. Her assignment was to recount a significant writing center experience in a way that would be helpful to consultants-in-training. Write a letter to Maloney, describing how the essay affected you, a member of its intended audience. Consider this an opportunity to try out your consulting skills, even though in this case you won't be face to face with the author. If you see weaknesses in the essay, explain how they lessened the essay's impact on you.

FOOTNOTES

[1]Perhaps these writers fear their skill will desert them if they try to dissect it. Legend has it that W.C. Fields juggled effortlessly until he tried to explain what he was doing, at which point he began to think about it, the balls fell to the floor, and he could never juggle again.

[2]Because so many good writers seek peer consultants, most colleges and universities now have "writing centers" rather than "writing labs" or "clinics." The term "writing center" also reinforces the social nature of writing, whereas "lab" implies a detached, impersonal transaction, and clinic" implies illness or trauma.

[3]Helping a writer get started is discussed in chapters 3 and 4.

Chapter 2

Getting to Know You

All of us who write work out of a conviction that we are participating in some sort of communal activity. Whether my role is writing, or reading and responding, might not be very important.
–Joyce Carol Oates

Consulting is first and foremost a personal interaction, whether it occurs face to face or via technology of some kind. Because of this strong personal dimension, you will sometimes play a key role not mentioned in chapter 1: that of host. You will be greeting and welcoming people, putting them at ease, finding out what interests them, getting them to talk about themselves. Being a gracious host in the writing center is more difficult than at a party, where people expect to relax and have a good time. Writers may be nervous, upset, or under pressure when they show up for an appointment. They may feel defensive or apologetic about their work, assuming that because you are a consultant, you effortlessly toss off grade A papers at a rapid clip. Here are some suggestions for getting consulting sessions off to a positive start.

Preliminaries

1. Introduce yourself and find out whom you're working with. An anxious writer may blurt out his problem even before he sits down: "This is due tomorrow and all I have is a bunch of notes." Even when a writer seems eager to get going, pay attention to him before turning to the paper. A response like, "Well then, let's get started. My name's Janet—what's yours?" creates a space for small talk if the writer feels like it, but also offers him the option of briskly identifying himself and getting right to work.

   If your writing center format involves working repeatedly with the same person, use some of your first session to get acquainted with the person, not just the writer. Find out what her major is, where she comes from, what her interests are. Remember what she tells you, even if you have to write it down in your journal.

2. Listen attentively when the writer talks about something besides writing. Informal talk may be a necessary preliminary to a fruitful session. The writer may need to "clear the decks" mentally before he can

concentrate on his draft. Small talk sometimes contains important information about details (missed classes, inadequate sleep, extracurricular demands) that are complicating the writer's job.

3. Identify and sympathize when you can. As a peer, you are eminently qualified for this role—when a writer talks about the stresses and strains of college life, you can say, "I know what you mean" or "That's happened to me too." But it's not part of your job—or part of your expertise—to offer advice or solutions to personal problems. If you are aware of support services that are available on campus, you might mention them, but beyond that, you're out of your depth.

4. Eventually move the conversation towards the student's writing. Sometimes a gentle nudge is enough: "You really *do* have a lot going on—let's see if we can at least make some headway on this assignment." If the indirect approach doesn't work, mention the time constraints you're under: "We've got 20 minutes before the next appointment—do you want to take a look at your draft now?"

5. Avoid a judgmental stance. Don't judge the writer for waiting until the last minute. Don't judge the assignment by saying that it's vague or confusing. Don't judge the teacher by declaring that his demands are unreasonable or his grading policy unfair. In particular, don't judge the paper by indicating the grade you think it deserves.

6. Respect privacy. Don't talk about teachers, consultants, or writers by name. If an incident involving one of these people is a good illustration of a point you're making, tell the story in generic rather than specific terms. This reassures the writer who is listening to the account that you will respect her privacy as well.

7. Be sensitive to personal and cultural differences. Although talking may seem as natural as breathing, in reality it is highly dependent on culture. Details like how much eye contact feels right, how close participants sit to each other, how long a silence is comfortable, vary a great deal from one culture to another. In general, American conversational patterns and rhythms are quicker and more aggressive than those of other cultures. It's easy to overwhelm someone from a different background by sitting closer, responding faster, or looking at him more searchingly than he is used to. In these matters, take your cue from the writer; in particular leave plenty of time for him to respond to your remarks, even if the silence seems unbearable to you.[1] This topic is treated in more detail in chapter 11.

8. Explain things. If this is a writer's first visit to the writing center, tell her how things work so she will know what to expect. Explain who you are and how you got there—if other people are present, introduce them and explain their roles. Describe time limits, appointment policy,

and any paperwork you will be doing or asking her to do. Make a follow-up appointment if it is in order, and offer to set it up during your shift if she would like to work with you again.

While Discussing Writing

1. Let the writer set the agenda and be in charge of the conversation. If you seize control of the conversation, the way a doctor does with a patient, the writer will sit passively, waiting for you to make a diagnosis and recommend a cure. To keep the initiative with the writer, ask what his concerns are or what he wants to concentrate on. If the answer is vague—"Everything"—re-frame the question, e.g., "Are you working on anything particular in this draft?"

2. Keep the writer involved. This point is intimately connected to the previous one: being in charge requires being involved. Some first-time visitors to the writing center expect to drop off a paper and pick it up a couple of hours later. They see the center as a fix-it shop; just as there's no reason to hang around while their car is getting a tune-up, they reason, their presence is not required to get their paper humming smoothly. Nothing could be further from the truth, of course, since consulting demands interaction. More to the point, it's not enough for a writer merely to be present in the flesh—she has to be fully engaged in the session.

   Here are some ways to encourage a high level of involvement from a writer.

   A. Pay attention to spatial relationships. The importance of spatial relationships explains the popularity of round tables in writing centers. A round table has no "head chair," does not intrude between two people the way a desk does, and does not suggest solitary activity the way a carrel does. Sit next to the writer, and the spatial relationship conveys the message, "partners."

   B. Be careful with the tools of the trade. Furniture doesn't guarantee equality—you can sit at a round table and still dominate the conversation. To guard against tyranny, disarm: hand the pen or pencil to the writer instead of wielding it yourself. Put the paper between you rather than directly in front of you, so that you lean towards each other to read it. If you're working at a computer, put the writer at the keyboard rather than sitting there yourself.

   C. Have the writer read the draft aloud. Karen Spear points out, "When writers hear their ideas in the presence of an audience, they understand themselves differently" (97). By reading his own work, a writer reinforces the fact that the draft belongs to him. This strategy also puts him in charge, because he can stop when he comes to a passage he wants to work on. It also helps him hear passages that "sound funny" even though they may look fine on paper.

D. If the writer is reluctant to read, you read the draft aloud. This is not as desirable as option C, but it is better than silent reading. Ask the writer to follow along as you read, so the material will be fresh in her mind and she can stop you to discuss a passage, clarify a point, or ask a question.

E. If the writer is reluctant to have his draft read aloud, the remaining option is to read it silently. You will have to work hard to overcome the limitations of this method. Silent reading is solitary and awkward, since we are not used to being silent in company. Silence seems to stop the clock. You may get nervous about taking so long to get through the paper, and the writer may get nervous wondering what you're thinking.

To mitigate the negative aspects of silent reading, ask the writer to read along with you. Break the silence with frequent comments: explain that you are skimming the paper to get an idea of its overall structure, remark on something you find interesting, ask permission to mark passages you'd like to come back to.

One excellent consultant developed a silent-reading strategy that looked extremely difficult but that he followed with apparent ease. He provided a running commentary of what he was doing—"I'm checking this first paragraph for a thesis statement—it's sort of like a map of where the paper will go. Okay, it looks to me like your thesis is... Is that right? Now I'm moving on to this paragraph to see if I can follow the way your ideas are put together and how you support your point. I'm having a little trouble figuring out what this paragraph is about—what's the main idea behind it?" This consultant had figured out how to begin discussing the paper AS he read it, instead of reading as a lengthy and awkward preliminary to discussion.

3. Work with the writer to establish priorities. It's frustrating and counter-productive to deal with all aspects of a text at once. In this regard, consulting is like writing: a writer can't search for precisely the right word at the same time that he's formulating a topic.[2] Your first source of information about priorities should be the writer: ask him what he'd like to work on. Be sure you understand what he means by a particular term—a writer who says he wants someone to proofread his draft may actually want general suggestions for improvement.

A second important source of information about priorities is the writing process itself. Both writing and consulting follow a top-down process, with the more global aspects of the paper—such as focus, organization, and development—taking shape before the smaller ones—such as final word choice and sentence structure.

Here is a general sequence of priorities to keep in mind as you read a draft and begin discussing it.

PRIORITIES IN READING A DRAFT

1. Ask the student what he or she would like to work on.
2. Ask which draft you're analyzing (first, second, final) and when the assignment is due.
3. Find out what the assignment is. If the student has a copy of the assignment, read it over together. Check the draft for APPROPRIATE-NESS. Does it meet the assignment specifications? Take the specified approach? Have all the necessary parts? Do everything that's asked? (Discussed in chapters 3, 4, and 10)
4. If #3 is in order, check the draft for FOCUS. Look for a central idea, either expressed or implied, holding the paper together. Is the idea appropriate, worthy of discussion, and limited enough to be discussed thoroughly? (Discussed in chapter 5)
5. If #4 is in order, check the draft for ORGANIZATION. Is each paragraph connected to the thesis? Are the paragraphs connected to each other in a logical way? Does each paragraph deal with only one idea? Are all the remarks about one idea located in the same paragraph (or of the idea is a complicated one, are all the remarks about it located in consecutive paragraphs)? (Discussed in chapter 6)
6. If #5 is in order, check for DEVELOPMENT. Are claims and statements supported by sufficient examples, details, and illustration? What do you want to hear more about? Where did the essay leave you feeling unsatisfied or disappointed? (Discussed in chapter 6)
7. If #6 is in order, check the introduction and the conclusion. Do they accurately reflect the body of the paper? Does the conclusion provide a sense of closure? Is it more than a repetition of the introduction? (Discussed in chapter 6)
8. If #7 is in order, check SURFACE FEATURES such as punctuation, grammar, sentence structure, and documentation. (Discussed in chapter 7)
9. If #8 is in order, check DICTION and STYLE (word choice, sentence structure, conciseness) (Discussed in chapter 8).
10. If the writer has a manuscript copy or polished draft, help proofread for last-minute typing or printing errors; also check the manuscript format. (Discussed in chapter 8).

This list is not a rigid form into which you must squeeze every consulting session. Nor is it, unfortunately, a sure recipe for success. It is a flexible set of guidelines to help you find a good place to start talking about a draft. Don't rush to get through the entire list of priorities in one session. Starting from the top, you will soon locate an area that requires attention. For instance, if the draft is not appropriate to the assignment, you might spend the session discussing how to get it back on track.

If the writer wants to discuss an item close to the end of the list (for instance, punctuation) and you identify a problem near the top of the list (for instance, lack of focus), let the writer decide: "I see what you mean about commas, but I also see other areas we could work on first—do you want to try to do both or shall we just fix the comma errors?"

4. Before the writer leaves, tie things up. No matter what wonderful potential for the draft is revealed by your conversation, a writer is likely to feel confused and discouraged if she leaves with no clear idea about what to do next. As the session draws to a close, take time to synthesize and reach some conclusions. With the writer, reflect on what's been accomplished and what's next: "I can really understand how your ideas hang together now, and we've worked on some of the comma errors too. Do you want to make an appointment for another session after you've added details and done another draft?"

For Better or For Worse®   **by Lynn Johnston**

ASSIGNMENTS

1. Read Kenneth A. Bruffee's "Peer Tutoring and 'The Conversation of Mankind,'" then do one of the following things:
   A. Write a two-part report on Bruffee's article. *First*, summarize the article in 100–200 words. Identify the focus of the article, using a

format like, "In this article, Bruffee argues that ..." or "This article shows that ...." Also explain how Bruffee support his focus, and how the major points of his argument relate to each other and to the focus. Don't use direct quotes or examples: a summary should reveal the underlying skeleton of a text, and examples are part of the fleshing out rather than the skeleton. *Second*, evaluate the article. How effectively does Bruffee make his point? What kinds of support does he use, and how persuasive are they? Can you think of evidence that contradicts his point? How could he have made his argument stronger? Do you agree with his point?

B. Write an essay about "the powerful educative force of peer influence," drawing from your own experience.

C. Do you agree with Bruffee's statement that "the powerful educative force of peer influence" is "largely... ignored and hence wasted by traditional forms of education"? In class discussion or in an essay, support your opinion with examples from your own education.

2. Read Jeannine A. Broadwell's essay, "Rehabilitating the Writing Center Junkie," then write an essay about how she might have prevented her disastrous experience with Randy. What did she do right in her sessions with Randy? Use relevant materials from your journal, readings, or class discussion.

3. To remind yourself of what it's like to be on the other end of a consulting session, take a draft to the writing center and work with a consultant on it. Write a journal entry about the session. How did you feel at the beginning? At the end? What did you notice about the consultant, now that you're preparing to become a consultant? What connections can you make between your session and material in chapter 2?

4. Bring a working draft of some kind to the next meeting and use it to role play with another member of the group. Take turns playing the role of consultant, assuming that you are working with a first-time visitor to the writing center. Discuss each other's drafts, keeping in mind the suggestions made in this chapter. Critique each other's performance as the consultant in the session.

FOOTNOTES

[1]Marian Arkin and Barbara Shollar have a simple suggestion for controlling the urge to break the silence: count to ten before you speak. This tactic gives the writer space to think, consider, and perhaps break the silence himself. They also suggest pausing before answering a question, so the writer can add to the question and mull over possible answers of his own (97).

²Peter Elbow explains that writing involves both creating and criticizing. Trying to create and criticize at the same time is like pulling in opposite directions, whereas shuttling back and forth between creating and criticizing is an efficient way to work towards a polished draft (8–9).

Chapter 3

Getting Started

I suffer as always from the fear of putting down the first line. It is amazing the terrors, the magics, the prayers, the straitening shyness that assails one.
—John Steinbeck

Most writers agree that getting started is the hardest part. Perhaps Red Smith put it most memorably: "Writing is easy. All you do is sit staring at the blank sheet of paper until the drops of blood form on your forehead." Many writers think they must produce text before they can talk about their work, a belief that traps them in a frustrating Catch-22: "I need to talk to somebody because I'm having trouble getting started, but how can I talk when I haven't written anything to talk about?" In this chapter we will explore effective ways to help students begin writing.

Why Is Starting So Hard?

Much of the difficulty of getting started can be traced to counterproductive myths about how writing takes shape. Here are a few of them.

MYTH: There is ONE right way to get started—and everybody knows it except me.

ON THE CONTRARY, the more alternatives you have, the better position you are in. Different kinds of writing, different audiences, invite different strategies. We will discuss many in this chapter. You and your colleagues will come up with others, and the writers you work with will add to the list.

MYTH: Know what you're going to write before you begin; have a plan for the entire paper before you start. For many years this myth was perpetuated by a model of writing which dictated that an outline precede even the roughest draft. It was assumed that outlining promotes strong organization and prevents digressions. Hidden beneath this assumption was another one: that writing merely records thinking, rather than extending or enriching it.

ON THE CONTRARY, we now know that writing is a powerful *mode* of thinking, not just a recording technique.[1] People write when an idea gets too complicated to follow in their heads and they want to push the envelope. E.M. Forster asks, "How do I know what I think until I see what I say?"

As the result of a shift in research methods, these days outlining is rarely presented as a compulsory preliminary to writing. The "Begin by Outlining" rule was based on a deductive approach, in which it was assumed that effective writing adhered to general rules. The deductive approach has been supplemented, and to some extent replaced, by an inductive approach based on observation and information-gathering. Inductive researchers say, "To discover how good writing is produced, let's find out what individual writers do and then decide what, if anything, they have in common." Their data reveal that for accomplished writers, an outline sometimes works and sometimes doesn't; that writers often use outlines *after* writing, to check for organization, rather than *before* writing, to predict how the text will develop; and that writers who begin with an outline use it as a rough guide rather than a rigid mold into which they shoe-horn all their ideas.

Writing without knowing exactly what you will say leaves room for surprise and discovery: what looks like a digression may turn out to be the idea you've been fumbling for all along. The pleasure of discovery is so keen that many writers claim it compensates for all the hard work; some identify it as the strongest impetus behind their writing. Gore Vidal says, "I never know what is coming next. The phrase that sounds in the head changes when it appears on the page. Then I start probing with a pen, finding new meanings....That's why I go on, I suppose. To see what the next sentence I write will be" (311).

MYTH: Don't write anything until you have something good enough to keep. This myth assumes that like talking, writing goes in one direction—forward—and that, to use movie-making terminology, you only get one "take."

ON THE CONTRARY, the beauty of writing is that you can keep going back and refining it, instead of having to get it right the first time. Novelist Amy Tan, whose first book *The Joy Luck Club* was a critical and popular success, describes the circuitous route she followed to come up with the idea for her next book, *The Kitchen God's Wife*:

> I wrote 88 pages of a book about the daughter of a scholar, who accidentally kills a magistrate with a potion touted to be the elixir of immortality. I wrote 56 pages of a book about a Chinese girl orphaned during the San Francisco earthquake of 1906. I wrote 95 pages about a young girl who lives in northeast China during the 1930's with her missionary parents. I wrote 45 pages about using English to revive the dead language of Manchu and the world it described on the plains of Mongolia. I wrote 30 pages about a woman disguised as a man who becomes a sidewalk scribe to the illiterate workers of Chinatown during the turn of the century.... I wrote with persistence, telling myself that no matter how bad the story was, I should simply go on like a rat in a maze, turning the corner when I arrived at it. And so I started to write another story, about a woman who was cleaning a house, the messy house I thought I should be cleaning. After 30 pages, the house was tidy, and I had found a character I liked. I abandoned all the pages about the tidy house. I kept the character and took her along with me to another house. I wrote and then rewrote six times another 30 pages, and found a question in her heart. I abandoned the pages and kept the question and put that in my heart (6–7).

If Tan had waited to write until she had something good enough to keep, she may well have remained a one-book author.

MYTH: When you write, follow the same chronology as your reader— the first sentence you write should be the first sentence he sees.

ON THE CONTRARY, although ideas in the polished draft should follow a logical sequence, the composing process may form a totally different pattern. The first paragraph of an analytic essay usually predicts the direction the paper will take—as E.M. Forster points out, you don't even know where you're going until you've traveled awhile. A dazzling first sentence may come to you and light your way through the entire text. When this happens, rejoice in your good fortune and make the most of it, but don't wait for inspiration to strike every time you start writing.[2]

Helping a Writer Get Started

1. Reassure the writer that getting started is hard for everyone, that it's a normal part of writing, not a sign of poor writing skills.

2. Inventory the writer's resources. It's encouraging for a writer to realize that he has a wealth of material to build on and is not really starting

from scratch. Merely talking about what he knows may trigger writing of some kind. Discuss the following aspects of the writing context:

- What topics he's considered writing about
- What he's already tried
- What usually works and why it didn't work this time
- What the assignment is
- What else is going on in the class
- What external factors may be complicating the writing

3. Take dictation. While talking, the writer may mention an excellent idea for a topic. Quietly jot it down—if you ask her to stop talking and start writing, she may lose her train of thought. Show her what you've written and explain that you've merely copied down what she has said. Without even realizing it, she has gotten beyond the blank page.

4. Describe alternatives. Realizing that there is no single right way of getting started is a tremendous relief, because it provides options: if A doesn't work, no sweat—let's try B. Based on what the writer has told you about the situation, suggest trying one of the activities below or another activity that has worked for you.[3] Unstructured activities appear at the beginning of the list. If the writer has not had success with a structured activity such as outlining, he can try something near the top; if the less structured activities haven't worked, he can move further down the list. Except for freewriting (which requires silence), get the activity started *during* your discussion; this way, you can offer support, and the transition from talking to writing will occur naturally and gradually.

Some Ways of Getting Started

Freewriting. This activity by definition gets rid of the blank page or screen: it consists of writing nonstop for a specified period of time. Writers who like structure get the screaming meemies if they freewrite much longer than five minutes, but others can keep it up for as long as ten or fifteen minutes. The only way to do this wrong is to stop writing; if a writer has no ideas, she should write, "I don't have any ideas,"and eventually, out of sheer boredom, she will think of something else and begin writing about it. At the end of the time limit, the page will be filled and the writer may have the germ of an idea.

Brainstorming. This was originally conceived as a group activity, but it can also be done solo. To brainstorm, the writer puts down *all* the ideas that come into his head in connection with the assignment, without judging, censoring, or deciding whether they will work. Like

freewriting, brainstorming is evaluated in terms of the amount generated, not the quality.

Listing. We're all comfortable with lists, because they're an integral part
of life: grocery lists, packing lists, to-do lists, invitation lists. Lists can
be random and and that's why they're low-stress—if we forget something, we just tack it on at the end. Listing for writing works the same
way: the writer lists possible points, ideas, or aspects of the topic as
they occur to her or as they come up in conversation.

Mapping. This activity is helpful for writers who conceptualize spatially
and feel that a list locks them into its sequence. Instead of putting ideas
one after the other, the writer scatters them arbitrarily across the page,
an arrangement which frees him to discover connections.

Clustering. A follow-up to listing or mapping, clustering consists of drawing lines to connect ideas that have something in common, or
re-grouping items that belong together. Clustering is less formal than
an outline, but like outlining, it makes a visible connection between
related ideas.

Experiment with thesis statements. E.M. Forster might object that it's too
early to decide what you have to say, but trying on several thesis statements for size can help a writer decide which approach is likely to
work better. For instance, if the student must write about a place that
reflects her sense of self, ask what places she is considering, then have
her write several alternative endings to the sentence, "In this essay I
will show that_____." Including the word "that" is important,
because it requires a more precise statement than, "In my paper I will
describe the trunk of my car." Using the first formula, the writer must
come up with something like "My essay will show that the trunk of my
car suggests I'm an extrovert who hates to be alone."

Design and fill in a chart. The type of chart will vary with the writing situation. For a comparison-contrast paper, the chart might be as simple
as a top-to-bottom line down the middle of the page, separating the
items or concepts being compared; and a side-to-side line across the
middle of the page, separating similarities and differences.

Make an outline. Outlines aren't the kiss of death, as long as they're one
alternative among many. A good time for an outline is after one or
more of the messier activities, when the writer wants to impose order
on an abundance of material.

Analyze the assignment. Re-read the assignment and use its language to
begin talking, listing, mapping, clustering, charting, or outlining. The
assignment provides a solid base for fluid activities like brainstorming
and freewriting. If the assignment provides alternative topics, ask the
writer which ones he's considering, and why.[4]

Examine the larger context. After discussing the assignment, move on to
the course, its goals, and the writer's notes from classes, readings, and
lectures. Does material from these sources flesh out lists, clusters,

maps, charts, or the outline? Going over this material may also raise questions the writer decides to answer in her essay, so it can help with organization and development, not just with getting started.

ASSIGNMENTS

1. Read Peter Elbow's essay, "The Loop Writing Process," then do one of the following things:
   A. Write a journal entry about reading Elbow's essay. Which methods do you think would work for you? Which ones wouldn't? Why or why not? What assumptions about writing underlie his suggestions? Do you agree with them?
   B. Try one or more of Elbow's methods while writing a paper. Report on the results.
   C. Elbow uses a two-step metaphor to describe the writing process he follows: a voyage out and a voyage back. Think about your own writing process, create a metaphor to describe it, then write an essay explaining the connection. You may want to think about a particular kind of writing; the process you use on a research paper may inspire a different metaphor than the process you use for writing a newspaper column, a poem, or a literary analysis.

2. Read James Tilt's essay, "The Marathon Session That Wasn't Quite a Session," then do one of the following things.
   A. Write a journal entry about reading the essay. What connections can you make between Tilt's unusual experience and the material in this chapter? Is there any other way to explain this writer's behavior, besides the explanation Tilt provides?
   B. Tilt's essay suggests that a positive environment can help a writer get started. Write an essay about places that help you write. Judging from your own experience, what qualities are needed for a good writing place? Does your writing center possess these qualities? If not, is there a way to introduce them?

3. In class, write a paragraph describing your favorite getting-started technique. Explain what it consists of and why you find it helpful. Read your paragraph aloud, listen to your classmates' paragraphs, then discuss the inventory of getting-started strategies the group has generated (as a memory aid, have someone keep a running list on the blackboard). If some of the techniques don't work for you, explain why and when they fail.

4. Write about a time when your usual way of getting started didn't work. What did you do? If you finally succeeded, to what do you attribute your success? Does your experience suggest ideas for helping other writers get started?

5. Check your journal for consulting sessions with a writer needing assistance getting started, and recount your experience to the group.

FOOTNOTES

[1]Toby Fulwiler explains that writing is a powerful mode of learning because it possesses three qualities: first, it is physical, focusing attention and actively engaging the writer in his subject; second, it is visible, providing a tangible product that records his ideas and makes refinement possible; third, it is personal, encouraging commitment to a point of view.

[2]This idea is discussed in greater detail in chapter 6.

[3]For a fuller description of these activities, consult any writing handbook.

[4]This strategy is discussed in more detail in chapter 5.

Chapter 4

Analyzing
an Assignment

Good writers cheerfully admit they need all the help they can get. Besides soliciting feedback from readers, they glean ideas and inspiration from the writing situation itself. Questions like "Who is my intended audience?" and "What's the context of this piece of writing?" remind a writer she's not composing for herself, working in a vacuum, or tossing her ideas into a void.

For a college writer, the assignment is the single most important component of the writing context.[1] Helping a writer analyze the assignment and keep it in mind while he works is a key aspect of consulting. As a student responding to assignments in your own courses, you are well-qualified for this job; conversely, the reading skills you hone during your training will come in handy for examining teachers' assignments as well as writers' drafts.

Although teachers may require early drafts or offer to read them, in many cases there is no discussion of the assignment from the time it is given out to the time the paper is due. Of course, an assignment gives direction on nuts-and-bolts matters such as page length and documentation format; however, the assignment is also a teacher's attempt to help the writer produce a successful paper, a product that will satisfy them both.

Two Schools of Thought

You may already have noticed that writing assignments vary widely from one discipline to another, one course to another, and one teacher to another (and—if you are a transfer student—one institution to another). Some assignments are quite detailed, e.g., "Write an 8–10 page paper presenting the arguments for and against drug-testing among college athletes. Include medical, ethical, and legal arguments, discuss both strengths and weaknesses of the arguments, consider counterarguments, and explain your own point of view. Incorporate at least 8 sources from academic or professional journals, using APA documentation."

Highly specific assignments like this one offer a good deal of direction about organizational matters. With a minimum of rearranging, the drug-testing assignment could be transformed into a working outline:

    I. Statement of the Issue
   II. Brief Description of Points of View
      A. Pro
      B. Con
  III. Medical Aspects of the Issue
      A. Pro
        1. Strengths
        2. Weaknesses
        3. Counterarguments
      B. Con
        1. Strengths
        2. Weaknesses
        3. Counterarguments
  IV. Ethical Aspects of the Issue
      A. Pro
        1. Strengths
        2. Weaknesses
        3. Counterarguments
      B. Con
        1. Strengths
        2. Weaknesses
        3. Counterarguments
   V. Legal Aspects of the Issue
      A. Pro
        1. Strengths
        2. Weaknesses
        3. Counterarguments
      B. Con
        1. Strengths
        2. Weaknesses
        3. Counterarguments
  VI. Conclusion: My Position

Some teachers feel that assignments that contain specific guidelines free writers to concentrate more fully on gathering material, critiquing arguments, and evaluating evidence. Another advantage of highly specified assignments is that they promote proficiency in particular writing formats: a case study for psychology or business, an ethnographic report for social science, a lab report for science, a rhetorical analysis for communication.

On the other hand, some teachers prefer to keep assignments fluid, believing that students write better about subjects that interest them, and that they need to learn how to formulate good topics. A literature teacher, for instance, might ask students to write about some aspect of *The Scarlet Letter* that interests them.

Calvin and Hobbes

by Bill Watterson

Consultants and Assignments

As a consultant, you can help writers make constructive use of assignments. Properly exploited, the assignment becomes an ally rather than an obstacle or a trial. In the preliminary stages of writing (perhaps as early as the "Getting Started" stage described in chapter 3), the assignment triggers questions that suggest a possible focus or thesis. Later in the process, the assignment becomes a combination checklist and map, moving the drafts towards a logical format and providing hints for development. Finally, when the polished draft is imminent, the assignment answers questions about manuscript preparation.

There are two ways to use assignments constructively: by analyzing the assignment itself and by examining the rhetorical context of the assignment.

Analyzing the Assignment

Teachers deliberate carefully about the language of assignments because they want to convey a maximum of meaning with a minimum of confusion. So a student needs to read the assignment just as deliberately, giving it the same kind of attention she would devote to a question that is going to be on the exam. Let's look at a college composition assignment[2] and see what information it yields.

> Write an essay in which you describe an event that has been significant to you. The event should not be one in which the significance is immediately clear; it should probably not be a milestone like graduation, getting your driver's license, winning the big game, or getting accepted to college. Nor should it be an event with obvious dramatic impact, such as the death of a friend. It should be an event that *you* put significance into, but that somebody else might pass off as unimportant. What you're looking for is a time in your life when something apparently ordinary meant, or came to mean, something important to you.

In order to succeed, your essay must eventually do two things: it must describe the event fully and in detail, so that your audience (your classmates) will understand what it was like to experience it. Second, it must explore the significance you eventually attached to it, and what elements in the experience contributed to that significance.

Step #1. Find the Operative Verbs

Students often complain to teachers (especially those who prefer non-specific assignments like the invitation to write about *The Scarlet Letter*), "I don't know what you want." The verbs in an assignment identify the actions a writer must complete to give a teacher what he wants. This assignment contains two operative verbs: "describe" and "explore." Describing an event involves more than recounting what happened; describing requires enough details to convey the experience vividly. "Explore" suggests probing beneath the surface rather than being satisfied with a superficial explanation of what the experience meant.

Here are some other operative verbs and suggestions for using them to shape writing.

- *Compare and contrast.* Analyze both the differences and the similarities between the items being examined. Since every characteristic a writer considers will be either the same or different, it takes some ingenuity to make a comparison-contrast approach fresh and lively: Roger Sale says that all too often comparison-contrast papers work like "big swinging gates" (83). The trick is to figure out what's interesting about the differences or similarities. Why does looking at these things together help the reader understand them better than if they were considered individually? To turn comparison-contrast into a thoughtful approach rather than a dry formula, have a writer try this: Begin with your gut-level, knee-jerk impression of the components you're comparing and contrasting. Quick, without mulling it over, are they more alike or more different? Whatever the answer is, the interesting material is probably on the other side of the equation. Think about how things that at first seem similar are different in pivotal ways, or how things that to the casual observer couldn't be more different are alike beneath the surface. The old adage has it that you can't compare apples and oranges. Why not? They have the same general shape, belong to the same food group, have skin, get put in lunchboxes, don't spoil readily at room temperature—you get the idea.
- *Evaluate.* Assess the quality or effectiveness of the item under examination. To evaluate, a writer must first decide how to measure quality or effectiveness—in other words, he must develop criteria. Then he must explain whether the item under examination meets the criteria, supporting his assertion by matching the item against the criteria. For instance, to evaluate the effectiveness of his college's affirmative action

program, the writer would have to decide what makes an effective pro-gram (increased minority presence in the institution, the absence of reverse discrimination, adequate support services, a low drop-out rate, etc.), then apply the criteria to his college's program.

- *Define.* Explain the meaning of a term, putting it into the category it belongs to, then listing the characteristics that distinguish it from other members of the category. An example can supplement and clarify a def-inition, but it is not sufficient by itself.

Step #2. Discuss/Define Pivotal Terms

In addition to operative verbs, assignments contain concepts or terms that must be discussed or applied. In the assignment above, the obvious pivotal term is "significant." The assignment assumes that meaning can spring from private and individual sources as well as from more public sources such as ceremonies and official milestones. That is why the assignment warns against choosing an event with obvious significance: with a subject like divorce, dan-ger, serious illness, or death, the significance is sitting right on the surface, so it's not necessary to "explore."

A less obvious pivotal term in the assignment is "event." This word steers writers away from lengthy experiences such as a trip, or a chain of events such as an athletic career. The assignment requires looking deeply at some-thing; if the subject is broad, too much time will be required to describe it, and neither reader nor writer will have the energy to explore its significance.[3]

Step #3. Follow Hints for Development

Besides obeying the verbs and grappling with pivotal terms, writers must include all the components listed in the assignment. This assignment clearly identifies two components that must be in place to satisfy the prompt: 1) describe the experience and 2) explore its significance. Two more components are implied: the writer must include detail in the description, then use that detail to explain the event's significance. In other words, detail is the link between the two components of the assignment.

Filling in the Rhetorical Context

An assignment often contains information about the framework in which the student is writing. In the significance assignment, an audience is specified: the writer's classmates, who were probably not part of his life at the time of the experience and did not share it with him. Keeping this audience in mind will help him decide how much background to provide (e.g., identifying other people involved in the event, explaining events that led up to it), and what kind of vocabulary is suitable.

Another aspect of the writing situation is the course out of which the assignment arose. What is going on in lectures, class discussion, and assigned readings? If this information is not included in the assignment, ask the writer about it. The significance assignment occurred immediately after students had read and discussed "Living Like Weasels" and "Once More to the Lake," essays in which Annie Dillard and E.B. White invest ordinary events with highly personal meanings. Prompting a writer to talk about reading assignments and class discussion may suggest a promising approach.

Another component of the writing situation is the purpose of the assignment, which the teacher may or may not explain. Thinking about purpose, even speculating or guessing about it, can transform an assignment from an empty exercise to a purposeful act.

A final aspect of the context is evaluation criteria. Criteria may be spelled out as part of the assignment or distributed early in the semester with the blanket statement that they apply to all assignments. If no criteria are mentioned in the assignment, ask the writer for additional information, then pay special attention to the criteria given the greatest weight by the teacher.

Working with Open-Ended Assignments

What about the professor who leaves the topic up to the writer, asking you to write about whatever interests you in *The Scarlet Letter*? Open-ended assignments leave room for creavity but contain little guidance or direction. Staring at a blank screen while thinking about *The Scarlet Letter* (and possibly finding nothing that interests you very much) presents the same challenges as getting started on any other kind of writing task. Try some of the strategies in chapter 3, combined with filling in the rhetorical context, described above. Also consult chapter 10 for advice on writing assignments in particular disciplines.

ASSIGNMENTS

1. Read the essay by Linda Flower and John R. Hayes, "The Cognition of Discovery: Defining a Rhetorical Problem," then do one of the following things:
    A. Write a dialogic notebook entry about the article and come to class prepared to discuss the two or three passages you found most interesting.
    B. Write an essay critiquing the article. What is Flower and Hayes' thesis? What kinds of evidence do they use to support it? Do their research methods have limitations or drawbacks? How compelling do you find their claim? Is it supported by your experience as a writer and a consultant? How does their essay help you work more effectively with writers and their assignments?

2. Read Elizabeth Foote's "An Experience to Remember," then critique the session she describes, referring to points discussed in this chapter (or earlier ones), points raised in Flower and Hayes' essay (or other readings), and your own experiences as a writer or consultant. How might you have reacted in the same situation?

3. Read the following early draft, written in response to the significant event assignment, p. 25. Do a spontaneous role-playing session or a written dialogue in which you use the assignment to help the writer strengthen the draft. With another group member taking the writer's role, read your dialogue in class. Listen to and critique the dialogues of other group members.

> I was a member of an organization called STOPP of Nashua, Students to Offset Peer Pressure. The group was formed about eight years ago by junior high guidance counselors, with only eight students. The purpose of the group was to reach out to the community and give students alternative activities to drinking and doing drugs. By my senior year in high school, the eight students had expanded to over three hundred.
>
> Over the six years that I was a member of this organization, I was active either working at the dances that we held or helping out with fundraisers, but I felt I could have done more. So my senior year I made a commitment to myself to become more active than I was in the previous years.
>
> Every year STOPP sponsors Red Ribbon Week, which symbolizes a week without drugs and every year our advisor selects a certain few to speak at the candle-light vigil that starts off the week. Last year I was one of those select few that was asked to speak. At first I was hesitant to do it but I reminded myself of the commitment I made so I agreed to go along with it.
>
> As many know, I'm not one that likes to stand in front of large groups and speak or even small ones. Especially this group where there were a couple hundred people, not to mention my parents, my brother, and all my friends were there.
>
> Even though I was extremely nervous I got up there and delivered my speech. At first I felt really uncomfortable but as I looked out into the crowd and saw my family smiling at me I felt like I was doing something positive for my city. After the first few seconds I was fine and when I was done I heard the applause from the crowd which made me feel extremely relieved.
>
> I hoped by giving my speech I had made a difference in someone's life, no matter how small that change is, and that was the purpose of my speech. Many people might think that people don't change just because they heard a speech but I feel that I might have made a significant change, hopefully positive, in at least one person.

4. Using an assignment you found difficult to respond to, write an imaginary dialogue in which a consultant helps a student with the

assignment. Also write a brief rationale explaining why you chose the techniques you did. Distribute copies of the assignment to group members, give them a few minutes to read it, then read your dialogue aloud with another group member reading the student's part. Listen to and critique the dialogues of other members of the group.

5. If your writing center keeps a file of course assignments, browse through them and write a journal entry about your observations. What did you notice about the differences between assignments? The similarities? Did you find some assignments more interesting or stimulating than others?

FOOTNOTES

[1]This chapter expands on Step #3 of "Priorities in Reading a Draft."

[2]I've selected an assignment of mine, because I can reconstruct the process I went through as I drafted it.

[3]See the draft in Assignment #3 for an illustration of what happens when a writer ignores the word "event."

Chapter 5

Finding a Focus

Although the hardest part of writing is probably getting started, as a consultant you may find your greatest challenge occurs soon after the writer has gotten started, producing an early draft you can't get a handle on. No matter how carefully you read, you can't find a point that holds it all together. This disorientation is dramatic proof that good writing must be focused; that is, it must be held together by a clear, interesting idea or point.[1] Writing handbooks favor terms like "thesis," "topic," or "hypothesis" when referring to the main idea of a text, but "focus" is a more accessible term because it draws on common visual experience. Anyone who has gone to a movie, watched TV, or riffled through a batch of photos knows about focus and why it's important.[2]

What Makes a Good Focus?

Ideally, the point a writer chooses as her focus is unifying, thought-provoking, and narrow enough to explore in depth. First, it has to hold the entire text together. It can contain contradictory elements, but all parts of the text must somehow relate to it. For instance, in a literary analysis, the writer can acknowledge that there is strong evidence to support different interpretations, and even decide that the interpretations are equally compelling. But all parts of the essay must relate to the writer's exploration and evaluation of the interpretations.

Second, the focus should be complex and interesting enough so that it requires discussion and exploration. An essay "proving" that Othello was a jealous man or that pollution is bad has a central idea, but not one that requires elaboration. If a reader's initial reaction to the main idea is "Really? How so?" then it's probably worth writing about. If her reaction is "Of course" (or in the current pop culture terminology, "Duh"), the idea won't hold up under examination.

Finally, the focus should be limited enough so the writer can explore it thoroughly. A five-page essay arguing that pollution is a pressing contemporary problem does not have a narrow enough focus. Even a five-page essay about one kind of pollution (e.g., "Water pollution in the Northeast is becoming more and more serious") is probably too broad. A focus such as "Recent attempts to reduce pollution in the Hudson River have not been as successful as engineers had predicted" is more manageable, and probably more interesting as well, because it can be discussed in some detail.

DUFFY®   **by Bruce Hammond**

Common Problems with Focus

Several factors may explain why writers, particularly students writing for professors, have difficulty with focus. They may feel unqualified to discuss the assigned topic or come to a conclusion about it. They may be uncertain about whether they understand the material or know how to evaluate it. They may be ambivalent, especially about a complex issue: "I don't know how I feel about the death penalty. When I read about a brutal crime I think I support it, but then I see a movie like *Dead Man Walking* and I change my mind."

You may not have enough information to identify the source of a writer's difficulty with focus, but as you begin working with him to develop one, think about what kind of problem it seems to be.

> *Belaboring the obvious.* This is what happens when the focus is not complex enough to require exploration. Its symptoms include the generous use of cliches ("America is a great country"), a tone of blustering certainty ("Everyone knows that exercise is good for you"), and circular logic ("It's obvious that rap lyrics are obscene, or people wouldn't be so upset about them").
>
> *Shifting foci.* An essay with this problem might begin by discussing the use of animals in medical research, then without warning or transition switch to the use of animals in developing cosmetic products.
>
> *Contradictions.* The writer may clearly announce a focus ("If we make society more equitable, sexist language will automatically disappear") then contradict his original position ("Women will never be truly equal while we continue to use words like 'bimbo' and 'broad'").

Helping a Writer Focus

Before you discuss focus, review the assignment. If it specifies a particular focus, ask the writer to trace the focus throughout the draft. Explain any difficulties you had recognizing the focus, and let him work on stating it more clearly, or in terms that are closer to those of the assignment.

What happens if the assignment doesn't specify a particular approach and the draft doesn't have an obvious focus? One strategy for getting the writer actively involved is especially helpful when the draft turns out to lack focus. Ask the author to complete, in writing, the sentence, "In my essay I show that...." If you perceive an effective focus in the essay and it matches the author's completed sentence, point out this congruence, then move on to other aspects of the draft such as organization or development (see "Priorities in Reading a Draft"). If there is no focus, an ineffective focus, or a focus that differs significantly from the completed sentence, together search the draft for passages where the focus is suggested or stated. If it is only implied, explain why you didn't see it, and ask the writer to express it more directly. If it doesn't yet appear in the draft, look for places and ways to introduce it. Point to passages you had trouble understanding, and repeat the questions you asked yourself as you tried to comprehend them.

If the writer can't complete the focus sentence, "In my essay I show that...," put the draft aside and ask her to tell you in her own words what she wants to convey. This approach works well with writers who feel they must "translate" their ideas into the complicated language they associate with college writing. Since the language is not natural to them, it obscures their meaning. But when they use the language they know well—the language of conversation—their point may come through quite clearly. Listen attentively, then repeat what the writer has told you, and ask if that is the focus of the essay. If you've interpreted correctly, you and the writer can return to the draft and begin adjusting it so it conforms to the newly identified focus.

If as the writer talks he begins to warm to his task, expanding on the focus and describing how the draft hangs together, serve as his scribe, jotting down what he says. Then show him how cogently he has laid out both focus and organization. Because you are merely taking dictation, there is no danger of your appropriating the paper.

When the paper vacillates between one focus and another, point out places where you were confused by the shift, and ask if there is a connection between the two approaches. Perhaps the focus shifted from animal testing in medical research to animal testing in cosmetic research because the writer feels animal testing is justified in one situation but not in the other. If so, she has several options. One is to write a transition between the two ideas, explaining the connection ("Many of the reasons given for animal testing in medical research do not apply to animal testing in cosmetic development"). Another option is to devote the bulk of the paper to the more interesting idea, briefly referring to the other idea for contrast ("Carefully supervised animal research for the development of life-saving medical procedures has much to recommend it, but blinding rabbits for something as trivial as sexier eyelashes is inexcusable"). A third option is simply to eliminate the less interesting idea, recognizing it as irrelevant.

When the draft contains contradictions, point them out, explain why they confused you, and ask if there's a way of reconciling them. If the writer has made a casual statement he doesn't wish to stand by, he can eliminate or qualify it ("Although changing 'he' to 'he or she' will probably not hasten gender equality, the elimination of sexist terms like 'bimbo' and 'broad' is an important step towards taking women seriously"). If the two statements can be reconciled, their reconciliation may turn out to be the most interesting part of the paper ("Although sexist language does reflect the sexism in our society, it also perpetuates that sexism. We must reform the language and the social conditions simultaneously"). Perhaps the contradictory statements define changes the writer experienced as he read, wrote, and thought about the topic; in that case, he could present them as stages in his evolving understanding ("I began this paper thinking that language merely reflects the sexism in our society, but I eventually decided that it also perpetuates that sexism").

If these focusing strategies fail, look elsewhere for a focus. Read through the draft together, searching for ideas discussed at some length. Ask the writer to identify the main idea behind each paragraph; if the same idea occurs several times, it might serve, with some adjustment, as the essay's focus. If the writer identifies this or some other idea as a potential focus, have her begin talking through the rest of the draft, re-shaping it to reflect the tentative focus.

Another possibility is to put the draft aside and return to the assignment, re-reading and analyzing it as described in chapter 4. Look at the operative verbs and key concepts, discuss the rhetorical context, and then ask the writer to talk about how she used them to prepare the draft. Be alert for a possible focus or thesis statement, and if you think you hear one, have the writer test it against the draft. Or after you've discussed the assignment, return to the draft, searching for places where the operative verbs and key concepts are addressed. This reminder of what the assignment involves may give the writer new ideas for a focus. The final possibility is to put the draft aside temporarily and treat this as a "Getting Started" situation, applying the ideas described in chapter 3.

ASSIGNMENTS

1. Read Jennifer Brice's "Northern Realities, Northern Literacies: The Writing Center in the 'Contact Zone,'" then do one of the following things:
   A. Identify the focus of Brice's essay. How would you complete the sentence, "In her essay, Brice argues that..."? Was the material about her personal experience with Alaska useful background, or

did you find it irrelevant to the consulting issue she is exploring? Does her focus meet the criteria described in this chapter? If not, does her focus work anyway? Should the criteria be changed or qualified?

B. Evaluate the effectiveness of the consulting relationship Brice describes. Do you think she should have persuaded Philip to develop a more conventional focus?

2. Read Lynette Gajtka's "I Am Eager to Begin," then do one of the following things:
   A. React to Gajtka's opinion that focus is important in consulting, not just in writing. In what ways are these two kinds of focus the same and in what ways are they different?
   B. Critique the focus of Gajtka's essay. Does one central idea hold it together? If not, how would you describe her focus problem? What suggestions would you make in a consulting session concerning this essay? If you wish, write an imaginary dialogue, a memo, or a letter to Gajtka.

3. Bring to class a piece of published writing that lacks a thesis statement, and be prepared to discuss it. Why do you think the author decided against a thesis statement? Is a thesis statement implied? How did the absence of a thesis statement affect you as a reader? Is the text focused, even though it lacks a thesis statement? Where does the focus come from? After discussing these examples, do you agree with the statement in the opening paragraph of this chapter, "Good writing must be focused"?

4. Read the following draft, then either improvise a role-playing session with another member of the group, or write and then read a dialogue in which you help the writer discover a focus. Listen to and critique the dialogues of other members of the group. The draft was written in response to the "significant experience" assignment, p. 25.

> Working at a local restaurant during the summer before my senior year in high school was a period in my life which was significant to me. This wasn't my first job. I had worked as a paper boy when I was younger and I had worked as a landscaper the summer before. However, this job was different than any other I had.
>
> I worked as a kitchen helper in the restaurant. Usually, my work day would start out by my having to wash dishes. When I had finished this, I would either sweep the kitchen floor or peel vegetables. My work day would last no longer than six hours. The work wasn't hard but it was boring. At the time, this job seemed to be nothing more than a nuisance. As I look back on it now, I see that it marked a turning point in my life.
>
> Working at the restaurant was my first "real" job. It was my first experience in the work force. I had new found responsibilities. I had

to pay for things that I used to take for granted. I now had a car which I was responsible for and I was even saving for college. I was using my money now for more than candy and the movies like I had when I was delivering papers.

The real significance of the job is that it marked an important transition in my life. In a sense, this job was the beginning of my adult life. It was my first step into a world where I controlled what happened to me.

That summer has passed like every other summer before it. But with that summer came my first step into adulthood.

5. In your journal, find an account of a consulting session involving a draft that lacked an effective focus. Write another journal entry analyzing the session according to the ideas in this chapter. After reading the chapter, do you have new ideas for how the session might have been handled? Which suggestions in the chapter wouldn't have helped? Why not? Can you add to the suggestions in this chapter? Share your original entry and your new thoughts with the group.

FOOTNOTES

[1]This chapter expands on Step #4 of "Priorities in Reading a Draft."

[2]In the hands of a master, focus becomes an interpretive tool, telling us what to pay attention to. A cinematographer may begin a scene with one character's face sharply focused and the other blurred, then sharpen the blurred image when that character becomes the emotional center of the action. Similarly, writers sometimes intentionally introduce fuzziness or ambiguity to convey uncertainty or complexity, or to engage readers in interpreting the material.

Chapter 6

Organizing and Developing a Draft

I love the privileges of form.
–Bernard Malamud

The kind of unifying and thought-provoking focus described in chapter 5 is necessary but not sufficient for good writing. Focus imposes unity, but beyond that a text must be organized, conforming to an order that allows a reader to comprehend it without undue effort. And a text must be developed: the writer must support points with details, examples, explanations, or other evidence. In this chapter we will discuss techniques for helping a writer add shape and substance to a draft that is focused but not clearly organized or adequately developed.[1]

Linear models of writing, which assume that writing proceeds in a straight line, describe organization as preceding development: first you figure out how to arrange your ideas, then you flesh them out. But these two qualities are so intimately related that working on one frequently has an immediate effect on the other. That's why we will discuss them together.

Writing as Connecting

> Only connect!...Live in fragments no longer.—E.M. Forster

Writing is all about connecting: connecting emotion to intellect, experience to contemplation, writer to reader, the general to the specific, the individual to society. So we value writing that cogently connects ideas to each other. Isolated insights, no matter how dazzling, do not persuade us or hold our interest for long. We want to understand how ideas fit together, how an argument or story proceeds from one point to another. When we talk about a draft's organization, we are considering how well its connections work. When we evaluate a draft's development, we are looking at how effectively it connects general statements to specific support.

Linda Flower and John R. Hayes points out that a "writer-based" draft, which is comprehensible only to its author, must change significantly before it becomes a "reader-based" draft, which readers too will be able to follow. Making adequate connections is a crucial step in moving from a "writer-based" to a "reader-based" text. It's often hard for a writer to determine where readers need connections, because he has them all in his head—even the ones that don't appear in the text yet. Overly explicit connections quickly become mechanical and tedious, making a reader feel her intelligence is being insulted. On the other hand, a reader may become confused, frustrated, or distracted by connections that are too sparse or too oblique. So one of the most useful things you can do as a consultant is explain where you become confused while reading a draft.

Organization

> That's what I really love best—putting things in their best and proper place, revealing things at the time when they matter most.—Eudora Welty

Connections drive writing on all levels—even grammar and punctuation are ways of clarifying relationships. But if you begin by paying attention to the larger aspects of organization, the smaller ones may take care of themselves; and even if they don't, they can be dealt with during editing.

When you are having difficulty figuring out how the parts of a draft fit together, your difficulty may be symptomatic of organizational problems on one or more of several levels. Consider each level, starting with the most general and working your way down, since a problem on one level usually seeps down to the levels beneath it.

Overall Pattern

Check first for the overall organizing pattern of the essay (e.g., chronological or reverse chronological, cause-effect, comparison-contrast, general to specific, specific to general, items in ascending or descending order of importance). Then check to see whether the pattern suits the assignment, and whether the writer's material fits naturally into it. A chronological pattern, for instance, works well for a narrative or other sequential topic, but not for a cause-effect or analysis assignment.

Here are some ways to talk about organizational problems on this level. Your goal, as always, is to help the writer discover and express her ideas, not to impose your ideas on her. Therefore, keep your questions open-ended, rather than trying to second-guess her with a question like, "Were you trying to set this essay up as a pro-and-con argument?"

"Your focus seems to be that Grant Wood is much more than a regional painter. That's interesting, because 'American Gothic' seems like such a regional icon."

- "But I'm having trouble figuring out how your ideas connect to each other."
- "Why did you decide to put your material in this order?"

- "Did you consider other ways of arranging your essay?"
- "Why did this one seem best to you?"
- "Is there a way to make this pattern clearer?"

Sequence from One Paragraph to Another

Check to see if the paragraphs proceed in an order that links them to each other and to the overall pattern of the draft. In a tightly organized text, reversing or otherwise tampering with paragraphs weakens the structure. Here are some questions to use on this level.

"I understand the point of this paragraph—that Wood experimented with post-Impressionism—and I understand the point of the next one—that he was a commercial success when he returned from Europe."

- "But I don't understand the connection between the two ideas."
- "Why did you decide to put these two ideas together? What connects them?"
- "Do you want to explain the connection in the essay?"
- "Is another paragraph more closely connected to the first one than the one following it now?
- "Do you need another paragraph to explain the connection?"
- "What would happen if you switched these two paragraphs?"

Overall Paragraphs

The paragraph is one of the simplest but most powerful organizational units at a writer's disposal. Although many published writers use (or abuse) paragraphs in unconventional ways,[2] the two basic rules for paragraph boundaries remain useful, everyday guidelines.

- Limit each paragraph to one idea.
- Gather all material related to a particular idea into one paragraph (or if it is a complex idea, into consecutive paragraphs).

GLOSSING: THE KEY TO PARAGRAPHING

Glossing consists of writing in the margin next to each paragraph the single idea that unifies it:[3] Although it is a simple technique, it helps to diagnose an assortment of paragraph problems, including the following:

More than one idea in a paragraph. The problem will become apparent when more than one idea appears in the margin next to the faulty paragraph. The writer can give each idea its own paragraph, even if it contains only one sentence at first. This "breathing space" provides room for further development.

One idea recurs in widely separated paragraphs. This problem will become apparent when the same gloss keeps popping up in the margins. A draft that repeatedly broaches the same idea but never explores it thoroughly makes a reader feel she going around in circles and getting nowhere. When glossing reveals this problem, the writer can gather all the related material into one paragraph, then re-shape, expand, and put the paragraph where it belongs. Surrounding paragraphs may also require some re-shaping and revision.

Shaky connections between paragraphs. Glossing also exposes weak connections between paragraphs; in this case, the statements in the margins will be unconnected to each other. Work with the author on rearranging paragraphs so that the connections are stronger: For instance, if: Paragraph 1 defines noise pollution, Paragraph 2 defines pollution in general, and Paragraph 3 discusses the seriousness of noise pollution, putting Paragraphs 1 and 3 together would probably improve the organization of the draft. Peripheral revision may also be necessary to integrate the rearranged material.

If a writer has difficulty writing out glosses, you can achieve the same results by talking your way through the draft, asking, "What idea or topic holds this paragraph together?"

Organization Within Paragraphs

Check to see that individual sentences within a paragraph follow an orderly progression. The following questions encourage more careful analysis of organization within paragraphs:

- "What connects this sentence to the one before and the one after it?"
- "What would happen if you changed the sentence order?"
- "Is there a better way to arrange these sentences?"
- "Do you need more sentences to make the connection clear?"

Adding Transitions

Once material has been arranged in a suitable order, help the writer reinforce the organization with transitional words, phrases, or sentences. Many transitions will occur naturally as she glosses and answers the previous questions. For instance, a writer might gloss Paragraph 1, "the financial costs of pollution" and then gloss Paragraph 2, "the psychological costs of pollution." In explaining why she chose that order, she might say, "The financial costs were more obvious, so I decided to get them out of the way first." With minor adjustments, her explanation could be shaped into a transition sentence like, "Less obvious but perhaps more serious than the financial costs of pollution are its psychological costs."

Transitional sentences like this one may be needed to express elaborate relationships, but sometimes a transitional word or phrase is enough to signal the connection between one idea and another. Any writing handbook will provide a long list of transitions arranged according to organizational type. Here's a short list:

Temporal order: first, second, etc.; then; consequently; finally
Continuation: in addition, also, similarly, likewise
Contradiction: conversely, however, but, alternatively, on the other hand
Cause-effect: therefore, because, for this reason
Summation: In conclusion, Thus we see
Illustration: for instance, for example, a case in point

Development: Filling in the Blanks

An observed detail has a resonance—a branching truth—that no generalization can match. —John Updike

The best way to improve the development of a draft is to make sure the organizational framework is solid. In the process of figuring out how the writer's ideas are connected, he will see that some of them are merely mentioned or sketchily described. In particular, when glossing reveals that one paragraph contains several ideas, teasing the ideas apart will produce a string of short, undeveloped paragraphs, each of which is a blank to be filled in with details and examples. When you get to this point in a consulting session, particularly one that is already fairly lengthy, you might suggest that the writer fill in the blanks on his own, then schedule another session to work on the next draft.

Here is a draft that illustrates the interdependence of organization and development. It was written in response to the significant event assignment, p. 25.

It was unbelievable! I could see everything perfectly clearly, without the feeling and sight of frames. Everything was in focus. I could see what people's faces looked like from across the store. Getting contact lenses was probably one of the most significant events in my life. To most people it might seem mundane and ordinary but it was something that had a great effect on my life. I had worn glasses for several years to see things at a distance such as reading the blackboard in school but that was all that I would use them for. I absolutely refused to wear them in any public place such as outside, in stores, in the halls of school, and any kind of social events. The reason that I refused to wear glasses other than when I absolutely had to was because I thought that they looked geeky and only nerds wore them. Since that time back in the seventh grade I have changed my perceptions about people who wear glasses but I myself am still not totally comfortable with them. Without my glasses I had a very hard time recognizing people and so it was hard to be social with people that I could barely recognize and meeting new people was even worse because I couldn't see what they looked like. One of the biggest parts of conversation between two people is facial expression and without glasses I was denied seeing the reactions of those to whom I was speaking. Not being able to read or get a feeling about what the other person was thinking or how they felt about what I was saying made it very hard to be outgoing.

Getting contacts seemed to clear up all of my problems. Wearing contacts was like seeing the world for the first time. Everything was clearer, I noticed details of things that I hadn't even known were there before. The best thing about getting contacts was the fact that I could now see the person I was speaking to. Meeting and talking to new people became so much easier as did everything else such as sports and other social activities. I made a lot more friends and became involved in many social activities that I otherwise would probably not have participated in. It was as if my entire personality had changed but it hadn't, it was just different because so much more could be seen that had been missing before.

The writer has selected an event that's ideal for the assignment: we want to know why getting contact lenses was so meaningful for him. He has also roughed out a focus: "This essay shows that contact lenses made a big difference in my social life." But the draft is very hard to follow, and it is frustratingly thin. Just as we are getting drawn into his transformation from introvert to social butterfly, the essay peters out. The most obvious problem with the draft is that it consists of two huge paragraphs, each containing many ideas instead of just one. This problem causes weak organization *and* skimpy development of the writer's promising idea, because the constricted format leaves no room for the details we crave.

What would happen if glossing were applied to this draft? The writer might initially argue that the paragraphs are already perfectly unified, with one idea in each one: the first paragraph is about life before contact lenses, and the second is about life after contact lenses. Although with the exception of the initial scene this description is fairly accurate, it isn't a careful enough gloss, because it doesn't identify the many ideas embedded in the two general topics. See how many you can find in the first paragraph, then read on.

The first paragraph, in addition to the introductory scene, includes the following overlapping ideas:

- My negative attitude towards glasses
- Subsequent changes in my attitude towards glasses
- Reasons for my negative attitude towards glasses
- Results of my negative attitude towards glasses
- The social consequences of my refusal to wear glasses
- The importance of good vision to social skills
- How my personality was affected by my refusal to wear glasses

Some of these ideas are echoed in the second paragraph, with the significant difference that the context is wearing lenses rather than refusing to wear glasses.

- The social consequences of my being able to see better (because of contact lenses)
    # I go to more parties
    # I'm more conversationally adept
    # I can play sports now and that's another social opportunity
- How my personality was affected by my wearing contact lenses
- Other benefits of wearing contact lenses

Once the writer sees how many ideas each paragraph contains, he can decide which ones are worth pursuing and which are irrelevant.[4] Separate paragraphs will allow him to provide the details a reader desires. What kinds of social cues did he miss when he didn't see well? What social opportunities passed him by? What difference did it make when he had access to those cues? What were the results? Most intriguing is the observation that his personality didn't really change, even though it seemed to; this cries out for exploration.

When the writer has gone as far as she can go with this fill-in-the-blank procedure, suggest that she return to the assignment to make sure all the specified kinds of support have been provided. Finally, read through the draft and tell her where the existing support doesn't seem adequate to you. What questions do you have that are not answered by the current draft?

Back to Square One?

As the author of the above essay continues to elaborate on his ideas, he may realize he no longer wants to talk all about life before contact lenses and then all about life after contact lenses. He may prefer to shuttle back and forth—for instance, describing events which occurred under similar circumstances, except that in one he couldn't see well and in one he could—so that the contrast will be sharper.[5] In other words, improved development may demand a change in organization. Is this a step backwards? Absolutely not—it's a positive sign that the writer is continuing to refine his ideas. Tinkering with organization and development can also shift the focus of a draft. This shift doesn't mean the initial idea was bad or the writer has done something wrong; it is merely an example of writing doubling back on itself to integrate new discoveries and perspectives. Elsa Graser explains the interconnectedness of the stages of writing this way:

> Think of three separate metal rings, interlocked, each able to move in its own plane, but not separable. As you twirl one ring backward and forward, for the moment you let the other two slip out of your attention; yet moving one ring, you may reveal a previously unseen aspect of the others. You know that moving one will cause the others to move, but you look at each separately. (5)

The Introduction and Conclusion

It may seem logical that what the reader sees first is also what the writer produces first. But there are good reasons to postpone writing the introductory paragraph until the draft is fairly advanced in terms of focus, organization, and development. One writer explains that when he attempts to write his introduction first, he feels like he's trying to pick up a box he's standing on. This is a wonderfully apt comparison: since the first paragraph predicts where the text is going, writing it before the rest of the text doesn't make sense. To use a less original analogy, it's like taking an exam at the beginning a course rather than at the end.

What an Introduction Does

Ideally, an introduction both draws a reader into the text and predicts what is coming. How much and how clearly it predicts is up to the writer. Traditionally, the introduction of an academic essay includes a thesis or focus statement, perhaps incorporating the key concepts of the assignment itself. Some authors like introductions that are puzzling, ambiguous, or mysterious, reasoning that the best way to draw a reader in is to appeal to his curiosity.[6] As you read this kind of draft, point out any difficulties you have with understanding the writer's point.

Here are some introductory moves to pique a reader's interest:

- A compelling quote. " 'Just like old times,' said Bob Bronstein, a former Green Beret, as he watched the Vietnam-era Huey helicopter come in low over his suburban home. 'Looks the same, sounds the same. In a minute it's going to smell the same. We better get in.' " (Liston, A3).
- An interesting example. "As she watched a crew put up press tables in soon-to-be-packed Gampel Pavilion one morning last November, Marsha Mann Ralph's basketball career flashed in front of her eyes. 'There are more people setting up chairs than came to my games,' she realized. On today's 215th anniversary of the passage of Title IX, Ralph's daughter is playing basketball in a world vastly different from the one in which her mother made All-America at North Carolina in 1975." (Huebner, D1).
- A story or anecdote. "A friend of mine, a young mother, was recently abducted when she made the mistake of trespassing on private property. She had no identification on her so no one knew that she'd left her children home alone and that they were incapable of summoning help. They starved, as far as I can tell, while I was unaware of the tragedy unfolding just a few feet away. Did I mention that my friend is the raccoon who lived in our chimney?" (Weltner, F2).
- A vivid physical description. "A teenage couple sits on a park bench talking and kissing. Slung over her shoulder is an M-16 rifle; over his, an Uzi." (Richman, D2)

FOX TROT   by Bill Amend

What a Conclusion Does

A conclusion should provide a sense of closure, a feeling of satisfaction that what was expected has been delivered. It is a bad sign if a reader's reaction to the final sentence is to turn the page over, searching for more. But although the conclusion should connect with the introduction, in a sense completing a circle, merely repeating or re-wording the introduction suggests that reading the essay has been a waste of time. A reader's reaction to the conclusion should be, "I see how this complements the introduction and how my understanding has been expanded since I read the introduction."

Helping with an Introduction and a Conclusion

Looking at the introduction and conclusion with the writer, consider the following questions:

- "Do the introduction and conclusion connect to each other?"
- "Do the introduction and conclusion accurately reflect the contents of the body of the draft?"
- "Have all the promises made in the introduction been kept in the body of the draft?"

If the answer to the final question is "no," the writer must decide whether the unkept promise is irrelevant—in which case he will change the introduction—or whether he wants to honor his promise by keeping the introduction and revising the draft.

A Good Time for an Outline

When the writer is satisfied with her introduction and conclusion, focus, organization, and development, suggest that she try to outline the draft. Although an outline can feel like a straitjacket early in the composing process, it is a good way to evaluate structure in an advanced draft. If the outline checks against the draft, it's time to move on to correcting, editing, and preparing a polished draft.

ASSIGNMENTS

1. Read Nancy Sommers' "Revision Strategies of Student Writers and Experienced Adult Writers," then do one of the following things:
   A. Write a dialogic notebook entry about the article and come to class prepared to discuss the two or three passages you found most interesting.
   B. Gloss the first five paragraphs of the essay, then discuss in class how well Sommers uses the organizational potential of paragraphing.
   C. Write an essay describing your concept of revision and your revision processes. To what extent does Sommers' analysis of student writers apply to you? If her analysis doesn't apply, how do you account for this discrepancy?
   D. Bruffee, Elbow, and Sommers all discuss the relationship between speech and writing. Write an essay comparing their ideas about this relationship. Where do they agree? Where do they disagree? Whose ideas do you find most persuasive? If you prefer, write a conversation in which they defend their ideas or try to reach consensus.

2. Read Joy Farmer's "The 20-Minute Solution: Mapping in the Writing Center," then try mapping with an assignment you are working on, or in a writing center session. Has Farmer overestimated the power of this method? Can you imagine a situation in which it might not work?

3. Read the following draft, written in response to the "significant experience" assignment, p. 25, then either spontaneously role-play with a partner, or write a dialogue showing how you would help this writer strengthen organization and development.

> As a member of my church's youth group, which consisted of nine high school girls, this past year I traveled to New York City and California to work with the homeless. While actually in both places I failed to see the significance of my work. Now in retrospect, I am beginning to realize the impact which I created.
>
> In setting out for my experiences I was asked what I expected from them. My reply was to make a difference in someone's life; not expecting that the difference would be made in my own. All the people we met had a different story to tell. The nine of us listened with eager ears to any one willing to share, each individual changing my life perhaps forever.
>
> Before this experience I thought that if you lived on the street that automatically meant that you were unhappy and unwilling to receive any kind of charity. I was proven wrong.
>
> One of our customers in New York City was a lady from Jamaica. Although she was without permanent shelter, she wore a huge smile on her beautiful face. What really shocked me about her was that when offered a pair of shoes she refused them; her reason being that they were not feminine enough.

I met another person who went by the name Money Grip. He told us that even the littlest baby in the street knew him. Although drunk at the time, he still had a lot to offer. His message to us was to listen to our mothers, be happy and most importantly stay in school. He was unlike the homeless people that I pictured in that he was trying to get out of poverty. He was tired of just receiving welfare and had a job interview for the next day. I now know that not all homeless people abuse the system due to laziness.

"Stingy" is another word I used previously to describe homeless people. Again I was proven wrong. While working at the clothes closet in Palo Alto, my friend met a gentleman who was playing a bamboo flute. She admired the music that was made by this delicate instrument which he had just made the previous evening. When it was time for us to leave he gave the flute to her thanking her for her kind smile.

Another man, by the name of Mike, befriended our group. One night he invited us out to experience his world. Mike used to have a high paying job, but due to illness lost both his job and house.

One place where Mike sleeps is the airport. He learned when and where he could sleep without being caught, wearing a suit and tie to appear like a businessman during a layover.

One time when waiting at a terminal a politician came up to ask him what he thought was the nation's biggest problem. Mike's response was homelessness. The politician was rather taken aback by his reply and asked him why he thought this. Mike told him that he himself was homeless. The policeman was totally shocked because Mike didn't look homeless. I guess this man and I shared the same mindset, all homeless wear ragged old clothes, are dirty, and smell bad. Both of us were proven wrong, because Mike was well dressed and groomed and I can still smell the clean scent of his cologne.

It took me awhile to realize the significance of those trips and I am still not sure if I totally realize the full impact it had on my life. I do know that it has changed my life for the better. I am more open-minded and realize how wrong stereotypes can be. I think it has taken me, as an individual, longer to figure out the significance of these excursions because we were such a close group; we worked together, shared together, laughed and cried together. Someday I'll be able to separate my self from the group and be able to analyze my own feelings but until then here is my most significant experience.

4. Bring in a text that has what you consider an effective introduction. Read the introduction aloud to your group, then explain why you selected it. What does it introduce? Why is it effective? Does it both draw the reader in and predict what is to come? Does it illustrate one of the introductory strategies in this chapter? If not, what strategy does it use?

5. Find a text in which the introduction and conclusion complement each other well. Write a brief essay analyzing how they complement each

other. How do they relate to the body of the text? How does the conclusion avoid merely repeating the introduction? How does the conclusion provide a sense of closure?

6. Check your journal for consulting sessions involving organization or development problems. Write another journal entry, reconsidering the session in view of material in this chapter. After reading the chapter, do you have other ideas about why the session worked or didn't work? Share both journal entries with the group.

FOOTNOTES

[1] This chapter expands on Steps #5, #6, and #7 of "Priorities in Reading a Draft."

[2] For instance, a writer might use a single-sentence paragraph, which is conspicuous for its shortness, to highlight a crucial point. Long, rambling paragraphs, in which one idea morphs into another, are a favorite device of stream-of-consciousness authors.

[3] Glossing is also an excellent study aid; because it is more detailed than outlining, it helps a reader expose the structure of a writer's argument without blurring subtle distinctions.

[4] Don't try to make these decisions yourself, no matter how obvious they seem. For instance, the remark about seeing a whole new world may sound clichéd, but the writer might spell out a deeper meaning in a later draft. Similarly, the observation that the writer no longer has a negative stereotype about people who wear glasses seems beside the point, but his new attitude may be connected to the fact that he no longer has to wear glasses himself.

[5] In the actual draft, the writer is content with the "bow and arrow" format, where the topic changes only once, and the switch is like shooting an arrow from one topic to the other. With more to say, the writer may decide he prefers the "ping-pong" format, switching back and forth between topics, imitating the rapid pace of a ping-pong game.

[6] The first sentence in the contact lens essay is a good example of a slightly puzzling beginning. What kind of frames? What is "it"? Some readers like this brief note of uncertainty, but others are impatient with it, labeling it a mistake rather than a conscious choice by the writer. What do you think?

Chapter 7

Correcting Surface Errors

*No iron can pierce the heart with such force as a
period just at the right place.—*
Isaac Babel

In this chapter, we move from the underlying structure and meaning of a draft
to linguistic features such as sentence structure, grammar, and punctuation.[1]
Of course, these two levels are intimately connected, since linguistic features
convey meaning. But switching from holistic consideration of a draft—focus,
organization, development—to more localized matters requires a shift in consulting strategy. It is like a film director's decision to move from a long shot to
a close-up. Now you will be reading closely, word by word, paying attention
to detail rather than concentrating primarily on the larger picture.

"Surface error" encompasses aspects of writing—punctuation, grammar,
sentence structure—that sometimes overlap and are easily confused. It's useful
to have a term that embraces them all. "Surface error" also describes how a
reader is affected by these problems: he may stumble over rough spots or
wander off a path that hasn't been made sufficiently smooth. Errors distract a
reader and prevent him from grasping the writer's point, like heavy static
drowning out music on the radio. And since surface features clarify relationships and connections, errors are confusing as well as distracting.[2] In short,
surface errors have consequences that are far from superficial.

Helping a Writer with Surface Features

As a consultant, you can be most helpful by explaining how error limits your
ability to understand and appreciate a writer's work. Here are some general
suggestions for dealing with errors.

1. *Fix all the same kinds of errors at once.* Ask the writer if you may
   mark places in the margin to which you'd like to go back. Scan the
   essay, using a simple notation system to flag different kinds of errors (S
   for sentence, P for punctuation, and so on). Then, instead of discussing
   the errors in the order in which they occur, discuss all examples of one

kind of error together. After going through three in a row, the writer will probably be able to correct the fourth one herself.

2. *Talk about patterns.* The marginal abbreviations used in Step 1 sort the errors into rough categories. Recognizing the patterns will help the writer understand how to fix the errors. The problem will seem more manageable if he realizes there are only four types of error rather than forty individual errors.

3. *Discuss the reasons behind errors.* As Mina Shaughnessy points out, errors are not random. There is usually a method, even a logic, behind them, and the more the writer explains her method, the better her chances of correcting it and avoiding error in the future. If one kind of error occurs several times, ask the writer to explain how she made that particular choice. Regarding a sentence fragment, for instance, she might explain, "The sentence was getting so long, I figured I ought to end it." This statement reveals that she is using a faulty definition of a sentence (a sentence of a certain length is complete), but it also shows that she understands a basic principle of style (Long sentences can be confusing). In this case, you might then compare the fragment to a long, complete sentence in her draft. On the other hand, if the writer of the fragment, "Because I was sick," explains, "I put a period at the end because the sentence has a subject and a verb," you could talk about how the word "because" affects the sentence.

4. *Use common language to discuss errors.* You don't have to be a grammar guru to help eliminate surface error. As a matter of fact, one of your assets as a peer consultant is your ability to de-mystify correctness by using accessible vocabulary rather than grammatical terms. For instance, it's more useful to point out that "Because I was sick" doesn't contain a complete idea than to explain that "because" is a subordinating conjunction.

5. *Don't pretend you know more than you do.* Half-remembered or inaccurately remembered rules can play at least as much havoc as complete ignorance. Besides, admitting that you don't know all the rules will make the writer feel less embarrassed about her error, and looking up the rule together will show her how to do it alone the next time.

6. *Ask questions, don't give a lecture.* Remember that although the writer's goal is to produce an error-free draft, your goal is to help him avoid errors on his own. Unlike questions intended to reveal what the writer wants to say, questions about surface errors are usually closed-rather than open-ended. They may actually have a "right" answer, even a "yes-or-no" format. Since correcting is rule-driven, these questions help the writer match his performance against the rules. Questions that accomplish this matching effectively don't have a wide variety of acceptable answers.

Sentence Fragments and Run-on (Fused) Sentences

These two errors are opposite sides of the same coin, and they frequently occur together. A sentence fragment ("Because I was sick") contains too little to qualify as a legitimate sentence, and a run-on or fused sentence ("I'm sorry my paper was late I missed the deadline I was sick.") contains too much. As the example in Step 3 above shows, it's important to understand why the error is occurring, because the reason will drive your discussion of how to fix it. Consult a handbook for a fuller definition of a sentence. In a nutshell, however, a sentence requires three things:

> A subject
> A predicate (verb, plus object if required)
> A clause with no subordinating word ("Because" is a subordinating word)

A fragment exists when a group of words punctuated as a sentence does not have these three components. A fused or run-on sentence exists when two or more groups of words with these components are run together (fused) without benefit of punctuation. However, unless the writer indicates familiarity with grammatical terms by using them, the best way to correct fragments or run-ons is to ask simple questions:

- "How many ideas in this sentence?"
- "If there's more than one idea, what's the best way to distinguish between them?"
- "Do you want to separate them completely, or is there a connection that you want to preserve?" The fused sentence above ("I'm sorry my paper was late I missed the deadline I was sick") could be re-written in a number of ways, depending on the degree of connection the writer wants to preserve.
    # I'm sorry my paper was late. I missed the deadline. I was sick.
    # I'm sorry my paper was late, but I was so sick that I missed the deadline.
    # I'm sorry my paper was late; I missed the deadline because I was sick.
- "Is the idea complete?"
- "If the idea is not complete, what's needed to make it complete?"
- "If the idea is not complete, would connecting it to another sentence make it complete?"

Reading aloud sometimes helps a writer identify a fused sentence, especially if she pauses at the point of fusion (after "late," in the sample above). You can then ask why she paused, and explain that when you read the sentence to yourself, you did not pause because no punctuation signaled a pause. Your reading the sentence aloud without a pause will illustrate how the two thoughts become tangled at the point of fusion.

What about an intentional sentence fragment? Accomplished writers sometimes use fragments for dramatic or poetic effect. For instance, here is a description in Annie Proulx's novel *The Shipping News* of the initial encounter between protagonist Quoyle and the woman of his dreams.

> **Then, at a meeting, Puddle Bear. Thin, moist, hot. Winked at him.** Quoyle had the big man's yearning for small women. He stood next to her at the refreshment table. **Grey eyes close together, curly hair the color of oak.** The fluorescent light made her as pale as candle wax. The eyelids gleamed with some dusky unguent. **A metallic thread in her rose sweater.** These faint sparks cast a shimmer on her like a spill of light. She smiled, the pearl-tinted lips wet with cider. She chose a cookie with frosting eyes and an almond for a mouth. **Eyed him as her teeth snapped out a new moon.** An invisible hand threw loops and crossings in Quoyle's intestines. **Growls from his shirt.** (12)

In the boldfaced fragments, subjects and verbs evaporate in the intensity of Puddle Bear's sensory assault.

Isolated sentence fragments in an otherwise error-free draft may indicate that the writer is using them intentionally, like Proulx. First verify that this is a choice rather than an error, then describe how the choice affects you as a reader; some readers find Proulx's unconventional style self-indulgent and annoying. If there are many fragments, do they lose their impact? Are some successful and others not? Do they begin to feel like a knee-jerk habit rather than an effective choice?

Dangling or Misplaced Modifiers

A sentence with a dangling modifier omits the term the modifier applies to. Example: "While relaxing by the pool, three motorcycles came roaring down the street." The modifier "relaxing" is meant to describe someone, but whoever it is, it's not in the sentence. As the sentence reads now, it's the motorcycles that are relaxing by the pool as they simultaneously roar down the street.

A misplaced modifier is positioned so that it seems to modify something it couldn't really modify. Example: "Abraham Lincoln wrote the Gettysburg Address while traveling to the battle site on the back of an envelope."

Reading the sentence aloud sometimes help the writer "hear" the faulty modifier: "Oh, that makes it sound like the motorcycles are relaxing by the pool." If this doesn't work, ask a simple question, such as "Who's doing the relaxing?" or "What happened on the back of the envelope?" Answering the question may make her realize what's wrong ("We were—oh, I left that out"). If necessary, explain why you were unable to tell who was doing the relaxing when you read the sentence. Illustrate your confusion by reading the sentence yourself, with no pause to separate "while traveling to the battle site" and "on the back of an envelope." Or explain how you originally interpreted the sentence: "When I read the sentence the first time, it sounded like the battle site was on the back of the envelope, or like Lincoln was traveling on the envelope, even though I knew that didn't make sense."

Once the writer understands the problem, your final question is, "How can the sentence be re-written to say what you really mean?" Be careful not to answer the question yourself—instead, encourage the writer to come up with his own revisions, and limit your role to pointing out problems you have with them.

Sometimes only a slight adjustment is needed, such as adding the missing element and changing a few words so the modifier no longer dangles: "While we relaxed by the pool, three motorcycles came roaring down the street" or "While relaxing by the pool, we heard three motorcycles roaring down the street."

But it's not always that easy, especially with a misplaced modifier. For instance, the revision, "While traveling to the battle site, Abraham Lincoln wrote the Gettysburg Address on the back of an envelope" takes care of the misplaced modifier, but now the meaning of "the battle site" is ambiguous, because it occurs earlier in the sentence than "Gettysburg Address." Changing the sentence to "While traveling to Gettysburg" clears up the ambiguity, but repeating "Gettysburg" is awkward. Revising the sentence to read, "While traveling to Gettysburg, Lincoln wrote his famous address on the back of an envelope" eliminates the repetition, but now the meaning of the phrase "address on the back of an envelope" is ambiguous, since it could also refer to Lincoln's other famous address, his street address. Wrestling with these alternatives suggests that the modifier was originally misplaced because it's so hard to find a satisfactory alternative. Can you come up with one?

Lack of Parallelism

A sentence lacks parallelism when words or phrases are put into forms that don't correspond to each other. Example: "The characteristics of Baroque art are movement, tension, and very dramatic." The first two components of baroque art ("movement" and "tension") are parallel, because they are both nouns. But the third component isn't parallel to the other two: it's an adjective.

Begin a discussion of parallelism problems by asking what belongs together in the sentence. Then look at the components and see if their forms match. Finally, have the writer decide how to make them match. In this case, the three components could become either nouns ("movement," "tension," "and "drama") or adjectives ("kinetic," "tense," and "dramatic").

Faulty parallelism frequently occurs with the terms "not only/but also." What comes after the first term should follow the same format as what comes after the second term. If the formats are different, the equation doesn't add up. Example: "Not only was Leonardo a great artist, but also a brilliant scientist and engineer." "Not only was Leonardo" does not have the same format as "but also a brilliant scientist." The simplest revision is probably, "Leonardo was not only a great artist but also a brilliant scientist and engineer." "Not only a great artist" has the same format as "but also a brilliant scientist." Have the writer explain what two things are being set against each other, see if the two formats match, and finally help him move the "not only" and "but also" terms around so that the formats do match.

Verb Problems

Tense Shifts

A tense shift error exists when one verb is in one tense and another verb is in another tense, even though both refer to the same time frame. Example: "When he is with Horatio, Hamlet seems warm and friendly, but when he interacted with Ophelia he was cold and distant."

Past and present tenses have different strengths, and tense shifts may occur when a writer tries to draw on both strengths at once. Telling a story in the present tense adds immediacy and excitement, as if it is still happening and nobody knows how it will come out. Past tense is the traditional narrative mode—"Once upon a time, there was"—and it conveys the impression that the action has been completed once and for all.[3]

In literary analysis, present tense emphasizes the reader's role, which occurs in the present each time the text is read. Past tense, on the other hand, emphasizes the author's role: the text was completed in the past and its form is now fixed, barring subsequent revised editions.[4]

How you help a writer with tense shifts depends on how many shifts occur. If most of the verbs are in one tense, the shifts may be a momentary lapse. Ask the writer, "Did these actions already take place, or are they happening now?" Use his answer to point out verbs that confused you because they suggest a different time frame.

If the verbs are almost equally divided between tenses, the writer may be ambivalent about which tense she prefers. Until she chooses a tense, there is no way of telling which verbs need to be corrected. Explain that you had difficulty figuring out when the events were taking place, and ask, "Do you want to make it sound like these events are happening now, or like they already happened?" Using her answer as a guide, work through the draft as she adjusts verbs to make them consistent with her choice. She may discover that the chosen tense isn't working well: " 'All of a sudden I begin to panic.' That feels funny. If I think I'm going to get mugged, why am I writing instead of running?" Encourage her to try the other tense and see if it works better. Unless the assignment specifies a particular tense, the tense itself is not as important as consistency.

Of course, if the action shifts from something happening now to something that happened in the past, changing verb tenses is not an error but a marker of the changing time frame. For example, "Yeltsin claims to be in perfect health, but the press was skeptical when he suddenly left yesterday's meeting without an explanation."

A writer may also shift from one tense to another to signal a turning point in the text. For instance, he may begin an essay in the past tense, giving background information and leading up to the central event, then shift to present tense to describe the event itself. Ask why he made the change, then check to see whether the shift accomplishes what he intended.

Faulty Verb Sequences

Verb sequences are faulty when a change in time frame is not indicated by the proper verb forms. For example, "I opened the envelope with shaking hands and read that I was selected for a full-tuition scholarship." Because all the verbs are in the past tense, it sounds like all the events happened in the same time frame. But this is inaccurate; the writer was selected for the scholarship before she opened the envelope and read the letter. Since "opened" is already in the past tense, a verb indicating an action that happened even earlier must go in the past perfect tense: "I had been selected for a full-tuition athletic scholarship."

To correct sequence errors, point out the verbs in question and ask, "Did these things happen at the same time, or did one happen before the other?"[5] Then explain why you could not tell this from reading the sentence on your own. When asked how to show that "selected" occurred before "opened," most native speakers will come up with the past perfect form ("had been selected"), even if they don't know what it's called.

MOTHER GOOSE & GRIMM   **BY MIKE PETERS**

Punctuation Errors

Emily Meyer and Louise Smith point out that punctuation errors arise from many sources besides the carelessness to which they are often attributed: half-remembered or erroneously remembered rules ("Never use a comma before 'and'"), unfamiliarity with certain kinds of punctuation, punctuating according to the rhythms of conversation or composing instead of the rhythms of reading, inability to distinguish between the "sounds" of similar kinds of punctuation (178–79).

Periods, semicolons, colons, dashes, and commas all direct the reader to pause when something in the text needs to be set off from something else. How much of a separation is needed and how long a pause to take is encoded in the punctuation itself. The longest pause is marked by a period, question mark, or exclamation point. The next longest pause is marked by a semicolon, colon, or dash, and the shortest pause by a comma.

Reading Aloud

Because pauses drive punctuation, reading aloud can help a writer identify punctuation errors. If he pauses at a point where no punctuation exists or doesn't pause where punctuation does exist, talk about the sentence. Is a pause needed there, or was he just stopping for breath? Would a pause help the reader understand the sentence, or is a pause frustrating and counterproductive at that point? How much of a pause is needed?

Unfortunately, the rhythms of speech are not identical to the rhythms of written prose, so reading aloud doesn't always solve punctuation problems. Notice how often a storyteller or radio announcer pauses after "but," "because," or "then"—points where the listener is left hanging, waiting to find out how things turn out. The speaker pauses in order to exploit her listener's desire for completion. Pausing makes dramatic sense, but it does not make semantic sense: it does not mark the end of a unit of meaning. As a matter of fact, adding punctuation at this point forces a reader to pause in a way that frustrates meaning instead of clarifying it. So the pauses indicated by reading aloud are not always reliable indicators of where punctuation belongs.

Another limitation of the reading-aloud method is that some writers don't pause when they read (especially if they are embarrassed by reading aloud and want to get it over as quickly as possible) and others don't hear the pauses they insert as they read. You can help by reading a problem sentence aloud after the writer has done so, then comparing the two readings. Explain why you became confused as you read, then discuss ways to punctuate so that the rhythm of the sentence supports its meaning.

Beyond Reading Aloud

Punctuation errors that can't be located through reading aloud can be handled in other ways. The basic strategy is the same as for sentence-level errors: work on one kind of error at a time, ask simple questions phrased in common vocabulary, and avoid grammatical terms whenever possible. Here are some questions to keep in mind as you work on punctuation:

- "Why did you decide to punctuate this sentence this way?"
- "How many ideas are in this sentence?"
- "If there is more than one idea, are they clearly separated from each other?"
- "How can you separate the ideas more clearly?"

Beyond Asking Questions: Need-to-Know Punctuation Rules

There is no easy way to handle punctuation errors that still exist after reading aloud and asking questions. Asking more questions at this point is liable to be frustrating to both you and the writer, particularly if he suspects he is guessing at an answer you already know. The cleanest solution is to explain the punctuation issue briefly and simply, then point out an error in the paper and help him use the rule to correct the error. Here's a brief dialogue that begins with a question, moves to an explanation of the rule, then ends with the consultant helping the writer apply the rule.

Writer (reading from draft): "I never answered a question, all I did was sit listening to my brother."

Consultant: How many ideas are in the sentence?

Writer: Two—not answering the question, and listening to my brother.

Consultant: I got that when I read the sentence too. Do you think the ideas are clearly separated from each other?

Writer: Sure, they're separated by commas.

Consultant: That's true, but I still had trouble figuring out how they hung together. Here's a sentence that gave me no trouble.

Writer (reading): "My mother did not know the answer, so she passed it on to my brother."

Consultant: Do you see how that sentence separates the ideas more clearly?

Writer: No, it looks the same as the other sentence to me. This one has two ideas: not knowing the answer, and passing the question on. The two ideas are separated by a comma. What's different?

Consultant: In this second sentence, you've used a connecting word, "so," not just a comma, and that helps me understand the connection better. A comma isn't strong enough to connect two ideas all by itself. You either have to make the punctuation stronger or give the comma some help.

Writer: What should I do now?

Consultant: Well, you know how to use connecting words because you did it perfectly in the second sentence. Can you think of a connecting word to add to the first sentence?

Writer: Would "so" work there too? "I never answered a question, so all I did was sit listening to my brother." That's what I meant.

Consultant: I understand the sentence better now, too. But there are other choices. How about making the punctuation stronger?

Writer: I guess I could make two sentences, since there are two ideas. "I never answered a question. All I did was sit listening to my brother."

Consultant: How do you like that?

Writer: It's okay, I guess. But the sentences are awfully short. It makes me sound like a second-grader.

Consultant: Yeah, the sentences *are* short, but they're not wrong. Are the ideas in the two sentences connected?

Writer: I think they are, and that's why I put them in the same sentence to begin with, but you said that's wrong.

Consultant: How are the ideas connected?

Writer: Well, one sort of re-states the other, but adds more information. It's almost like saying the same thing in two slightly different ways.

Consultant: Try putting them back together, and see what punctuation you might use.

Writer: "I never answered a question (pause) all I did was sit listening to my brother." The only thing I haven't tried is a semicolon.

Consultant: You could use a semicolon there. It connects the two ideas by putting them in the same sentence, but it's stronger than a comma. What do you think?

Writer: I don't know. I never use semicolons. I think I'll go with the "so" this time.

Consultant: Okay, great. Let's take a look at another sentence, and see how it compares to these two.

User-Friendly Punctuation Rules

Here are simple punctuation rules that explain common errors. When a writer is having problems with a particular kind of punctuation, you may want to consult a writing handbook together. In general, however, a writer learns most about surface errors by correcting her own, extrapolating the rules from her experience or having them provided on a need-to-know basis. Limit explanations to the boldface passages when you can, and use the additional material only if it's needed.

Commas: Use a comma when you want your reader to pause briefly so that she can understand the sentence without going back and reading it again. For instance, commas mark the end of one idea and the beginning of another, a shift from introductory material to the main idea of a sentence, or an interruption of the main part of the sentence by less important information. Sometimes a comma marks a pause that changes the meaning of a sentence drastically. "Her husband who is an attorney was at her side" implies that she has more than one husband, and the one who is an attorney was the one who was at her side. "Her husband, who is an attorney, was at her side" means that she has only one husband and that he is an attorney and was at her side.

Comma splices: A comma is not strong enough to hold two sentences together all by itself; trying to do this creates a comma splice. If you want to connect two syntactically complete sentences[6] because the ideas are closely connected, use stronger punctuation, or add a connecting word to the comma. The dialogue on p.57 illustrates a comma splice and two possible corrections.

Semicolon: Think of a semicolon as a weak period; use it to connect two syntactically complete sentences that you want to keep together because their ideas are closely related. For example, "I never answered a question; all I did was sit listening to my brother." A semicolon also works like a strong comma, indicating a slightly longer pause in a sentence that already contains commas. For example, "Their data reveal that for accomplished writers, an outline sometimes works and sometimes doesn't; that writers often use outlines *after* writing, to check for organization, rather than *before* writing, to predict how the text will take shape; and that writers who begin with an outline use it as a rough guide rather than a rigid mold."

Colon: Think of a colon as saying, "Details to follow." Use it to introduce an expanded explanation (possibly a list) of what came before. Example #1 "My husband and I have employed three wonderful young women over the last four years to care for our two toddler boys: a German au pair and two board-certified British nannies." Example #2: "Writing without knowing exactly what you will say leaves room for surprise and discovery: what looks at first glance like a digression may turn out to be the idea you've been fumbling for all along." Use a colon only after a syntactically complete sentence. ("I had lots on my mind that day: my finals, my dismal social life, and my money problems" but NOT "On my mind were: my finals, my dismal social life, and my money problems").

Apostrophe: An apostrophe indicates a contraction (don't) or when combined with the letter "s" it indicates possession (the boy's book). This sounds simple, but apostrophe errors are extremely common, even in published texts, because an apostrophe is NOT used with possessive pronouns, which already show possession by definition ("That book is *yours*," "The house lost *its* roof during the storm"). It's confusing to distinguish between the contraction "it's," which requires an apostrophe ("*It's* a beautiful day in the neighborhood"), with the possessive pronoun "its," which does not ("Virtue is *its* own reward").

The issue is further complicated by plural nouns: what happens when the word already ends in an "s" because it's plural? The solution here is to form the plural first (singular "dog," "child"; plural, "dogs," "children"). Then form the possessive. If there's already an "s," add only an apostrophe ("the dogs' tails"), if there's no "s," add apostrophe plus "s" ("the children's school").

ASSIGNMENTS

1. Read Mina Shaughnessy's introduction to her book *Errors and Expectations*, then do one of the following things:
   A. Summarize Shaughnessy's essay, then evaluate its effectiveness. How does she attempt to try to win you over to her point of view? What kind of evidence does she present? What IS her point of view?

B. Imagine this situation: The National Writing Center Association is publishing an anthology aimed at undergraduates preparing to become writing consultants. The association has enough money to include twenty-five essays. As a stellar consultant, you have been appointed advisor to the editorial board, and your job is to read Shaughnessy's essay and recommend whether to include it in the anthology.

Write a report in a suitable format, presenting and justifying your recommendation. In what ways is Shaughnessy's text relevant to writing center consultants? Is it relevant enough to put it into the top twenty-five articles? What factors argue for or against including it? Keep in mind your audience. What does the editorial board expect of you as an advisor? What do they expect of your report? What are their needs as readers?

If you prefer, select another reading and argue for or against its inclusion in the anthology.

2. Read the following paragraph, which is part of a draft describing a car accident. You may see many ways in which the paragraph could be improved, but let's assume the writer just wants to correct surface errors. Spontaneously role-play with a partner, or write a dialogue showing how you would work with the writer to correct surface errors. If you a write a dialogue, also write a brief rationale of the strategies you employed.

> Nothing happened to the very first car it left without a scratch on it, fortunately. My car and the car that I hit had extensive damage. As the two of our cars collided my hood began to compact as did the rear of his car. His license plate was readable in my bumper because of such force that our cars collided at. My sister was in the passenger seat neither one of us were wearing seatbelts. My sister was thrown from her seat into the windshield, nothing happened to me. As her head came in contact with the windshield the glass shattered and she fell to the floor unconscious. When the commotion finally came to a halt, I got out of my car and went to the nearest phone called the police and then tried to contact my parents. I was unable to reach them, I began to panic.

3. Select a surface feature you don't understand thoroughly. Read about it in a handbook, then write a dialogue in which a consultant assists a writer having problems with this surface feature. Don't forget that the consultant shouldn't sound like the handbook!

4. Check your journal for consulting sessions dealing with surface errors. Write another journal entry reconsidering the session in view of material in this chapter. After reading the chapter, do you have new ideas for how the session might have been handled? Share your original entry and your new thoughts with the group.

FOOTNOTES

[1]This chapter expands on Step #8 of "Priorities in Reading a Draft."

[2]For instance, erratic punctuation makes it hard to count the people in this sentence (and this household): "My husband and I have employed three wonderful young women over the last four years to care for our two toddler boys, a German au pair and two board-certified British nannies."

[3]However, the present tense is becoming so common in contemporary fiction that Lynne Sharon Schwartz says it "has gone beyond stylish to positively *de rigueur*" (232).

[4]Roger Sale explains, "We do not say, '*The Sound and the Fury* was' because it was, is, and will be, and like every other book it 'is' every time someone starts reading it" (166).

[5]A time line sometimes makes the sequence more concrete. Draw a line with an arrow at one end to indicate the direction in which time is moving; have the writer put X's on the line to indicate when the opening, the reading, and the selecting occurred.

[6]To be syntactically complete, a sentence must have all the requisite parts: subject, verb, and a clause with no subordinating word. However, these parts don't automatically make it semantically complete, because it may still not express a complete thought. For instance, "I had a lot on my mind" is syntactically complete, but some readers might judge it semantically incomplete because it doesn't explain what the writer had on her mind.

Chapter 8

Editing, Proofreading, Preparing a Polished Draft

I usually write to a point where the work is getting worse rather than better. That's the point to stop and the time to publish.
—John Dos Passos

This chapter describes the final steps in readying a text for its reader: editing, proofreading, and preparing a polished draft.[1] Editing encompasses the choices that go beyond correctness, adding personality and individuality—in essence, style—to a text. The choices call for fine-tuning, finding exactly the right word, the right sentence structure, the right balance of predictability and variety. For many writers, editing is the fun part. As Henry Miller explains, "I write a thing any old way, and then, after it's cooled off...I set at it with a fresh eye. Then I have a wonderful time of it. I just go to work on it with the ax" (170).[2]

Why Edit Last?

Writing handbooks usually recommend editing for style before correcting errors. But when discussing a draft with its author—as opposed to composing a draft of your own—correcting before editing makes sense for several reasons. One reason is purely pragmatic: it's extremely important to produce an error-free draft—probably more important than crafting a graceful, elegantly written draft. The ideal, of course, is a draft that is both correct *and* elegant, but since errors probably have more serious consequences than a lackluster style, it is prudent to deal with the errors first. Editing after correcting also makes sense from a procedural point of view: if new errors arise during editing, they will probably resemble the ones you've already discussed, and will be that much easier to deal with.

Finally, there's a psychological reason to postpone editing: it's very hard work. Once a writer has labored to get each word in a sentence precisely right, she will be understandably reluctant to decide it doesn't belong in the essay at all, or must be moved and then re-edited in its new position.

Editing is a little like juggling, since both require keeping several things going at once. Nonetheless, you needn't be an octopus to help a writer edit effectively. Aspects of style are so intertwined that a single change can effect several kinds of improvement at once. For instance, combining two choppy sentences will clarify connections, add sentence variety, and reduce wordiness. The most important aspects of style to attend to during editing are sentence-level and word-level sense, variety, conciseness, and gender-neutrality. Pick and choose among them, depending on the draft you're reading.

Sentence-Level Sense

A principle of functionalist architecture is that form follows function: a barn should look like a shelter for animals and crops, not like a temple. Form follows function in writing too, with the complexity of a sentence matching the complexity of its contents. For instance, in William Faulkner's "Barn Burning," a convoluted sentence conveys a young boy's tangled sensations, emotions, and impressions as his father is tried for arson.

> The store in which the Justice of the Peace's court was sitting smelled of cheese. The boy, crouched on his nail keg at the back of the crowded room, knew he smelled cheese, and more: from where he sat he could see the ranked shelves close-packed with the solid, squat, dynamic shapes of tin cans whose labels his stomach read, not from the lettering which meant nothing to his mind but from the scarlet devils and the silver curve of fish—this, the cheese which he knew he smelled and the hermetic meat which his intestines believed he smelled coming in intermittent gusts momentary and brief between the other constant one, the smell and sense just a little of fear because mostly of despair and grief, the old fierce pull of blood. He could not see the table where the Justice sat and before which his father and his father's enemy (our enemy he thought in that despair; ourn! Mine and hisn both! He's my father) stood, but he could hear them, the two of them that is, because his father had said no word yet:
> "But what proof have you, Mr. Harris?" (499)

This long, mind-bending sentence perfectly suits its content. Breaking it up into more conventionally organized sentences would destroy the contradictory, all-at-once quality of the boy's experience.

When unsuitable sentence structure keeps you from understanding what a writer means, ask her to read the draft aloud.[3] Any sentence she stumbles over is likely to make a reader stumble too. Stop and talk about these sentences, as well as those you found unclear as you listened. Explain what is difficult about the sentence for you, and if the writer is unable to solve your difficulty, ask one or more of the following questions.

- "Can you think of another way to say what this sentence means? What would happen if you wrote the sentence the way you just explained it?"
- "Is the sentence too complicated to convey your meaning effectively? How can it be simplified?"

- "Is the sentence too simple to convey your meaning? What does the sentence leave out that is essential to your meaning? How can you add what's missing?"
- "Would the meaning be clearer if you connected this sentence to another one? How might you connect them?"

Sentence-Level Variety

Most writers have a preferred sentence format they automatically fall into when they're concentrating on something else. This is an efficient method for producing an early draft, because like any other "default mode," it kicks in automatically, freeing the mind for more pressing matters. However, varied sentence structure is an important aspect of style. Too many long, elaborate sentences exhaust a reader's patience—even Faulkner begins with a short, brisk sentence. A string of short, simple sentences quickly becomes choppy and boring. If varied sentence structure is not part of a writer's composing process, help him add variety during editing.

Reading aloud is the simplest way to detect lack of variety—the sentences will sound repetitious in rhythm, vocabulary, and form. As a writer edits to improve sense, she may also achieve sentence variety as a by-product of the clearer connections and explanations she adds. If this doesn't happen, locate a passage with varied sentence structure, and point out how much more interesting it sounds than the unvaried passage. If all the sentences are short and simple, ask the writer to find connections between ideas. If the sentences are long and elaborate, ask her to find places where the ideas can be separated.

Here are some questions to help a writer achieve sentence variety:

- "Is one of these ideas less important than the other or are they equally important?"
- "How could you show that they are equally important?" (suggests the use of coordinating words like "and," "but," "so")
- "How could you show that one is less important?" (suggests the use of subordinating terms like "after," "although," "because," "since," "though," "unless," "until," when," "while"; also suggests the possibility of embedding additional information in a sentence, using terms like "that," "which," "whom")

Like sentence fragments intentionally used for dramatic effect, repetitious sentence structure can have a powerful impact when it's done with care. Charles Dickens' opening to *A Tale of Two Cities* is a familiar example.

> It was the best of times, it was the worst of times, it was the age of wisdom, it was the age of foolishness, it was the epoch of belief, it was the epoch of incredulity, it was the season of Light, it was the season of Darkness, it was the spring of hope, it was the winter of despair, we had everything before us, we had nothing before us, we were all going directly to Heaven, we were all going directly the other way.... (1).

Ask a writer who consciously uses repetition what her goals are. Then, re-read the passage in a receptive spirit, and see if the repetition has the desired effect. If it doesn't work for you, explain why not, as objectively and clearly as possible. Don't argue or try to get the writer to change her mind; remember, the draft is her property, not yours. If she uses the repetition strategy several times, point out which ones work for you and which don't. Maybe the novelty wears off after the first time, or maybe the writer carefully considered her initial decision and then became less discriminating as she went on.

Word-Level Variety

Repetitious sentence structure is often exacerbated by monotonous vocabulary, as in this paragraph:

> **I became aware** that I could contribute to the world. I broke out of the cocoon in which I had spent my childhood. **I became** more outgoing and comfortable expressing my own opinions. **I was determined** not to return to the shell that had enclosed me for eight years. **I was aware** for the first time that I had a voice in this world, and at that moment, **I became determined** to use it.

Every sentence begins with "I," every sentence except the last one is approximately the same length, and several words ("became," "aware," "determined") are frequently repeated. The interesting image of the cocoon, which is maintained over two sentences, is blurred by the generic vocabulary in the rest of the passage.

If reading aloud does not help a writer identify repetitious vocabulary, point out examples and explain how they affect you. Don't suggest changes yourself, but act as a sounding board for the changes she comes up with. The obvious one-stop-shopping spot for expanded vocabulary is a thesaurus, but this resource should be used with caution. Its format, in which a word is followed by its so-called synonyms, puts an invisible equal sign between the words and suggests they are interchangeable. This equation ignores subtle but crucial differences in nuance, connotation, and degree of formality.[4] A writer achieves effective diction (word choice) by choosing carefully from the words he knows through reading, writing, and listening. Vocabulary building by means of a thesaurus is like studying the *Cliff Notes* instead of the work itself.

Conciseness

Sometimes a writer resorts to wordiness because she is trying to write a paper of a specified length ("Write a ten-page essay on an ecological issue that interests you") before she has generated enough ideas and information. Wordiness can also result from an author's attempt to "dress up" ideas she suspects are too simple or obvious. In some cases, wordiness is an intermediate stage in the composing process, a way of moving beyond the difficulty of getting started.

Pick your consulting strategy to fit the kind of wordiness you are dealing with. If thin development is the cause, treat it as a development problem, using strategies described in chapter 7. If the writer is insecure about the quality of his ideas, examine the ideas more carefully. If they don't hold up under scrutiny, work on focus, organization, or development, using chapters 6 or 7. If the ideas are solid, reassure the writer, then point to passages where wordiness bogs the essay down. This procedure also works well if wordiness is a vestigial remnant of the writer's composing process.

Questions to ask when editing for conciseness include the following:

- "Are there any empty words in this passage? If you were paying $25 a word, which ones would you cut?"
- "Is there a simpler, more concise way to state this?"
- "What difference would it make if it were stated more simply and concisely?"
- "Would anything essential be lost if it were stated more simply and concisely?"

Conciseness is not an absolute good, and the briefest version of a sentence is not always the best. Consider the sentence, "In Paulo Freire's essay, 'The Banking Concept of Education,' Freire contrasts two kinds of teaching." "Paulo Freire contrasts two kinds of teaching" is extremely concise. But the writer may feel that something important is lost in this version, because Freire's title is the focus of his own analysis, so he wants the reader to be familiar with it in advance. For this writer, the most concise version that does not omit essential information might be "In 'The Banking Concept of Education,' Paulo Freire contrasts two kinds of teaching."

Gender-Neutral Language

One final area to call a writer's attention to during editing is gender-neutral language, that is, language that treats both genders the same way rather than privileging one over the other. Gender-neutral language establishes the writer's credentials as a fair person and demonstrates that he uses language carefully. Here are some aspects of gender-neutral language to keep in mind.

Gender-Neutral Pronouns

The most unavoidable gender issue in English is pronouns, specifically the third person singular pronoun referring to an unknown or unspecified person. Until recently, one used "he," with the understanding that "he" in this sense referred to either a male or a female. This usage, with this understanding attached, is called the common gender pronoun. However, research in the 1970s revealed that readers did not interpret the common gender pronoun as referring to either a male or a female; for most readers, the pronoun suggested a male (Martyna). So the sentence "Every student needs his own study space" can be seen as reinforcing the sexist stereotype that the average student is male, and that a female student is an aberration.

There are a number of alternatives to the common gender pronoun. Here are some of them:

- Use both male and female pronouns: "Every student needs his or her study space" or "her or his study space."
- Make the sentence plural: "All students need their own study space." Pluralizing doesn't work very well here, since the point is that the *individual* needs space.
- Omit the pronoun completely: "Every student needs individual study space."
- Alternate between male and female pronouns. In this book, I alternate between male and female pronouns, usually shifting for each paragraph.

Gender-Neutral Professional Labels

Terms like "woman doctor" and "male nurse" perpetuate gender stereotypes by implying that it's the norm (and hence, more "natural") for a one gender to assume this profession. Choose gender-free terms when possible ("flight attendant," rather than "steward/stewardess," "mail carrier" rather than "mailman"). It's not always easy to find gender-free alternatives to long-standing terms with a sexist bias. For instance, all the alternatives to "chairman" have limitations: "chairperson" is awkward, "chair" could refer to a piece of furniture, and "director" may not accurately describe the duties associated with the position.

Parallel Treatment of Men and Women. Include the same information when describing men and women—for instance, don't give a man's educational background but a woman's marital status. Use their names in the same way too: "Austen and Fielding," or "Jane Austen and Henry Fielding," not "Jane Austen and Fielding."[5]

Avoiding Sexist Assumptions and Demeaning Stereotypes. "Vice presidents and their wives are invited to the reception" is based on a sexist assumption—unless it refers to a company in which all the vice-presidents are in fact men—because it assumes that the norm is male vice-presidents. "Ask your mother to bake cookies for the party" assumes that women do the baking in every family, and that mothers bake cookies rather than buying them on their way home from work. Casual cliches like "Isn't that just like a man!" "Women—who can understand them!" "Women drivers," and "You pitch like a girl" are based on demeaning gender stereotypes.

When a writer's language is not gender neutral, point out several examples and help the writer consider alternatives if she wants to make changes. Don't conduct a consciousness-raising session or try to make the writer "see the light." Discuss gender-neutral language as an aspect of audience awareness, and expand the discussion to include language that stereotypes or demeans on the basis of race, ethnicity, class, appearance, etc.

Preparing the Polished Draft

The term "surface error" is useful for the reasons explained in chapter 7. In addition, it complements the term "polished draft," since a surface free from obstacles or bumps might well be described as "polished." When helping a writer check his polished draft, be attentive to the following things:

Manuscript Specifications

Ask the writer if she has been given specifications as part of the assignment or part of her coursework. If not, consult a writing handbook for guidance on issues such as heading, title, numbering pages, format, margins, and spacing.

Polished Draft Etiquette

These user-friendly features are gestures of common courtesy towards a reader:

- Number the pages
- Double space and leave generous margins, for ease in reading and commenting
- Make sure the type is dark enough to read without strain
- Remove the leader holes from computer paper and tear the sheets apart rather than leaving them connected
- Attach the pages to each other, using a paperclip, staple, folder, or binder. Some teachers have strong preferences in this area, but in the absence of instructions, make a common-sense decision (folder or binder for a longer paper, staple or paperclip for a short one). Don't hand in loose pages or pages crimped together by means of folded corners.

Proofreading

This is a final opportunity to catch and correct errors, not the time to edit a sentence or add new material in the margins. As a consultant, limit yourself to pointing out errors, not fixing them. Printing a corrected copy of a word-processed text is so easy that there is no excuse for submitting a hand-corrected draft, but if reprinting is not possible, neat, hand-written corrections are preferable to unmarked errors.

ROBOTMAN® by Jim Meddick

A Note on Spelling

When you notice spelling errors while proofreading, ask the writer if she has used the spellchecker on her computer. If she hasn't, suggest that she do so, or even better, log on and do it together as part of the session. Writers sometimes think that a spellchecker is a substitute for proofreading and will find and fix all their misspellings. This is decidedly not so.[6] Spellcheckers with limited dictionaries don't encompass complex, technical, or specialized vocabulary. Most programs don't check words that are in a language other than English. Few of the current generation of spellchecker address the following problems:

- Misspelled proper names
- Incorrect choice between homonyms (words that sound the same but are spelled differently): "He is **two** serious."
- Typing error that results in a properly spelled word :"That is **them** question."

ASSIGNMENTS

1. Read Richard Lanham's "Who's Kicking Who?" then do one of the following things:
   A. Evaluate Lanham's description of student writing. Is it out of date, or are today's students writing like the students he described in 1987?
   B. Find an example of bloated writing and compute its lard factor. Does your experience support Lanham's point that the lard factor often conceals fuzzy meaning? How would you re-write the passage to trim the lard and sharpen the meaning?
   C. Are there some situations in which what looks like bloated writing is actually the best way to express an idea? If so, provide an example and explain how all the words are necessary.

    D. Lanham suggests that students write like this because teachers encourage them to. Do you agree? Support your opinion with evidence from your own experience.

    E. Analyze the tone of Lanham's essay. What kind of relationship does he establish with his reader? What factors contribute to this relationship? Why does the title contain a grammatical error? How were you affected by the comment about physical satisfaction and premarital sex?

2. Read Kathleen Higgins' "A Little Trip to the Writing Center," then do one of the following things:
    A. Using Higgins' essay as a model, compose a text in which your writing speaks up and describes what it is like to be edited or otherwise changed.
    B. Write a dialogue in which you help Higgins edit her essay.
    C. Analyze the effectiveness of Higgins' metaphor of a text as a family. What works in the metaphor? What doesn't?

3. Write a dialogue in which you help the writer of the contact lens essay (p. 41) or the summer job essay (p. 35) edit for style.

4. The essays by Nancy Sommers and by Linda Flower and John R. Hayes assume that metaphors direct and limit our thinking process, and that picking the wrong metaphor can handicap our ability to think effectively.
    A. Compare their essays on this level: do both essays persuade you that the metaphor under discussion is counterproductive? If not, why are you not persuaded?
    B. Describe and analyze a metaphor you find counterproductive or limiting. It can be a metaphor for writing, but it doesn't have to be.

5. Survey textbooks in other classes for their policy on gender-neutral language, then report on your findings. Are some disciplines more concerned with gender-neutral language than others? Does the gender of the author affect these decisions? What other factors go into such decisions?

6. For fun, write a dialogue in which you attempt to talk Faulkner or Proulx (p. 52) out of their unconventional styles.

7. Check your journal for consulting sessions involving editing or other subjects discussed in this chapter. Based on your experience, do you have advice to add to the material in this chapter? Share your original entry and your new thoughts with the group.

FOOTNOTES

[1]This chapter expands on Steps #9 and #10 of "Priorities in Reading a Draft."

[2]However, other writers dread editing. Virginia Woolf draws a clear distinction between writing, which gives her pleasure, and "the repulsiveness of correcting that nauseates me" (166). It's clear from the rest of the passage that she means editing, not correcting surface error.

[3]Many writers begin at the end of the text and edit backwards, reading the last sentence first. Inverting the order helps them evaluate each sentence individually, rather than being distracted by the momentum of the essay as a whole.

[4]*Roget's Thesaurus* offers "heavens" and "firmament" as synonyms for "sky," but a sentence like "There's not a cloud in the sky" would be significantly altered by either of these substitutions.

[5]Parallel treatment is the rationale behind the title "Ms." Before this term was coined, the social titles for women, "Miss" or "Mrs.," revealed their marital status, whereas the social title for men, "Mr.," does not. This discrepancy suggests that a woman's marital status is essential to her identity, whereas a man's marital status is not.

[6]One of Ann Landers' correspondents volunteered the following illustration of her spellchecker's limitations:

> I have a spelling checker, it came with my PC.
> It plainly marks four my revue mistakes I cannot sea.
> I've run this poem threw it, I'm sure your pleased too no,
> Its letter perfect in it's weigh, my checker tolled me sew.

Chapter 9

Working with Teachers' Comments

Mysterious abbreviations in the margins, cryptic comments between the lines, paragraphs on the final page—transforming this welter of professorial feedback into a blueprint for better writing is the aspect of consulting we will consider here. As a consultant, you can help a writer realize that this kind of feedback is a benefit rather than a threat. Then you can work with her to extract as much information from the comments as possible, using the information to improve the final product.

Types of Commenting Policies

Some teachers require submission of a working draft so students won't postpone writing until the night before the polished draft is due. Both writer and reader can concentrate on a working draft without the distraction or discouragement of a grade. Some teachers make working drafts optional, providing written comments or responding to them orally during conferences.

Some teachers make comments on the polished draft and permit revisions, perhaps advising or requiring revisions of drafts that receive a low grade. Others make comments on the polished draft but do not allow revisions, reasoning that the writer will put the comments into practice when she writes her next assignment.

Some teachers require correction of surface errors, while others make corrections themselves, believing that after seeing the corrections, the writer will avoid these errors on the next assignment.

The type of policy a teacher adopts depends on her reasons for providing feedback. Teachers assume the labor-intensive task of responding to student drafts because they want to achieve one or more of the following goals:

- To meet institutional or departmental requirements that faculty respond to writing in addition to grading it
- To assist the student in completing the assignment successfully
- To make the polished draft more enjoyable to read

- To encourage the production of multiple drafts
- To remind students to keep the audience in mind
- To give the writer practice in responding to feedback
- To model useful, constructive feedback
- To clean up the paper and fix the mistakes
- To demonstrate the correct form, so the student will get it right the next time
- To justify or explain the grade
- To help the student understand the course material, the criteria being applied, or the type of writing the assignment represents
- To encourage revision, even after evaluation, so that the draft's (and the writer's) potential is more fully realized.

Student Problems with Teachers' Comments

Intermediate feedback from a final reader is very helpful when assessing what is working in a draft and what still remains to be done. But for a variety of reasons, teachers' comments—no matter how constructive and sensitively phrased—often appear daunting rather than enabling to student writers.

First, insecurity or emotional issues may interfere with a writer's ability to interpret comments objectively. A teacher may comment encouragingly about an area he finds exciting and full of potential ("I never thought of that interpretation—what examples support it?"), but the student may see the comment as indicative of deficiency in his writing or even his thinking ("If he never thought of it, I must be wrong, no matter how many examples I can provide"). Because writing is so closely connected to feelings and thoughts, it is easy to take criticism of one's work as criticism of oneself. The comment, "This is an interesting idea, but it requires more analysis" might be interpreted as, "I'm a hopeless case—I can't even analyze my own ideas."

Writers sometimes have cognitive problems with teachers' comments as well. The writer may not understand what the teacher's comments mean. Perhaps the comments are general rather than specific ("Your paper is still undeveloped"). Perhaps they are couched in technical or specialized language the writer is unfamiliar with ("Your hypothesis is not verifiable"). Perhaps they are ambiguous ("Example?" could mean "Is this a good example?" or "Are you presenting this as an example?" or "Where is the example?" or "Can you provide an example of this point?").

Finally, writers sometimes have procedural problems with teachers' comments. They may understand the comments but not know how to implement them. In particular, they may not know where to start. Figuring out what comes first is especially difficult when some comments point out surface errors and editing problems, and others identify problems with assignment requirements, focus, organization, or development.

Emotional problems may evaporate as the writer gets to work and begins to feel she is in control. In the meantime, empathize and acknowledge that you've had similar feelings and experiences. Sometimes a writer's introductory remarks about her feelings provide a good transition to the working session:

Writer: I worked really hard on this paper, but my grade was the same as on the last one, and I wrote that in an hour. I feel like a jerk, like I wasted my time, and my teacher hardly commented at all.

Consultant: Well, let's take a look at what she did write. Maybe this was a harder assignment, and if you hadn't put in more work, your grade would've dropped.

Once you move to reading the comments, mention positive points the writer may have overlooked or underestimated. Don't let negative misinterpretations go unchallenged:

Writer: My teacher's corrections are almost as long as my paper. I must have made a million mistakes.

Consultant: But he starts out by saying your interpretation is one of the most thoughtful he's ever come across. And then he makes three concrete suggestions for strengthening your argument. Have you decided if you want to write another draft?

Helping a Writer Work with Teachers' Comments

Although working with a draft-plus-comments can feel like reading two papers at once, your first step is the same as in any other consulting situation: find out what the writer wants to accomplish. He may want to analyze the comments so he can do better on the next assignment. He may want to revise the paper and improve his grade. Maybe he hasn't decided what to do, and wants to discuss the alternatives. Obviously, each of these goals dictates a different kind of conversation.

After finding out what the writer's goals are, look together at the draft, the teacher's comments, and the assignment. Depending on the goals and the comments, here are some ways to facilitate the writer's job.

Help Interpret the Comments

As you work through the comments, encourage the writer to explain what they mean. If she doesn't understand them or is unable to explain them, look at the assignment for possible explanations. If the comment uses writing terms you think you understand, explain them in your own words. For instance, if the teacher points out that the essay does not have a thesis statement and the writer does not know what a thesis statement is, introduce her to the "This essay shows that..." formula. Then search the draft for possible thesis statements, using strategies from in chapter 5. If the comments refer to course material the writer does not understand, class or lecture notes may provide enlightenment. If none of these leads pans out and you are unable to figure out what a particular comment means, suggest that the writer ask the teacher about it.

Apply General Comments to Specific Passages

Perhaps the writer understands a comment but doesn't see how it applies to his writing. For instance, the teacher may have commented that the paper is not adequately developed, and the writer may counter that he has provided all the support he can think of. If the teacher has mentioned or marked particular sections of the paper as undeveloped, turn to those sections and ask questions that encourage elaboration ("What made you come to this decision? Reach this interpretation? Make this generalization?"). If individual passages are not marked, read through the draft together, letting the writer explain how he supports each point, and keeping an eye out for points he skips or does not support thoroughly.

Point Out Patterns

Because teacher comments are so varied and occur in so many places,[1] even a writer who is energized and motivated by them may have a hard time figuring out where to start. It doesn't necessarily make sense to start at the beginning, because the most general remarks may occur in the summary comments at the end of the paper. So the first step in figuring out how to proceed is to put the comments into some kind of order, sort them into categories, and deal with each category separately.

1. First distinguish between comments about the overall adequacy of the draft (these comments suggest revision), and comments about specific sections, passages, or words (these comments suggest editing or correcting).
2. Then match notations in the margin with similar comments at the end of the paper. The marginal notations provide examples of the end comments, and the end comments may clarify marginal notations that are extremely brief.
3. Group together all comments describing a particular problem (for instance, all the places in the draft where a transition is needed). If a teacher points out that overall organization is unclear, individual paragraphs are not connected to each other, and many sentences are short and choppy, all three comments are calling for more careful connections between parts.

Set Priorities and Select a Plan of Action

Once the comments have been sorted, setting priorities becomes much easier. For instance, the first sorting method (revision vs. editing) suggests that revision should come before editing. When revising, search the teacher's comments for ideas about possible changes, plugging in relevant questions and procedures from chapters 4, 5, or 6. Then turn to editing and correcting, using the teacher's comments to locate and deal with errors and editing problems. Be sure to scrutinize the entire draft for errors—a teacher may mark only the first few examples of an error, holding the writer responsible for finding and fixing those that follow. New errors may also crop up during revision.

To build on the second sorting method (end comments linked to marginal comments), shuttle between an end comment and the marginal notations connected to it. Again, not all examples may be marked, so encourage the writer to read through the entire draft with a particular end comment in mind. If the teacher points out that paraphrased material has not been documented, the writer must find and document all paraphrased material, whether the teacher has marked it or not.

The third sorting method (group similar comments together) organizes material so that all examples of one particular problem can be discussed together, a process you are already familiar with from chapter 7.

Responding to a Response Draft

When a writer has already made changes in response to teacher comments, help her make sure the new draft is as effective as possible. If both drafts are available, together skim the early draft, then read the comments and the revised draft, having the writer point out changes and explain how they take the comments into account. Stop her whenever you don't understand the connection between the change and the comments, and discuss whether she wants to explain the connection, or whether there's a more effective way to respond to the comment. When you've finished the draft, turn to the comments, and make sure that the writer has dealt with each comment she wants to respond to. Of course, a writer is free to ignore a comment, but you should verify that this is a conscious decision rather than an oversight.

Even if it is undertaken in response to teacher comments, a successful revision is more than a series of reactions. Changes to one section affect the entire text, like ripples spreading across a pond when a pebble is dropped into it. So after looking at the draft and the comments as described above, evaluate the new draft for focus, organization, and development, returning to the strategies described in chapters 5 and 6. This is also the basic format to follow when a writer revises a polished draft for her own reasons and in the absence of teacher response.

ASSIGNMENTS

1. Read Lil Brannon and C. H. Knoblauch's essay, "On Students' Rights to Their Own Texts: A Model of Teacher Response." Then do one of the following things.

A. Write a dialogic notebook entry about the article and come to class prepared to discuss the two or three passages you found most interesting.

B. The writer described by Brannon and Knoblauch has found a way to make his assignment personally satisfying. Write about a time when you were able to do this. How did you make the assignment fulfilling and creative, at the same time that you met the teacher's specifications? What aspects of this experience might help other writers do the same thing? How can you use these ideas in your consulting?

C. Brannon and Knoblauch say that readers—especially teachers—are willing to grant professional writers final authority over their a text, working hard to understand it and assuming that if a rule is broken it is done intentionally and for a good reason. Bring in a brief passage from a published writer that you think a student writer would probably not get away with. Read the passage, then explain what the writer has done, why he has done it, and whether it works. What would a student writer be told if she produced a passage like this?

2. Read James Harrington's "In Defense of Thesis Statements," p. 223. After reading this chapter, what is your reaction to the session Harrington describes? Would you have proceeded differently? Discuss your opinion in class, write a memo or letter to Harrington responding to his essay and the session it describes, or write a dialogue in which you and Harrington analyze the consulting strategies he used and discuss possible options.

3. Re-read teacher comments you've received on your work, in this class or others. Considering these comments in light of this chapter, which seem prompted by a particular purpose or combination of purposes? Do some of the comments seem prompted by purposes that aren't on the list?

4. Put yourself in this situation: a friend of yours, who has decided he wants to be a college teacher, is taking an education theory class. For this week's assignment, he must formulate a policy for responding to student writing. Write a letter to your friend, describing your best or worst experience with teacher response to your writing[2] and making recommendations based on that experience. If you describe your worst experience, make your recommendations more constructive than, "Don't do what I had done to me." If it helps you make your point, incorporate material from this chapter, the Brannon-Knoblauch essay, or your experience in the writing center.

5. Check your journal for consulting sessions involving teacher comments. How do the details of the session connect to information in this chapter? After reading the chapter, what are your thoughts on the

strategies used in the session? Would you recommend doing things differently? Share your original entry and your new thoughts with the group.

FOOTNOTES

[1]Some teachers put comments in both margins, using one margin for surface and editing issues and the other for comments on focus, organization, and development.

[2]Interpret the word "response" as broadly as you like, to include conferences, grading policy, assignments, class discussion, etc.

Chapter 10

Specific Kinds of Writing

To begin reading with a pen in my hand, discovering, pouncing, thinking of phrases, when the ground is new, remains one of my great excitements.
—Virginia Woolf

Before you begin this chapter, take ten minutes to list all the writing you've done as part of your college coursework. Don't forget to include in-class writing, essay exams, journals, lab reports, and study questions.

When your ten minutes is up, you should have before you convincing proof that college writing comes in a dizzying assortment of shapes and sizes. A major challenge of consulting is to shape each session, not only to the needs of individual writers, but also to the wide-ranging requirements of different kinds of writing. Although this entire book attempts to provide guidelines flexible enough to be shaped to individual writing tasks, in this chapter we will focus specifically on particular types of writing and the consulting issues they raise.

Writing about Reading

Glance back at the list you've just made and you will see that the vast majority of writing tasks is connected to reading. You may be asked to summarize a reading to prove your comprehension of it; to analyze a reading, showing how it is put together; to evaluate it; to use it as a model for your own text; to compare it to another reading; or to apply its principles to a new situation.

ROBOTMAN® by Jim Meddick

Before discussing the challenges of writing about reading, let's take a look at the reading-writing connection. It's often assumed that this connection is a sequential one: first you read, then you write. Another common assumption is that a writer is active, generating new material, whereas a reader is passive, receiving and "consuming" what the writer has created. Actually, both reading and writing demand highly active engagement, because they generate meaning and discovery as they go. And rather than occurring sequentially, they are recursive, one inspiring the other, one triggering the other, one looping back on the other again and again. Consider the following:

Reading Is Writing

Readers write *as* they read, taking notes, scribbling in the margins, keeping a reading log or dialogic notebook. But in addition, as readers proceed through a text, they unconsciously ask the same questions that the writer asks while composing. What is the focus? How is this connected to that? What evidence is there for this statement? What makes me doubt this statement? What is the effect of this word/sentence/paragraph? As readers recapitulate the writer's actions, they complete and interpret the text.

Writing Is Reading

The origin of a text often lies in another text: while reading, the reader is moved to write. As the author generates text, she constantly reads and re-reads what she's written, gathering momentum from the words on the page. In her capacity as writer, she also puts herself in the reader's place, attempting to gauge the effect of her text.

Although reading and writing are intimately connected, a writer wishing to integrate other texts into his own draft must balance two activities that pull in opposite directions: he must distinguish the various texts from each other, but he must also blend them into a harmonious whole. The desired result is like a fabric in which individual threads remain distinct but form a coherent overall pattern.

As a consultant, you can help a writer achieve this tricky balance between distinguishing and blending by asking questions like these:

1. *Is there enough background information?* The draft[1] should be free-standing, so that the reader does not have to consult other texts in order to understand it. If the assignment specifies a reader familiar with the text, less explanation is necessary than if it specifies one unfamiliar with the text. For the latter kind of assignment, you will probably have the advantage of being a member of the target audience. Point out passages you don't understand, and as the writer explains them to you, she will generate additional background information to include in her draft.

2. *Are the attributions clear and careful?* Using the draft as your only guide, can you identify the writer's sources and locate the passages or information he discusses? If not, explain where you would get stuck or what information you are missing.

3. *Are the voices clearly labeled?* Can you tell where statements, opinions, and quotes in the draft come from and who they belong to? Is it clear when the writer is presenting her opinion or interpretation, and when she is re-stating someone else's?

   Point out places where you're not sure whose voice you hear. Frequent tags such as, "Bruffee explains ," "According to Trimbur," "Shaughnessy supports her point by..." "Broadwell disagrees, pointing out..." help sort out the voices. When the writer shifts to her own ideas or reactions, that requires a label as well, such as, "A recent session made me question Sommers' description of student writers."[2] Besides keeping the voices distinct, labels provide smooth transitions from one point to another.

4. *Are the voices clearly distinguished?* Be alert for passages written in an elaborate or sophisticated style that differs significantly from the style of the paper in general. These passages may have been inadvertently copied from the source. Point out a problematic passage, explaining that it sounds different from the rest of the paper; then ask the writer to try to recall whether he made up the wording or transcribed it. If he has brought his notes, an early draft, or the text, he can re-trace his steps rather than guessing. Most attribution errors are due to misunderstanding or oversight (for instance, copying the text word for word while taking notes, then forgetting to paraphrase or use quotation marks).

   If the passage is a quote, help the writer decide whether to preserve the exact words of the source or paraphrase them. If he decides to keep the language of the source, remind him to use quotation marks and recheck the text to guarantee accuracy. If he decides to paraphrase, remind him that the material must still be documented.

5. *Is there a good reason for each quote?* Early drafts are often top-heavy with quotes and skimpy on analysis and interpretation. Writers over-quote because they are in awe of their source, because they aren't sure they understand the material, because they want to avoid plagiarism, or because they are uncertain about how and when to paraphrase.

   Whatever the reason for over-quoting, the results are unfortunate. To go back to our textile analogy, a draft stuffed with too many quotes is like a crazy quilt awkwardly stitched together, rather than a fabric with an integrated design. Over-quoting obscures a writer's focus, threatens organization, and leaves little room for development. Long quotes are particularly disruptive, severely testing the reader's concentration and the writer's organizing skills. Over-quoting also dilutes the impact of material that deserves to be quoted.

How much quoting is too much? To some extent, the answer to this question varies with the context. A literary analysis may require many quotes, since its focus is the language itself, whereas a review of scientific literature may use no quotes at all, since it aims to convey the gist of the readings rather than specific language.

To help a writer avoid over-quoting, go through the draft together and let her explain her reasons for quoting a particular passage. Some solid reasons for quoting rather than paraphrasing include the following:

- Because the language is the object of investigation, for instance in the analysis of a poem or other literary work.
- Because the statement is controversial, and the writer wishes to show that the ideas have not been exaggerated or misrepresented
- Because the statement is extreme or objectionable, and the writer wishes to divorce her opinion from the source's opinion.
- Because the quote is central to the writer's argument.
- Because the language itself (rather than the idea) is remarkable or noteworthy.
- Because there is no other way to express precisely the same idea.

When a writer persuasively justifies a quote, continue through the draft, looking for quotes that might be paraphrased without loss of meaning or impact.

If the writer is over-quoting because he doesn't understand the source, encourage him to talk out his difficulties, re-read the material he doesn't understand, or schedule a conference to discuss the material with his instructor. If the writer is worried about plagiarism or uncertain about how to paraphrase, work together on a quote he wants to put into his own words. Explain that the paraphrase must differ significantly from the original in both vocabulary and sentence structure, and that a paraphrase, because it represents someone else's ideas, must be documented.

It may also be useful to work together trimming a long quote. The writer can decide what part of the quote is essential for her purposes, then paraphrase the non-essentials—or even eliminate them provided the meaning is not changed. See Assignment 4 for practice in quoting, paraphrasing, and attribution.

6. *Is there a clear connection between the voices?* Writers learning to incorporate texts into their drafts often have difficulty synthesizing. Early drafts may resemble club sandwiches, with alternating layers of source material and original material, but no interaction between the two. In a well-synthesized draft, the relationship between a writer's draft and her sources is symbiotic: the sources help the writer make

her point more forcefully, and the writer's point casts new light on the sources.

To help a writer synthesize material more effectively, point out passages where the connection between the writer's draft and his sources is not clear to you. Perhaps the material from the source is irrelevant and can be cut. If the writer feels the material is relevant, help him decide how to make the connection clearer: through transitional phrases, sentences, or paragraphs; stronger organization; or additional supporting detail. The section of chapter 6 dealing with organization may be helpful.

Besides being clearly connected to the writer's ideas, source material must be grammatically integrated into her sentence structure. Here is a quote which isn't integrated into the writer's sentence: "Lutz defines doublespeak as, 'Doublespeak is a blanket term for language which pretends to communicate but doesn't.'" When you notice problems with grammatical integration, treat them as an aspect of editing, after you've discussed the larger issues of focus, organization, and development.

Helping Writers with Research Papers

Like other assignments, a research paper needs a clear, interesting focus; solid organization; adequate development; an error-free surface, and a suitable style.

Focusing a research paper is particularly challenging. Gathering and interpreting sources may absorb so much time and energy that the writer neglects to establish a point of her own to hold it all together. In the absence of such a point, the research paper becomes a pointless exercise, the kind Ambrose Bierce describes as "moving tombstones from one graveyard to another." Use the strategies in chapter 5 to help a writer develop a focus.

Organizing a research paper is challenging because of the large amounts of material and the differing points of view involved. Each source has its own method of organization, which the writer must master to gather the material he needs. But then the material must be rearranged to fit into the writer's text and relate coherently to the other sources. Use the strategies in chapter 6 to help a writer with problems of organization.

What obviously distinguishes research papers from other kinds of writing is that rather than working with texts that have been provided, the writer has to go out and get them. This academic hunting and gathering involves many skills: identifying a promising area of investigation, discovering what's been written on a subject, figuring out which sources relate to the topic, actually laying hands on them, and interpreting them without benefit of class discussion.

As a consultant, don't try to pass yourself off as an expert on research methods. Teachers refer their students to reference librarians for up-to-date research procedures, and so should you. Technology is changing so rapidly in this area that staying on the cutting edge has become a specialty of its own.

Documentation De-Mystified

Besides research technique itself, the largest source of anxiety about research is documentation. You would never guess it from looking at book-length guidelines, but the rationale for documentation is simple: it lays the trail for a reader to follow if he wishes to consult a writer's sources. Documentation permits collaboration between readers and writers past and present. It is fueled by the optimistic belief that knowledge is progressive: that a writer, standing on the shoulders of those who have preceded her, can see further than if she were standing only on her own two feet. What a writer gains from this model of knowledge-building is a piggy-back effect: discovering one good source unlocks the door to all its sources as well. The price a writer pays for this bonanza is that before he presents his own ideas, he must read what's already been written on the subject. Documentation is proof that he has met this requirement and earned the right to join the conversation.

Documentation consists of both in-text and end-of-text components, with in-text material keyed to the corresponding end-of-text entry. This is a neat arrangement: parenthetical in-text documentation barely disturbs the surface of the text, and complete information is presented only once, rather than being repeated, as footnoting frequently demanded.

When a writer asks for (or obviously needs) help with documentation, find out as much as you can about the procedure she's been following so far. Is she consulting guidelines, drawing on a dimly remembered high-school format, or just winging it? If she's following guidelines, were they assigned or did she select them herself? If she selected them, how did she make her choice? With the writer, check the assignment for documentation directions.

When the assignment doesn't specify a documentation format, help the writer choose one. The two most common formats, MLA and APA, are easy to use and appear in virtually any writing handbook. MLA (Modern Language Association) is widely used in the humanities (including literature, philosophy, religion, fine arts). APA (American Psychological Association) is used in education, geography, political science, psychology, and sociology, and closely resembles formats used in specific sciences. Once the writer has decided on a format, he can begin applying the guidelines to his draft.

Documentation guidelines list rules for documenting different kinds of sources, as well as examples of the rules in action. Encourage the writer to consult the guidelines constantly, marking, highlighting, paper-clipping, or annotating to make them as user-friendly as possible. If she hasn't begun documenting, find a passage in her draft that requires documentation, then watch and listen as she follows the guidelines to formulate the citation. If she's done some documentation already, turn to the first citation in the draft and ask her to explain how she formulated it, pointing out the section of the guidelines she used. In this way, you can determine what aspects of documentation the writer understands and where the problems are coming from. Some of the most common problems are the following:

1. *The writer is using an inappropriate example or rule.* Documenting a journal article according to the rule for documenting a book will omit important information about the article, such as the page numbers and volume number. When the writer is using the wrong rule or example, ask him what kind of source he is documenting; then have him search the guidelines for the applicable rule. If the guidelines don't include a rule for the precise kind of source he is working with, help him find the category that comes closest, then work together to adapt the format.
2. *The writer is misinterpreting an example.* Used alone, examples can be confusing or misleading. For instance, it's hard to tell whether "Ed." in a sample citation is a man's first name or indicates that the text has an editor. The only way to be sure is to consult the rule as well as the example. Rules and examples provide a useful double-check against each other.[3]
3. *The writer is not connecting in-text and end-of-text material.* Encourage the writer to write out both kinds of documentation at the same time, even though it may be tempting to postpone end-of-text documentation until the rest of the draft is complete. Doing both parts at once makes it easier to connect them correctly, and the writer is less likely to omit something from the end-of-text documentation.

Writing in the Disciplines

Sooner or later, every consultant finds himself in a situation which raises the question, "How can I help a writer when I know nothing about his topic?" There are two ways to deal with this challenge. One is the traditional academic route: arm yourself with knowledge, learning as much as possible and chipping away at the number of subjects you know nothing about. The rest of this chapter will help you in this quest, providing brief introductions to commonly encountered kinds of academic writing.

But this approach can take you only so far. No matter how hard you work and how smart you are, you can't possibly cover all branches of knowledge, even superficially. After all, majors learn about their discipline by taking many courses, and much of it they learn tacitly, in ways they aren't even aware of. If you are busy pursuing your own major, you won't be able to duplicate this immersion process.

The second approach is to master the art of working comfortably and constructively with material you're unfamiliar with. Many consultants feel that their ignorance of a writer's subject matter is an asset, not a handicap. They say that in such a situation, ownership of the paper remains firmly where it belongs—with the writer. Knowing more about his subject than the consultant gives the writer an area of expertise, even if he feels tentative about his writing skills. Being less informed than the writer is especially helpful when dealing with a poorly organized draft. An informed consultant attempting to read supportively may be supplying missing connections and interpretations without realizing it. But an uninformed consultant can work only with what the text already contains, so she will become confused by missing transitions or fuzzy organization, and will have to ask questions.

However, being familiar with the conventions and expectations of particular kinds of writing frees you to devote more time and attention to the writer's work. The rest of this chapter gives brief descriptions of common kinds of academic writing.[4] Read it for deep background, but remember that a teacher's directions and specifications, because they've been tailored to the course and the assignment, always take precedence over general guidelines.

Social Sciences

The social sciences include anthropology, economics,[5] education, political science, psychology, social work, and sociology. Technical vocabulary is part of social science writing style. Since some readers are interested in only one section of a text, each section is self-contained, with its own heading, introduction, and conclusion. In undergraduate courses, the most common social science assignment is the *case study*, which describes a problem and presents solutions or treatments. The sections of a case study are "statement of the problem, the background of the problem, the methods or processes of the solutions, the conclusions arrived at, and suggestions for improvement or future recommendations" (*Writing* 106).

Sciences

The purpose of most undergraduate writing in the sciences is to convey information rather than to persuade or interpret. Scientific style reflects the high priority placed on accuracy and objectivity in this area of study. Passive verbs ("The liquid *was measured*") are preferred over active verbs ("I *measured* the liquid") because the object of the experiment is more important than the experimenter. Third person nouns and pronouns, which convey objectivity, are preferred over first or second person pronouns, even when the writer has conducted the experiment herself.

Humanities

Unlike social science texts, which consist of self-contained parts separated by headings, humanities essays are unified and organized through transitions rather than headings. First person pronouns are acceptable when expressing an opinion or personal response, but otherwise third person pronouns are preferred. Present tense is preferred ("Berlioz fully *exploits* the orchestra's range of color and tone"), except when referring to a sequence of completed events, such as the history of a piece of music or the writing of a text ("Berlioz *confused and alienated* most of his contemporaries"). An author's full name is used the first time he is referred to, and his last name is used in subsequent references.

Some common types of writing for the humanities are listed below, in alphabetical order.

> *Annotated bibliography:* full citation for each source, followed by a summary and concise evaluation. Material in the summary should not be repeated in the evaluation.
>
> *Bibliographic essay:* survey of research in a particular field, including evaluation of individual entries and comparison of the entries in terms of their usefulness and limitations. Include citations in the discipline's preferred documentation format
>
> *Book review:* summary and personal evaluation of a book; include title, author, and publication information.
>
> *Concert review:* summary and personal evaluation of a performance; include date and location of performance, artist(s), representative pieces performed (including composers and dates if known). Place any of this material in cultural or historical context if it is relevant.[6]
>
> *Literary analysis:* analysis of some aspect of a work of literature such as narrator, point of view, plot, structure, character, theme, setting, imagery, symbolism. The most common problems in literary analysis papers are the following:
>
> > • *Unsupported interpretation.* The writer's interpretation must be supported with passages or details from the text. Although formal documentation is not necessary when only a single text is being discussed, the reader must be able to locate the supporting material easily, through the page numbers, line number in a poem, or act and scene number in a play. To help a reader support her interpretation, locate an unsupported assertion in the draft and ask what in the text supports her statement.
> >
> > • *Plot summary to no purpose.* Plot summary to no purpose is what you get when you ask a five-year-old to tell you about the movie he just saw. The summary lasts as long as the movie did— or at least it seems to—because the young narrator has no powers of selection. In literary analysis, information about the plot can be a persuasive way of supporting the writer's interpretation; however, runaway plot summary soon swamps a paper and obscures its focus. Glossing (chapter 6) is useful for identifying runaway plot summary—if a paragraph is doing nothing more than recounting a sequence of events, ask the writer what the paragraph has to do with the focus of the paper. She can then cull from the paragraph the details that support her point, re-writing to make the connection clear.
>
> *Philosophical analysis:* description and evaluation of a philosophical theory. The analysis should do the following:

- Distinguish the theory's assumptions from its conclusions
- Explain how the assumptions do or don't support the conclusions
- Follow the theory to its logical conclusions
- Evaluate objections to the theory as well as arguments in its favor[7]

Reaction paper: description and explanation of personal reaction to a work, usually written in the first person.

Visual art analysis: description and evaluation of a work of art, often including discussion of its historical, cultural, or aesthetic context. Provide the title of the work, artist (if known), medium, provenance, and museum accession number (if any). Describe size, material, and state of preservation. Include analysis of elements such as line, shape, color, and texture.[8]

ASSIGNMENTS

1. Read Jean Kiedaisch and Sue Dinitz's essay, "Look Back and Say 'So What?': The Limitations of the Generalist Tutor"; then do one of the following things:
   A. Write a dialogic notebook entry about the article and come to class prepared to discuss the two or three passages you found most interesting.
   B. Design a customer satisfaction questionnaire like the one Kiedaisch and Dinitz used for their research. Compare your questionnaire with those designed by other members of the group. What problems do you see with implementing a questionnaire like this?
   C. If your writing center has videotape capabilities, arrange to have one of your sessions videotaped, as Kiedaisch and Dinitz did. Was the session affected by your knowledge that it was being taped? When you watched the video for the first time, did it reveal anything that surprised you? Do you plan to make adjustments in your consulting as a result of viewing the video?
   D. Write an essay explaining your position on the effectiveness of the generalist tutor, drawing from this article, this chapter, and your own experience. Do David, Michelle, Jill, and Joanne offer useful lessons in what not to do? Can you turn these lessons into positive suggestions about consulting with writers across the disciplines?

2. Read Mike Pytlak's essay, "Seeing the Light," then do one of the following things:
   A. Evaluate Pytlak's essay as an illustration of consulting proficiency. What consulting principles does he apply? Does he overlook or violate any? Would you have handled the session differently? Using this book as your source, document the principles you discuss.

Follow either MLA or APA guidelines and be sure to include both in-text and end-of-text components. Be prepared to explain why you chose MLA or APA.

B. Write a dialogue in which Mike, Melissa, and Crystal enact the session described in the essay.

C. Using essay or letter format, evaluate Pytlak's essay as a text. His assignment was to recount a significant writing center experience in a way that would be helpful to consultants-in-training. To what extent does his essay work for you, a member of its intended audience? Pay attention in particular to the unusual tone of the essay. Did it confuse or alienate you at first? How did the religious imagery affect you?

3. Describe and analyze a writing situation that was challenging because you were writing in a new context, or because you mistakenly assumed that the rules of one context applied to another.

4. Here is an excerpt from Niccolo Machiavelli's *The Prince.*

> Men nearly always follow the tracks made by others and proceed in their affairs by imitation, even though they cannot entirely keep to the tracks of others or emulate the prowess of their models. So a prudent man must always follow in the footsteps of great men and imitate those who have been outstanding. If his own prowess fails to compare with theirs, at least it has an air of greatness about it. He must behave like those archers who, if they are skillful, when the target seems too distant, know the capabilities of their bow and aim a good deal higher than their objective, not in order to shoot so high but so that in aiming high they can reach the target (22).

Here is how several writers incorporated the passage into a political philosophy essay for which they were told to use MLA documentation format. Write a dialogue in which you help one student with documentation format. If you wish, generate more text so that there will be a context for Machiavelli's material. Try to get the writer to identify her error, solve the problem, and formulate a rule that will prevent the problem in the future. With another member of your the group, read your dialogue aloud. Critique the dialogues of other group members.

> *Student A:* It occurred to me the other day that men nearly always follow the tracks made by others and proceed in their affairs by imitation.

> *Student B:* Machiavelli explains that men nearly always follow the tracks made by others and proceed in their affairs by imitation.

> *Student C:* Machiavelli said, "Men nearly always follow the tracks made by others, even though they cannot entirely keep to the tracks of others" (22).

> *Student D:* Machiavelli wrote, "Men nearly always follow the tracks of others...." (22)

> *Student E:* Machiavelli wrote, "Men...always follow the tracks made by others and proceed in their affairs by imitation...." (22)
>
> *Student F:* Machiavelli pointed out that people almost always pursue the tracks of others (22).
>
> *Student G:* plays it safe and quotes the entire passage, adding (22).

6. In an oral presentation, analyze a type of writing you've become familiar with through your major. If possible, use multiple copies or an overhead transparency of a sample text to illustrate the characteristics of the genre. Include relevant aspects such as organizational patterns, types of support, style (active vs. passive voice, sentence structure, vocabulary), how much background material to include, documentation format, preference for quotes vs. paraphrase, what should be included and what should be left out. What consulting strategies would you recommend when responding to this kind of writing?

7. Using APA format, decide how to cite a classmate's unpublished essay in a research paper on peer consulting methods. Include in-text and end-of-text documentation, as well as a brief explanation of how you used the guidelines to work out the citation.

8. Follow the directions for Assignment 7, but this time use MLA format to decide how you would cite an entry from your journal.

9. Check your journal for consulting sessions involving a research paper or writing in a discipline. After reading this chapter, has your perception of the session changed? Do you have new ideas about how the session could have been improved? Share your original entry and your new thoughts with the group.

FOOTNOTES

[1] To prevent confusion in this section, the word "draft" will be used to refer to the student's text.

[2] If "I" is not considered appropriate, a writer can signal the shift with a statement like, "Elbow's suggestions are interesting, but some are impractical for a writer with a deadline."

[3] However, a sample end-of-text documentation page is extremely helpful, because it provides quick visual clues about spacing, indenting, and title format.

[4] Unless indicated, descriptions are drawn from *Writing in the Disciplines.*

[5] For a lively description of economics style, see Donald McCloskey, "Economical Writing," *Economic Inquiry* 24 (1985): 187–222.

[6]I am grateful to Professor Daniel Lamoureux of Stonehill's Fine Arts Department, whose "History of Music" handout provided information for this entry.

[7]I am grateful to Professor Carole Rovane of Yale University, whose class handout, "Writing Philosophy Papers," was the basis for this entry.

[8]For additional information, consult Sylvan Barnet, *A Short Guide to Writing about Art*. NY: Harper Collins, 1997.

Chapter 11

Specific Kinds of Writers

It is essential for a consultant to remember that each writer is different. In view of this fact, I felt ambivalent as I wrote this chapter, since it assumes similarities between writers who belong to a particular group. I hope this chapter will make you feel ambivalent too, because then, even as you read about the common needs and concerns of these writers, you will stay alert to the crucial differences between them—differences in language skills; personality; ethnic, geographic, family, social, economic, and educational background; and the multitude of other factors that make each writer unique.

Working with ESL Writers

Most ESL (English as a Second Language) writers have *learned* English through formal study rather than *acquiring* it the way children learn their native language. Children learn to speak by watching, listening, imitating, making mistakes, and eventually correcting themselves into competence. In the process, they master elaborate rules unconsciously, without learning the rule itself.[1] On the other hand, formal language study involves memorizing rules and then practicing them in order to become reasonably proficient. Non-native speakers rarely acquire the fluency of native speakers—and when they do, it is almost always in a situation where they must use the language in order to be understood.

Writing in a non-native language presents the additional challenges of spelling, punctuation, a more formal style, and less forgiving rules of grammar than speaking requires. Even professionals who have been writing in a second language for many years have native-speaking readers edit their work for occasional lapses, particularly with idioms.

From the non-native student's point of view, working with a peer consultant is not just a way to improve her writing, but also a powerful learning opportunity. By its very nature, a consulting session fosters language acquisition rather than mere learning. First, all the student's language skills are exercised, since working with a consultant involves speaking, listening, reading, and writing. Even more important, it is a situation in which the student needs something and must communicate with a native speaker to obtain it.

For a consultant, working with an ESL writer is in many ways identical to working with any other writer. For instance, it makes sense to gather as much information from an ESL writer as possible—he may already understand what aspects of English give him the most trouble. Finding out what he already knows about himself as a writer saves time and puts him in charge.

As in any consulting session, begin with the overall aspects of an ESL writer's draft, such as appropriateness to the assignment, focus, organization, and development. The importance of these criteria may puzzle a writer whose culture values other qualities in writing. For instance, in some cultures, it is considered rude and abrupt to announce one's point immediately; the preferred format is a lengthy discussion of the context or problem, followed by the presentation of one's point. In other cultures, explicitly stating the point anywhere in the essay is considered an insult to the reader's intelligence. Students from a culture that prizes gradual revelation—or no revelation at all—will not take naturally to the English convention of an early and explicit thesis statement. In some cultures, stating a point once and then moving on to another point is considered inadequate and inelegant; the force of an argument depends on the number of ways it can be reasserted. Students from a culture like this may not understand why repetition is considered a flaw. Many Asian cultures prize tradition over originality: one makes a case by repeating the wisdom of the ages; attribution is not necessary, because this wisdom is a common heritage rather than one person's intellectual property. Students from these cultures will require a sensitive introduction to the notion of attribution and documentation, along with an explanation of the reasons behind these practices.[2]

Sometimes working with ESL writers involves paying increased attention to techniques that work well with all writers. In particular, it's crucial to put ESL writers at ease, since what they are doing—expressing themselves in a language that is not their mother tongue—is a high-anxiety, risk-laden endeavor. They may need extra time, and longer silences, to shape their thoughts into words before they speak. Some ESL students may also need extra encouragement to speak up or ask questions. Asian students, because their culture places a high value on expertise, may feel that as a consultant you deserve their silent respect. In some cultures, questions are considered rude, so you may have to be inventive in eliciting them. It's probably not enough to ask, "Do you understand?" Ask follow-up questions or have the writer explain things in his own words. Even better, have him do something that requires application of the concept you're discussing.

Body language is another aspect of behavior that can put an ESL writer at her ease—or not. There are vast differences between what is acceptable in one culture and another in terms of physical proximity and eye contact. You can't, of course, learn enough to become fluent in the body language of every writer you work with, although you should learn what you can about a culture that is well-represented among your writing center's clientele.[3] From a practical standpoint, your best bet is to take your cue from the writer, letting her make the choices. If you are already sitting down, she can select a chair that allows a comfortable distance between you. If she does not look at you during conversation, don't take it as a sign of boredom, hostility, or distraction—follow her lead insofar as you comfortably can.

The particular consulting methods that are most effective with ESL writers derive from the theory of error analysis: the belief that error, rather than being a sign of deficiency or carelessness, is essential to the process of mastering new material. Errors are systematic and can be explained; as "clues to inner processes" and "windows into the mind" (Kroll and Schafer, 136), they contain the seeds of their own correction. If you have not already done so, read Mina Shaughnessy's introduction to her book, *Errors and Expectations*, for a more thorough explanation of error analysis.

Format to follow with ESL Writers

1. Follow "Priorities in Reading a Draft," and when you get to Step #8 (correcting), skim the paper and note the three or four most common kinds of error. Discuss all the examples of one kind of error together, identifying them with marks in the margin—don't forget to ask the writer for permission first.

2. Pick one error and point it out to the writer. Listen carefully as he thinks out loud about the error. He may be able to identify and correct it on his own; if not, ask him to explain the process or rule he used.

3. Try to identify the reason for the error. Here are some likely possibilities:
   - Interference from the writer's native language. For instance, Russian contains no articles, so an omitted article may result from interference.
   - Hypercorrection. For instance, the writer knows that "ed" signals the past tense in English, so he adds "ed" to "went" to produce "wented."
   - Overgeneralization of a rule or applying a rule to an exception. For instance, the writer knows that "s" signals plural nouns, so he adds "s" to "child" to produce "childs."
   - Misunderstood or incompletely understood rules. For instance, the writer knows that the past tense of "go" is "went," so he writes "He has went."
   - Using the wrong rule. For instance, the writer knows that "s" signals the plural, so he adds "s" to the verb "describe," and produces "They describes."
   - Forgetting or not knowing the rule.

- Transcription errors, i.e., errors caused by the physical act of writing. The writer will automatically correct this kind of error when he reads the passage aloud. Point out the discrepancy between what he's said and what he's written, so he can correct the written version.

4. Discuss the reason for the error, then have the writer fix the error and all others of the same kind. You may need to discuss exceptions to the rule ("It doesn't make much sense, but it's 'shrimp' in both the singular and the plural,") point him in the direction of the right rule ("So you add 's' to most nouns to form the plural, but you don't add 's' to verbs even if the subject is plural"), jog his memory ("Do you remember how possession is shown in English?"), or explain a rule that he doesn't yet know. Most ESL students are familiar with grammatical terminology from their formal study of English, so use these terms if they are comfortable for you. If you're not sure of the rule, look it up together in a handbook. By doing this, you will give the writer additional practice in reading, and reassure him that competent writers don't have all the answers either.

5. As the writer begins correcting the errors associated with a particular rule, point to places where she has successfully observed the rule: "All these articles are correct, so you must be getting a good feel for when to use an article." Talking only about errors is like teaching archery by shouting "Miss!" but never shouting "Bulls-eye!" Besides, looking at places where the writer has succeeded may help explain what she's having trouble with ("I used an article with 'house' and with 'love' because they're both nouns and I'd use an article in Spanish. How are they different from each other in English?").

6. At the end of the session, have the writer jot down a short list of his most frequent problems. Suggest additions to the list only if there are major omissions. Then encourage him to formulate simple rules in his own words and to use them when correcting his work in the future.

Aspects of English That Are Difficult for ESL Students

The aspects of English that a particular student finds most troublesome are closely related to his native language, whose rules may differ from the rules of English.[4] For instance, Russian and Japanese students find articles difficult, because their native languages contain no articles whatsoever. Chinese students find plurals confusing, because Chinese nouns don't change in the plural—the presence of a plural number is the only sign needed. Here is a list of areas that are difficult for many ESL writers.

Word Order. Every language has rules for where to place words in relationship to each other and in the overall structure of the sentence. The basic English word order (subject, verb, object; all adjectives before the noun they describe) may be difficult for writers whose native language possesses a different order (in German, the verb goes at the end of the sentence; in French, some adjectives precede the noun and others follow it).

Plurals of Nouns. As mentioned above, some languages don't have plural endings for nouns. Irregular English plural forms are also puzzling: "dogs" and "books," but "children" and "geese."

Articles: Some languages have no articles; other languages, including the Romance languages, use more articles than English does, for instance with abstract nouns such as "love" (in French, "l'amour"). ESL writers also have difficulty figuring out when to use "the" and when to use "a."

Verbs. The English verb system is extremely complex, making it difficult for non-native speakers to choose the correct tense. There are also many irregular verbs (I am, you are, he is, they are, I was, you were). And then there's the tricky problem of auxiliary verbs, resulting in errors like, "He has went."

Prepositions. Some languages have verbs with the preposition built in, so it's difficult to decide when a preposition is required. Even more problematic is the fact that many English prepositions are idiomatic and don't accurately describe physical relationships. Why do we ride "in" a car but "on" a train?

Idioms. By definition the meaning of an idiom differs from that of its components, so it is doubly puzzling to someone who must look up individual words in a dictionary. Most idioms can't be explained logically (Why do we "take a bus"? What does it mean to "put up with" something?) Your best bet is to acknowledge the arbitrary nature of the idiom, give the correct form, and assure the writer that the more he speaks and listens, reads and writes, the faster the idioms will become second nature to him.[5]

Working with Writers Who Speak a Nonstandard Dialect

Students who speak a nonstandard dialect of English such as Black English Vernacular (BEV) are like ESL speakers in that Standard English is a second language for them. However, mastering Standard English for BEV speakers can be more emotionally complicated than it is for ESL speakers.

A Japanese student is unlikely to consider his native language inferior to English, but a BEV speaker may feel apologetic or defensive about her primary language. This feeling is reinforced by the widespread opinion that BEV is a primitive, error-laden, and inferior version of Standard English. Linguists insist that BEV is a dialect of English complete with strict rules that competent speakers must observe. In some ways, the rules are subtler than those of Standard English. For instance, BEV uses one tense for a habitual action

("She be studying") and another tense for an action taking place right now ("She study"). In Standard English, "She is studying" must do double duty, conveying both these meanings.

In actuality, no language or dialect is superior to another. In view of this fact, "nonstandard" is an unfortunate word. Although the intended meaning here is purely quantitative—one dialect is called standard because more people speak it than the dialect designated as nonstandard—an evaluative connotation may still come across, since "standard" also means a level to measure up to. Efforts to adopt the value-neutral term "Language of Wider Communication" (LWC) have not been successful so far (Weaver 111).

Speakers of nonstandard dialects may also feel conflicted about mastering Standard English interpreting it as a betrayal of their culture, an act that will distance them from family and friends. In fact, Standard Written English is not *anybody's* native language, because nobody speaks it. All users of Standard Written English speak something else, either BEV or a relaxed, oral version of English, which permits run-on sentences, sentence fragments, shifts in person and tense, and lack of agreement.

As a consultant, keep these undercurrents in mind when working with nonstandard dialect speakers. Discuss errors objectively, pointing out that they are based on differences between two language systems, not on objective criteria of correctness. The general procedure for working with ESL writers applies to nonstandard dialect speakers as well.

Working with Learning-Disabled Writers

According to the Learning Disabilities Act of 1968, a learning disability is "a disorder in one or more of the basic psychological processes involved in understanding or in using spoken or written language" (qtd. in Neff 82). If you work frequently with learning-disabled writers, take advantage of the information and expertise available to you through your counseling center, study skills office, or learning disabilities specialist.[6]

Your attitude when working with learning-disabled writers is extremely important. Because they need additional time to process language, they are often assumed to be slow or even mentally deficient. This is hardly ever the case—most learning-disabled people test at average or above average intelligence. Be cheerful, cooperative, and supportive in providing additional time and in repeating material. If you have just finished discussing something and a remark reveals the writer does not remember it, don't assume she hasn't been paying attention; some learning disabilities include difficulty retaining information. To give a learning-disabled writer extra time, book double appointments or find out how to waive your center's normal time restrictions. The learning disabled have the same legal rights as the physically disabled, including access to alternative forms of education (e.g., oral exams, use of a word processor for in-class writing, additional time for tests, permission to tape lectures, etc.).

```
        h              w        w      "W            l k
Onegay, Jo n anp Bop   n  froa  a k.    hatwo      ou i e
        e t            l               ulpy
 t o  a                    n'tk          r
  op op y?, Boq  ske  John. "I do   ow, J    ed ed,
    t          a   p            n      onh   li
           k                  I        o      c
hatwo lpyo li e ot go?" It in   mi ten  yw at   g a
w    u   u              h k   gh     j      hin
        sd c  l y       c
 o i  nTV, e  e ia l  fiw e   av es me do  ron. "Wow,"
m v eo                anh     o      dc
              q  n!      g                e k  e
saip Jonh, "Po c     hat  eati   Let's    c t
           or   W  a r   pea!        ch    h
 uq   r t  e               o
c  qoa  o s e fim y m the    gh s    he stalt im  e wetn
    d        o      rpou t   met              esh
s   in                 u       n
 hodb  g." "Look," hey e  ep, "af l    pit's  r il e
                       ll     lpoxa       O v  l
 e          yf a  r              u        t'sc  k
R pqenqocker! M    o  te!"    eat!" Bopsho  eq, "Le   o t:
              v  i     "Gr          t         o
         i r wa
udi      c o      nqs  e woh ti truns
   nt hem    vea     e              tou."
```

Trying to read this passage, you will experience the kind of difficulty a dyslexic reader faces when deciphering normal typeface (Almeida).

Because learning-disabled writers do not process language through normal channels, the key to consulting with them is to exploit other channels. In deciding how to proceed, don't forget that the writer is an important source of information. Many learning-disabled students have developed creative and sophisticated coping strategies on their own or with the help of experts. Here are some general suggestions:

- Present the material in alternate ways.
- Reinforce one channel with simultaneous use of another channel (for instance, read and point, talk and write).
- Get the writer physically involved.
- Adapt to the writer's learning style. Writing consultant Shoshona Beth Konstant developed consulting strategies based on four basic learning styles, and found that they work especially well with learning-disabled writers. Even though you may not be qualified to identify a writer's learning style, you can observe which strategies work best, then use more of the same kind.

Visual Learning Style. Use visual rather than purely textual presentations: charts, diagrams, pictures, and graphs. For instance, when working with a text, point to passages while discussing them, or write on a blackboard. Write in different colors for different kinds of material. Connect material visually, circling it or drawing arrows. Try graphic getting-started strategies such as mapping or clustering, rather than purely textual strategies such as listing or thesis statements. Have the writer make a chart, graph, or other record of the contents of your session.

Auditory Learning Style. Talk everything through. When working with a text, read aloud as you look at it. Discuss the major points of the draft or the reading. Suggest that the writer talk aloud to herself as she writes or studies, tape recording classes and lectures if it is permitted.

Kinesthetic Learning Style (through touch). Kinesthetic learners learn through their fingertips and the rest of their bodies, so make the writing as physical as possible. For starters, have the student do all the writing. Suggest that he re-copy text when he decides to make a change. Encourage him to manipulate text physically: for instance, by letting individual pieces of paper represent points he wants to make, then moving them around to decide where they belong.[7] Use gestures instead of, or in addition to, writing and speaking.

Multi-Sensory Learning Style. Present information in as many ways as possible. Do two things at once, a strategy that is effective with learning-disabled writers regardless of learning style. Develop nonverbal systems if the verbal ones don't work—use colors, gestures, or symbols to keep track of different ideas in your discussion or the writer's draft.

In her excellent article "Learning Disabilities and the Writing Center," Julie Neff points out that consultants may be called on to model or demonstrate aspects of composing when learning-disabled students can't envision them unaided, to participate in the physical act of transcribing text, and to take a more active role in correcting surface errors than they normally would (87).

ASSIGNMENTS

1. Read Judith K. Powers' "Rethinking Writing Center Conferencing Strategies for the ESL Writer," then do one of the following things:
   A. Write a dialogic notebook entry about the essay, and come to class prepared to discuss the two or three passages you found most interesting.
   B. Write a journal entry about reading Powers' essay. How did you deal with phrases like "a Socratic rather than a didactic context," "cultural informants about American academic expectations," and "benign neglect"? Do you agree with Powers that collaborative consulting strategies do not meet the needs of ESL writers? Do you feel comfortable with the role of "teaching 'ESL students' writing as an academic subject"?

    C. Write a dialogue with an ESL writer, in which you become a "cultural informant about American academic expectations" without taking over the job of writing his paper for him.

    D. Evaluate an idea from Powers' essay by applying it to your own experience with ESL writers in the writing center, in classes, or in other contexts.

2. Read (or re-read) Jennifer Brice's "Northern Literacies, Northern Realities," then do one of the following things:

    A. Compare Powers' concept of consultant-as-cultural informant to the relationship Brice establishes with Phillip. Has Brice decided against being a cultural informant for Phillip? If so, what role has she chosen instead? Does reading Brice's essay change your attitude about Powers' thesis? Work these ideas out in an essay or in an imaginary dialogue between Powers and Brice.

    B. Choose an ESL or ethnic population represented in your institution, gather information about their cultural values, and write an analysis like Brice's. Describe the culture's values and how they might complicate the task of writing for college; then suggest consulting methods to help these writers balance the values of their culture and those of the institution.

    C. Evaluate your writing center as a "safe house." Are there ways to make it more like the "safe house" Brice describes? If not, what factors make this move impractical or difficult? If the changes *are* practical, would there be disadvantages involved in making the changes? Are the benefits worth the price?

    D. Consult your journal for a session involving a writer from another culture. Analyze the session, applying the techniques Brice recommends. If other techniques were used, what are they and how well did they work?

3. To gain an appreciation of the difficulties ESL writers face, compose a short essay about some aspect of your first day in college, observing the following rules:

    • Add a "t" to all verbs that begin with a consonant, unless they consist of three syllables.

    • Start every adjective with the letter "e."

    • Do not use "the," "a," or "an" with nouns. Instead, use the word "human" before all nouns referring to humans, and "not human" after all others.

    • Do not use tense markings on verbs. Instead, use the word "yesterday" for events that happened within the past week, "tomorrow" for events that will happen within the next week, "long time ago" for events that happened within the past year but not within the past week, and "long time from now" for events that happened at any other time and the past or future.

- Put the subject at the very end of the sentence.[8]

When you've finished, write a wrap-up comment about how paying attention to these rules affected your writing process. Did the experience give you any new ideas about working with ESL writers?

4. To illustrate how elaborate the rules of English are, work several others in your group to formulate the rule for when to use "the," when to use "a," and when to use no article at all. No fair using a handbook! Keep generating examples that aren't covered by your rule, modifying the rule so it takes all the examples into account. Finally, check a handbook to see how close you've come to the "official" version of the rule.

5. Write a dialogue illustrating some suggestions for working with learning-disabled writers (e.g., presenting material in a variety of ways, simultaneously using several modes of reinforcing material, adapting to different learning styles). Be sure to include at least one situation in which your first attempt to explain something doesn't work.

6. Check your journal for consulting sessions with writers who belong to a group discussed in this chapter. How do the details of the session connect to information in this chapter? After reading the chapter, what are your thoughts on the strategies used in the session? Would you recommend doing things differently? Share your original entry and your new thoughts with the group.

FOOTNOTES

[1]For instance, adjectives follow a particular order in English. Native speakers effortlessly observe this rule, even though they have never learned it. How would you combine these terms: "sheep," "healthy" " "ten," "Scottish"? When you've gotten the answer, use it to figure out the rule. Now think about how much work it would be to apply that rule every time you used more than one adjective to describe a noun.

[2]The study of cultural differences like these is called contrastive rhetoric—for more information, see both Leki and Kaplan.

[3]Xia Wang's "Tutoring across Cultures," *Writing Lab Newsletter* 19.1 (Sept. 1994): 12–15, includes detailed information about Asian attitudes towards nonverbal behavior.

[4]For more information, see Leki, 108–121.

[5]News commentator Daniel Schorr describes going for drinks with a student from a Russian language institute, who was learning English in order to become a translator in the diplomatic corps. The student, who took great

pride in his mastery of American idioms, hoisted his glass and toasted, "Here's mud down the hatch!" (*Weekly Edition,* PBS, July 20, 1997).

[6]For general background, an illuminating case study, and consulting tips, see Neff.

[7]Eudora Welty takes great pleasure in the physical sensation of moving text. She says, "I revise with scissors and pins. Pasting is too slow, and you can't undo it, but with pins you can move things from anywhere to anywhere, and that's what I really love best..." (290).

[8]I am grateful to Erika Mitchell, formerly of Stonehill's Foreign Language Department, whose handout "Proofreading ESL Papers" was the basis for this exercise.

Chapter 12

The Virtual Writing Center: Computer-Assisted Consulting

We make our tools, and our tools make us.
–Anon.

Computers are undeniably part of the academic world, and likely to remain so. New dorms boast network connections for computers in every room and provide computers in common areas. Some colleges provide incoming students with computers, while others direct students to bring them as part of their gear. Computer literacy requirements are becoming a staple of the core curriculum. Many writing teachers demand that assignments be word-processed rather than typed, so that writers can shape evolving text without retyping every word.

Computers are also an integral part of the writing center scene.[1] It is a rare session indeed that does not include at least the shadow presence of a computer. During a single shift you might read a hard copy of a draft prepared on a word processor, lean over a writer's shoulder to discuss work she is revising onscreen, conduct an electronic rather than a face-to-face session, then take a break and talk shop with other consultants via an electronic discussion group. If your writing center is also a computer lab, you may be expected to help students with word processing and software matters, in addition to reading and responding to their writing.

Writing centers use computers in a multitude of ways: to gather and interpret data for operations and long-term planning, to track payroll and attendance figures, to connect to the library, the career services office, the registrar, and other resources, and to conduct on-line research. But as a consultant, you will probably find computers most useful—and perhaps most problematic—as writing and consulting tools.

Writing with a Computer

Word-processing programs are far and away the most common form of computer use by writers. Many writers have become so used to word processing that they would no more think of composing longhand or on a typewriter than they would consider scratching letters on the ground with a pointed stick. The main difference between word processing and handwriting or typing is ease of text manipulation. On a word processor, the writer can make multiple corrections with a single keystroke, move text instantly, delete, save several versions of a text, and salt away material for use at another time. The fluid nature of word-processed text takes the risk out of experimenting—it can always be changed back if it doesn't work. The ease with which text can be changed encourages scrupulous proofreading, correcting, and attention to detail. In addition, some writers find the computer screen gives them enough psychological distance from their text to recognize its flaws.

But the computer's advantages are not unmixed blessings. Granted, computers make the physical act of writing easier and faster; but faster isn't necessarily better. For some writers, the physical act of writing is an essential part of the creative process. Virginia Woolf revised by retyping her manuscript from the start, "a good method, I believe, as thus one works with a wet brush over the whole, and joins parts separately composed and gone dry" (68). Pablo Neruda observes that poetry he writes longhand is "more sensitive; its plastic forms could change more easily" (59) than a poem composed on the typewriter. Nora Ephron takes exception to computer editing in particular: "Word processors make it possible for a writer to change the sentences that clearly need changing without having to retype the rest, but I believe that you can't always tell whether a sentence needs work until it rises up in revolt against your fingers as you retype it" (442).

When text is easy to transcribe, a writer can also easily get carried away, spinning out yards of meandering prose, then neglecting to go back and shape it. Russell Baker's "The Processing Process" wittily illustrates this danger: two or three sentences into his computer-fueled style, the reader feels like the sorcerer's apprentice, desperately searching for a shut-off valve to quell the raging torrent. At the other end of the writing process, ease of editing (combined with intriguing features like the thesaurus, dictionary, "find and replace" command, spell-checker, style checker, and grammar checker) may cause a writer to begin editing too soon, before she's adequately explored, rearranged, focused, and developed his material.[2] The mesmerizing text glowing on the screen can blind the proud writer to serious flaws in the text. It LOOKS so good that it must BE good.

Writers' Attitudes Towards Computers

The range of writers' attitudes about computers is bracketed on each end by Annie Dillard, who states, "The computer makes writing into play again," and by Leslie Epstein, who counters, "The computer lets you write badly for the same reason that it lets you write easily: it removes resistances." A happy medium between these two extremes permits a writer both to exploit the strengths of computer technology and to compensate for its liabilities. A word processor is one of many tools at a writer's disposal, along with the favorite pen that slips naturally between the fingers and the notepad that's just the right size, shape, and design. Properly used, these tools can aid in the completion of a task, but none of them guarantees excellence or success. Today's computers have changed greatly from their early, room-sized ancestors, but one characteristic remains the same: Garbage in still produces garbage out.

Students bring an assortment of attitudes about computers to the writing center. Some are technophobic, convinced that they'll never catch on or that the computer will sap their creativity. Others are zealots who hail the computer as a wonder drug to cure all their writing ills.

When working with a technophobe, discuss his anxiety as you would any outside problem that makes writing more difficult. Point out that even if word-processed texts are required in a course, he can write out early drafts by hand, and postpone word processing until it's time to prepare the polished draft. Refer to your own experience: if it took you awhile to become comfortable onscreen, this fact will encourage him. If you adapted to word processing quickly, explain what you liked about it. Suggest that he bring up his text on the computer and make some changes while you watch; then, if you're familiar with the software, share tips and shortcuts. However, don't let computer talk take over the session entirely. Guidance in this area is probably available from other support services on campus, or as part of the software itself.

When working with a computer enthusiast, begin in the usual way, discussing the draft and asking questions about passages that require more attention to focus, organization, or support. To break the hypnotic spell of onscreen text, work from a hard copy, encouraging her to mark it up with marginal notations, arrows, cross-outs, and other visual reminders that the draft is imperfect and in flux. Some writers prefer to work on their text at a terminal, making changes as the discussion gives them ideas for improvement.[3] In this case, encourage her to "mess up" the text onscreen by glossing or making notations to herself in boldface, italic, or a different typeface (e.g., **add citation, better word needed, example?, Does this belong here? Re-write this sentence. Is this true?**). These embedded reminders take advantage of the fluid text (messages can be deleted as jobs are completed), let the writer transcribe rapidly when thoughts are flowing rapidly,[4] prevent premature editing, remind her that the text is still in process, and provide a checklist of editing suggestions.

In addition to word processing, a multitude of specialized software programs are available to help writers generate ideas, organize material, correct surface errors, or edit for style. Meyers and Smith point out that these programs possess some of the same advantages as consulting sessions: writers work at their own pace on their own texts, receiving rapid feedback they can put into practice immediately (315). We won't discuss individual programs here, since you will learn about those used in your writing center, either as part of your training or through the program itself. Run a text of your own through any program frequently used by the writers you consult with. Besides receiving a new perspective on your writing, you will gain hands-on experience with the program's limitations and options. For instance, a style checker will identify sentence fragments as errors, but a writer may decide she needs a fragment for dramatic effect. Software programs often contain commands that permit a user to override corrections or even turn off undesired features.

Consulting via Computer

Not only is a computer a valuable writing tool, but its networking capabilities allow consultants to reach out and touch writers in need of feedback, colleagues in their own writing center, and fellow-consultants around the globe.

There are three basic ways to collaborate with writers via computer:

1. Electronic mail (E-mail) sends messages to and from a specified person or persons. The message is unread until the recipient checks for new messages, so this kind of communication is asynchronous, i.e., sender and receiver can participate at different times.
2. Electronic bulletin board (AKA discussion group) is a group whose membership is defined by a particular interest or shared characteristic. Messages can be "addressed" to a particular member, but they are transmitted to all members (although some have private mail options). Like E-mail, bulletin boards are asynchronous.
3. Electronic chat room, like a bulletin board, transmits messages to all participants; unlike E-mail and bulletin boards, chat rooms are synchronous, i.e., all members must be available at the same time.

Online Consulting

Many campuses are experimenting with online writing labs (OWLs) in an attempt to reach writers unable to come to the writing center site, as a first step in getting students to the site, or in rare cases, as a substitute for a physical site. What are the tradeoffs between electronic consulting and face-to-face encounters? How does the absence of physical cues such as body language and tone of voice affect the writer-consultant dynamic? Does the technology throw up a barrier between the participants, or does it create a useful buffer zone?

Lurking beneath these questions is a more fundamental one: to what extent does our mode of expression shape and determine what we express? New technologies change the way we use language (and perhaps even the way we think). Researchers have thoroughly analyzed the effects of writing, which makes language visible; the printing press, which makes widespread literacy feasible; the radio and the telephone, which transmit audible language to a listener miles away; and the answering machine, which creates uncertainty about whether the listener is actually listening. The most notorious example of electronic communication shaping language use is the phenomenon of "flaming," or transmitting emotionally inflammatory messages the sender would not dream of conveying through any other medium. Given these precedents, it's not surprising that online consulting differs significantly from face-to-face consulting.

Its supporters claim that electronic consulting boasts many advantages, the most obvious being convenience. Online consulting usually occurs via E-mail, because only the consultant and the writer are involved.[5] Since E-mail is asynchronous, the consultant and the writer don't have to arrange a mutually convenient time or turn up at the same place. This fact puts writing center services within the reach of a new clientele: those who are ill, physically disabled, or otherwise immobilized, those taking correspondence courses or attending classes at satellite campuses of an institution with a centralized writing center, those whose schedules don't coincide with writing center hours.

In addition to the convenience of asynchronous consulting, some researchers claim that electronic communication levels the hierarchies that class, gender, and race impose on face-to-face exchanges, and that it elicits more participation from quiet or shy students who rarely speak in class (Spooner 6). Supporters also say the interactive, dynamic quality of on-line consulting encourages true collaboration (Crump "Some" 6) and builds writing proficiency because the exchanges actually occur in writing (Mitchell).

Michael Spooner summarizes the major limitations of electronic consulting. Although he finds online sessions ideal for disseminating generic material such as style sheets, bibliographies, and grammar tips, he maintains that face-to-face consultations are preferable for discussing a writer's work, because physical cues are so important in deciding how to respond to him, as well as to his writing. He also fears that writers may interpret a consultant's online remarks as a final evaluation, like a teacher's end comment on an assignment, rather than as the opening move in a process of collaboration and discussion. Finally, he points out that ethical problems are exacerbated by electronic consulting: ease of editing may tempt a consultant to make corrections rather than eliciting them from the writer, and ease of combining texts may tempt a writer to incorporate a consultant's comments into the draft itself (7–8).

Stuart Blythe warns that a critical approach to electronic consulting or any other technology must address not only logistical issues (Can we do this? What's the best way to do this?) but also theoretical issues (Do we want to do this? What do we gain and what do we lose? Can we compensate for the losses?) One theoretical aspect of online consulting—what we gain and lose—has been given a great deal of attention. But so far not much is available in the way of guidelines for electronic consulting.

Some tentative guidelines for online consulting can be extrapolated by working backwards from a description of its problems. For instance, Jeffrey Baker compares two hypothetical consulting sessions, one face-to-face and one electronic, dealing with the same writer and draft. Baker finds it difficult to discuss conceptual problems electronically. Asking questions is impractical, he says, given the time lag that may occur between sending a message and receiving a reply. But transmitting comments rather than questions is danger-ous, because the comments can so easily be used to appropriate the text or to re-shape it in the consultant's rather than the writer's image. It would seem that one solution is to make electronic consultation synchronous, arranging a time when writer and consultant are both at their terminals.[6] This would allow the consultant to ask the open-ended questions that work well in face-to-face conferencing, receive a reply rapidly enough to keep the exchange going, and provide useful feedback in a timely fashion. Another possibility would be to make electronic consulting available only for editing issues, or to require that an electronic conference be followed up by a face-to-face confer-ence, a sequence which occurred voluntarily in the consulting situation described by David Coogan. For the most part, however, electronic consulting is a capability we are still learning how to use.

Electronic Bulletin Boards for Consultants

Bulletin boards fill a variety of needs, serving as support groups, information sources, and sounding boards. When you need rapid feedback from many knowledgeable people, a bulletin board is the way to go. Imagine how long it would take to identify and track down a long list of experts, send out individ-ual letters, and wait for them to reply. A letter may wait for weeks in the mailbox or post office if the addressee is away, but online correspondents can check their electronic mail no matter where they are. Both E-mail and bulletin boards encourage an informal style many participants find attractive and accessible. "In an interactive network environment, where orality and literacy converge," Eric Crump writes, "conversation and debate come alive and so do the conversants" ("On-line" 3).

The electronic bulletin board for writing centers, WCenter, was established in 1991 at Texas Tech University. You can subscribe by following the normal procedure for sending an E-mail message, using the address: LISTPROC@ listserv.ttu.edu. Leave the subject line blank, and on the first line of the mes-sage space, enter "Subscribe WCenter <your first name> <your last name>. The monthly journal *Writing Lab Newsletter* frequently runs "From the Net," a feature consisting of WCenter exchanges on topics of current interest.

In-house bulletin boards can serve many of the same purposes as staff meetings. Valerie Balester, who set up Staff Contact at Texas A & M

University, found it convenient for conveying information about scheduling, budgets, paperwork, and other operational matters; she used the private mail option for communicating confidentially with individuals. Consultants used the bulletin board to solve scheduling problems, critique existing procedures and suggest new ones, share in each other's consulting trials and triumphs, discuss course material, describe consulting styles and beliefs, and swap consulting tips.

ASSIGNMENTS

1. Read David Coogan's "Towards a Rhetoric of On-line Tutoring," then do one of the following things:
   A. Keep a dialogic notebook and come to class prepared to discuss two or three passages you found interesting. What sections did you have difficulty understanding? How did you handle them? What points did you grasp? Can you generate one thesis that covers the entire essay, or do you need different thesis statements for different sections?
   B. Select a point that Coogan (or one of his sources) makes, and write an essay testing it against your own experience.
   C. Investigate and report on the procedure a student at your institution must follow to have an E-mail session with a consultant. Are you better off than Coogan and the other consultants at SUNY were when he wrote his essay?
   D. Choose someone in your group whose work you've responded to in person. Have an E-mail consultation, both exchanging drafts and responding via computer. Compare the two sessions, paying special attention to the aspects of online consulting Coogan describes. Were these aspects diluted by the fact that you already knew each other? Write a report on your findings, then compare them with your partner's findings. If you wish, collaborate on a joint report.

2. Read Russell Baker's "The Processing Process," then do one of the following things:
   A. Use Baker's text to illustrate how a writer's language is affected by the word processor. What happens to word choice, sentence length, punctuation, paragraphing, organization, attitude towards the reader? What is it about word processing that encourages each aspect of this style?
   B. Write a response to Baker, defending the word processor as a writing aid. Explain how it has helped you improve your writing. If you can figure out a way to do it, let your text illustrate your point, as Baker makes his text illustrate the dangers of composing on a word processor.

3. Generate guidelines for online consulting, and explain the reason for each one. Are there drawbacks to the guidelines? How can they be minimized?

4. Print out several E-mail messages you've sent to different people and several you've received from different people. Use them to formulate a description of "the e-mail style." How does it compare to conversation? To writing on paper? What are its advantages and disadvantages? What does it do well, and what does it do poorly? Does it help or hinder a writer's ability to succeed in more traditional writing situations?

5. Have a synchronous electronic consulting session with a member of your group, then have an asynchronous session. Compare and contrast the two experiences.

6. Look through your journal, keeping in mind the statement, "It is a rare session indeed that does not include at least the shadow presence of a computer." Does your journal support or contradict this statement? Report to the group on a session in which a discussion of computer issues figured prominently.

FOOTNOTES

[1]Margaret Mitchell of Southwest Missouri State University gives computers partial credit for the growing acceptance of writing centers among faculty. Questioned on the results of computer-assisted instruction, faculty frequently described the same positive outcomes observed in writing centers: students write more, learn from each other, and initiate their own learning strategies rather than waiting for guidance from an authority figure (11).

[2]The definition of "premature editing" varies widely with the individual. Some writers do a great deal of editing as they write, mulling over word choice and sentence structure because these subtle distinctions help them shape their thoughts more accurately.

[3]Pamela B. Farrell reports that many writers working with both consultants and computers think of the computer as "a third party or neutral ground" and thus find it psychologically easier to revise at the computer (29).

[4]Meyer and Smith suggest another way to keep up with the rapid flow of ideas: dim the screen brightness so the text becomes invisible and editing is impossible (331). Sheridan Blau experimented with invisible writing by having experienced writers use carbon paper and empty ballpoint pens. The writers reported that invisible writing helped them concentrate on more complex writing tasks, although it neither helped nor hindered when they were composing simpler texts (299).

[5]Of course, conferencing can also occur via a networked discussion group or teleconferencing arrangement, in which case the draft and exchanges between writer and respondents are transmitted to all members of the group. Writing teachers sometimes build this kind of interaction into a course, so students can give and receive multiple responses to working drafts.

[6]WebConferencing allows two people to view an electronic text simultaneously but at different locations; only one person can make changes to the text at a time, but they can take turns doing so.

WORKS CITED

Almeida, David. "Class and Faculty Workshop Handout." N. Easton, MA: Stonehill College, n.d.

Arkin, Marian and Barbara Shollar. *The Tutor Book*. NY: Longmans, 1982.

Baker, Jeffrey. "An Ethical Question about Online Tutoring in the Writing Lab." *Writing Lab Newsletter* 18.5 (1994): 6–7.

Balester, Valerie. "Electronic Discourse for Writing Consultants." *Writing Lab Newsletter* 18.9 (1994): 10–12.

Berthoff, Ann. *Forming, Thinking, Writing: The Composing Imagination*. Montclair, NJ: Boynton/Cook, 1982.

Blau, Sheridan. "Invisible Writing: Investigating Cognitive Processes in Composition." *College Composition and Communication* 34 (1983): 297–312.

Blythe, Stuart. "'Networked Computers + Writing Centers = ?'" Thinking about Networked Computers in Writing Center Practice." *Writing Lab Newsletter* 17.2 (1997): 89–110.

Crump Eric. "Some Thoughts on Michael Spooner's Thoughts," *Writing Lab Newsletter* 18.6 (1994): 6–8.

_____. "Online Community: Writing Centers Join the Network World." *Writing Lab Newsletter* 17.2 (1992): 1–5.

Dickens, Charles. *A Tale of Two Cities*. NY: Knopf, 1906.

Elbow, Peter. *Writing with Power: Techniques for Mastering the Writing Process*. NY: Oxford, 1981.

Ephron, Nora. "Revision and Life." *Discovering Language*. Ed. William Vesterman. Needham, MA: Allyn & Bacon, 1992. 440–443.

Faulkner, William. "Barn Burning." *The Faulkner Reader*. New York: Modern Library, 1971. 499–516.

Flower, Linda. "Writer-Based Prose: A Cognitive Basis for Writing Problems." *College English* 41 (1979): 19–37.

Farrell, Pamela B. "Writer, Peer Tutor, and the Computer: A Unique Relationship." *Writing Center Journal* 8.1 (1987): 29–33.

Fulwiler, Toby. Writing across the Curriculum Workshop, Boston University, Boston, MA: January 1987.

Graser, Elsa. *Teaching Writing: A Process Approach*. Dubuque, IA: Kendall/Hunt, 1983.

Huebner, Barbara, "Title IX Not Completed," *Boston Globe*, 6/23/97, D1.

Kaplan, Robert. "Cultural Thought Patterns in Inter-cultural Education." *Composing in a Second Language*. Ed. Sandra McKay. NY: Newbury, 1984. 43–62.

Kinkead, Joyce A. and Jeanette Harris, eds. *Writing Centers in Context*, Urbana, IL: NCTE: 1993.

Konstant, Shoshana Beth. "Multi-Sensory Tutoring for Multi-Sensory Learners." *Writing Lab Newsletter* 16.9/10 (1992): 6–8.

Leki, Ilona. *Understanding ESL Writers: A Guide for Teachers*. Portsmouth, NH: Boynton/Cook, 1993.

Liston, Broward, "Medfly Spray Alert." *Boston Globe* 6/27/97, A3.

Lotto, Edward. "The Lehigh University Writing Center: Creating a Community of Writers," in Kinkead and Harris: 78–96.

Machiavelli, Niccolo. *The Prince*. Trans. Harvey C. Mansfield. Chicago: University of Chicago Press, 1985.

MacLeish, Archibald. Interview with Benjamin Demott. *Writers at Work: The Paris Review Interviews*. Fifth Series. Ed. George Plimpton. NY: Viking, 1981. 21–48.

Martyna, Wendy. "What Does 'He' Mean?: Use of the Generic Masculine." *Journal of Communication*. 28.1 (1978): 131–38.

Meyer, Emily and Louise Z. Smith. *The Practical Tutor*. NY: Oxford, 1987.

Miller, Henry. Interview with George Wickes. *Writers at Work: The Paris Review Interviews*. Second Series. NY: Viking, 1963. 165–91.

Mitchell, Margaret. "Initiated into the Fraternity of Powerful Knowers: How Collaborative Technology Has Ethically Legitimized Writing Centers." *Writing Lab Newsletter* 19.7 (1995): 11–13.

Neff, Julie. "Learning Disabilities and the Writing Center." *Intersections: Theory-Practice in the Writing Center*. Eds. Joan A. Mullin and Ray Wallace. Evanston, IL: NCTE, 1994. 81–94.

Neruda, Pablo. Interview with Rita Guibert. *Writers at Work: The Paris Review Interviews*. Fifth Series. Ed. George Plimpton. NY: Viking, 1981. 49–73.

North, Stephen. "The Idea of a Writing Center." *College English* 46 (1984): 433–46.

Perry, William. *Forms of Intellectual and Ethical Development in the College Years: A Scheme*. New York: Holt, 1970.

Proulx, Annie. *The Shipping News*. NY: Simon and Schuster, 1993.

Richman, Evan. "Children in a Land of Conflict." *Boston Globe* 6/22/1997, D2.

Sale, Roger. *On Writing*. NY: Random House, 1979.

Schwartz, Lynn Sharon. "Remembrance of Tense Past." *Writers on Writing: A Bread Loaf Anthology*. Eds. Robert Pack and Jay Parini. Hanover, NH: Middlebury College Press, 1991. 232–247.

Spear, Karen. *Sharing Writing: Peer Response Groups in English Classes*. Portsmouth, NH: Boynton/Cook, 1988.

Spooner, Michael. "Some Thoughts about Online Writing Labs." *Writing Lab Newsletter* 18.6 (1994): 6–8.

Tan, Amy. "Angst and the Second Novel." *Publishers Weekly* 5 April 1991: 4–7.

Vidal, Gore. Interview with Gerald Clarke. *Writers at Work: The Paris Review Interviews*. Fifth Series. Ed. George Plimpton. NY: Viking, 1981. 281–311.

Weaver, Constance. *Teaching Grammar in Context*. Portsmouth, NH: Boynton/Cook, 1966.

Weltner, Linda. "Mother Nature's Children." *Boston Globe* 6/26/97, F2.

Welty, Eudora. Interview with Linda Kuehl. *Writers at Work: The Paris Review Interviews*. Fourth Series. Ed.George Plimpton. NY: Viking, 1974: 273–94.

Williams, Joseph. *Style: Ten Lessons in Style and Grace*. NY: Scott Foresman, 1981.

Woolf, Virginia. *A Writer's Diary*. NY: Harcourt, 1953.

Writing in the Disciplines. Fort Worth, TX: Harcourt, 1995.

Readings

Peer Tutoring:
A Contradiction in Terms?

JOHN TRIMBUR

Over the past several years, I've asked the peer tutors I train and supervise to describe their initial expectations when they started tutoring. This request was at first a matter of personal curiosity, but I've found that their descriptions have given me some important leads in thinking about the aims of peer tutor training. Harvey Kail says that peer tutors teach us how to train them. I think he's right. Let me describe my tutors' expectations and what I think the implications are for tutor training.

The undergraduates who become peer tutors in writing centers begin with a combination of high hope and nagging doubt. For one thing, the tutors want to share their enthusiasm for writing with their tutees, to make their tutees into committed writers. Matt, for example, thought "my major objective would be to fire up my students to want to attack their writing assignments." This enthusiasm, of course, can lead to unrealistic expectations. "My expectations when I started tutoring," Ellen wrote in her tutoring log, "were to turn all the students I tutored into 'A' students." And at times this enthusiasm can take on a positively evangelical quality. Geoff thought his task was "to save the English language from apparently inevitable decline."

Mixed in with these hopes, realistic and otherwise, are the considerable doubts tutors feel about their ability to tutor effectively. They are often insecure about their mastery of rhetoric, style, grammar, and usage. Despite (or maybe because of) their good intentions, tutors aren't always sure they'll be able to help their tutees write better. This combination of enthusiasm and uncertainty is familiar to experienced writing center directors who train peer tutors. We all face the problem of making sure that peer tutors' initial expectations don't backfire on them. I've seen it happen. Tutors are delicate mechanisms, without the protective coating and resiliency most of us develop as professionals. So there's the risk tutors' initial expectations will be shattered, leading to disappointment or even cynicism. When their hopes are not realized, when tutoring sessions don't go well or when tutees' grades don't go up, tutors may start to blame the students they work with. More often, the tutors blame themselves, and their feelings of inadequacy can turn into a debilitating sense of guilt about not getting the job done.

The problem, however, is not just the tutors' ego-investment. The problem concerns what the tutors have invested their energy doing. Tutors' initial standards for defining the aims and evaluating the results of tutoring are predictably conventional ones, informed by the prevailing reward structure that makes grades the central measure of success in higher education. It certainly helps to explain that peer tutoring is more interested in the long-term development of a tutee's writing ability than in the short-term results of any given writing assignment. As Stephen North put it so well, the job of tutoring is to produce better writers, not just better writings. But the mode of production tutors are most familiar with is the traditional academic mode of teaching and learning, a hierarchical structure in which the teacher passes down knowledge to the students and then measures how much the students received. This traditional model invariably shapes, to one extent or another, tutors' initial expectations—and can lead to considerable confusion about their work as peer tutors.

What is a Peer, What is a Tutor?

There's a certain irony operating here because the tutors' hopes and doubts about their work as peer tutors come in part from their own success as undergraduates. As a rule, tutors are highly skilled academic achievers: they are independent learners, they get good grades, they know how to "psych out" a course, they are accustomed to pleasing their instructors. Since they're used to performing successfully for evaluation, new tutors tend to measure learning by grades and to expect that tutoring will raise their tutees' grades, if not win them "A's."

At the same time, however, the traditional model of teaching and learning tells new tutors that they are not qualified to tutor, to pass down knowledge to their tutees. As any faculty opponent of peer tutoring will tell you, students do not possess the expertise and credentials—the professional standing—to help their peers learn to write. According to prevailing academic standards, faculty traditionalists are correct: peer tutoring doesn't make much sense. If anything, peer tutoring looks like a case of the "blind leading the blind."

Now most of us involved in writing centers have developed good arguments to counter our unreconstructed colleagues. Kenneth A. Bruffee makes a telling point when he argues that peer tutoring replaces the hierarchial model of teachers and students with a collaborative model of co-learners engaged in the shared activity of intellectual work. As writing center directors and peer tutor trainers, we may feel secure about the significance of collaborative learning and the way it redefines learning as an event produced by the social interaction of the learners—and not a body of information passed down from an expert to a novice. But for the undergraduates who become peer tutors, the insecurities linger. Rewarded by the traditional structure of teaching and learning, tutors have often internalized its values and standards and, in many respects, remain dependent on its authority.

In other words, new tutors are already implicated in a system that makes the words "peer" and "tutor" appear to be a contradiction in terms. How, many good tutors want to know, can I be a peer and a tutor simultaneously? If I am qualified to tutor, then I am no longer a peer to those I tutor. On the other hand, if I am a peer to my tutees, how can I be qualified to tutor? To be selected as a peer tutor in the first place seems only to confirm the contradiction in terms by acknowledging differences between the tutors and their tutees. The tutors' success as undergraduates and their strengths as writers single them out and accentuate the differences between them and their tutees—thereby, in effect, undercutting the peer relationship. Appointment to tutor, after all, invests a certain institutional authority in the tutors that their tutees have not earned. For new tutors, the process of selection itself seems to set the terms "peer" and "tutor" at odds. It induces cognitive dissonance by asking new tutors to be two things at once, to play what appear to them to be mutually exclusive roles.

In practice, new tutors often experience cognitive dissonance as a conflict of loyalties. They feel pulled, on one hand, by their loyalty to their fellow students and, on the other hand, by loyalty to the academic system that has rewarded them and whose values they have internalized. On a gut level, new tutors often feel caught in the middle, suspended in a no-man's-land between the faculty and the students.

The tutors' loyalty to their peers results from their shared status as undergraduates. Both tutors and tutees find themselves at the bottom of the academic hierarchy. Tutors and tutees alike confront a faculty who control the curriculum, assign the work, and evaluate the results. This common position in the traditional hierarchy, moreover, tends to create social bonds among students, to unionize them. Undergraduates have always banded together to deal with the emotional and cognitive demands of college, and, in one respect, peer tutoring simply institutionalizes and accords legitimacy to the practices of mutual aid students have always engaged in on their own.

But if peer tutoring programs are efforts by educators to tap the identification of student with student as a potentially powerful source of learning, peer tutoring can also lead to the further identification of peer tutors with the system that has rewarded them, underscoring the tutors' personal stake in the hierarchical values of higher education. New tutors feel not only the pull of loyalty to their peers. They may also feel the pull of competing against their peers and of maintaining the sense of cultural superiority the academic hierarchy has conferred on them. Tutors such as Geoff, whom I quoted earlier, may see themselves as missionaries on a crusade to save their college by bringing literacy to the masses. They may in fact wind up sounding like our most conservative colleagues. Geoff, for example, went so far as to suggest that the way the writing center could improve student writing was to picket the admissions office to raise entrance standards.

Now I don't mean to smirk at one tutor. All writing center directors have encountered peer tutors who are "bossy" and competitive know-it-alls unable to extricate themselves from the authoritarian attitudes and behaviors of the traditional academic hierarchy. Besides, at the other extreme are those peer tutors who use their superior learning, in this case out of loyalty to their peers, to co-author student papers, who cross the boundaries of the writing center and enter the realm of ghost writing and plagiarism. If you're like me, you may find the latter aberration from the norms of peer tutoring—a misguided sense of student solidarity—somewhat easier to correct and perhaps more forgivable. But the point is both instances threaten to subvert the educational promise of peer tutoring.

These aberrations, of course, are extreme, and happily they are rare. The vast majority of the peer tutors I've trained and supervised have handled the conflicting loyalties they experience with considerable grace and common sense. The usefulness of looking at these extreme instances is that they illustrate the social pressures peer tutors are likely to feel. In fact, we might say that to become a peer tutor is to invite these pressures. Peer tutoring invariably precipitates a crisis of loyalty and identity for the undergraduates who join the staff of a writing center. This crisis, I would argue, is a potentially fruitful one for students. And for writing center directors and peer tutor trainers, it is our unique responsibility to help tutors negotiate this crisis and put the terms "peer" and "tutor" together in practical and meaningful ways.

Models of Tutor Training

Let's take a look now at what peer tutors' initial expectations—the hopes and doubts and conflicting loyalties—suggest for tutor training. There is at present a considerable body of literature and accumulated experience in training peer tutors. As Nathaniel Hawkins points out, this work contains a problem similar to the one I've just outlined. The dilemma for tutor trainers, Hawkins says, is "whether to emphasize the tutor's role [as peer and co-learner] or his knowledge of grammar and theory" (9). We have, on the one hand, a model of tutor training that emphasizes the tutor component of the equation. This model regards the peer tutor as an apprentice and often designs training courses as an introduction to teaching writing. The book list for such a course may well look like ones used in a practicum for graduate teaching assistants—Tate's bibliographical essays, *Research in Composing,* Grave's *Rhetoric and Composition,* and so on. The second model emphasizes the peer component. This model casts peer tutors as co-learners. Bruffee's Brooklyn Plan is no doubt the seminal influence here, with its focus on the dynamics of collaborative learning and on the peer tutors' activity as writers and readers. Its goal is not so much to produce expertise as it is to produce an experiential knowledge of the process of peer critiquing and co-learning to write.

Each of these models, of course, has something to recommend it. We want tutors to know about writing and to be competent in talking to their tutees about the composing process. At the same time, we want them to be capable of collaborating with their peers and of making their own experience in writing and receiving criticism accessible to their tutees. If the tutors are not well trained, they won't be able to help their tutees. But, as Bruffee argues, if they are "too well trained, tutees don't perceive them as peers but as little teachers, and the collaborative effect of working together is lost" (446). Maybe, then, we need what Marvin Garrett calls a "delicate balance"—just the right amount of expertise and theory mixed with just the right amount of peership and collaboration.

If you expect me, at this point, to offer a tutor training program that balances the peer and the tutor components, you're going to be disappointed. Let me explain why. At a recent conference on peer tutoring, a colleague suggested that the apparently contradictory nature of peer tutoring could be resolved by helping tutors develop the judgment to know when to shift roles from that of tutor to that of peer and back again. Tutoring, that is, is a balancing act that asks tutors to juggle roles, to shift identity, to know when to act like an expert and when to act like a co-learner. What seems to me the case, however, is that making role shifts or balancing contrary identities is precisely what peer tutors cannot do. Peer tutors do not possess a strategic ego center outside their experience as peers and tutors from which to maneuver—to make such shifts or to achieve such balances. Rather they are peers and tutors simultaneously. In fact, I would argue that we should think of the terms "peer" and "tutor" not so much as roles to be played but as social pressures that converge on peer tutors, leading to the conflict of loyalty and identity crisis that inhere in peer tutoring. Tutor training, then, is not so much a matter of learning what roles to play as it is a matter of learning how to negotiate the conflicting claims on the tutors' social allegiances.

Training and Timing

The two models of tutor training—the apprentice model and the co-learner model—reproduce at the professional level the contradiction of terms "peer" and "tutor" that students experience at a gut level. The tilt of tutor trainers toward either the peer or the tutor component of the equation carries important implications not only for tutor training but also for the design and function of peer tutoring programs in writing centers. To follow the apprentice model and emphasize expertise and theory is to conceive of peer tutoring as an arm of the writing program, a way to deliver state-of-the-art instruction in writing to tutees. To follow the co-learner model and emphasize collaboration and experiential learning is to conceive of peer tutoring as a semi-autonomous activity that contributes to the formation of a student culture that takes writing seriously.

I don't pretend these two models can be easily reconciled. It may be the case, however, that the contradictory nature of the terms "peer" and "tutor" will make more sense if we stop talking about them in spatial terms, as roles to balance, and talk about them instead as a temporal sequence to be played out. I want to suggest a rather messy solution to tutor training that incorporates elements from both models but at different stages. What I have in mind is a sequence of tutor training that treats tutors differently depending on their tutoring experience—in short, that treats tutors developmentally. This developmental sequence would begin with a Bruffeesque approach to the peer tutors as collaborative learners. Given the way the traditional hierarchy influences new tutors' expectations and definitions of their activity as tutors, they initially need concrete and practical experience co-learning. Most peer tutors have had important experiences collaborating in everyday life but rarely in academic contexts. So they need practice if they are going to be effective co-learners. To my mind, this stage is the most significant because it demands that students unlearn some of the values and behaviors—the competitive individualism of traditional academics—that have already rewarded them and shaped their identities as students. They need, in effect, to relinquish some of their dependence on faculty authority and conventional measures of success (the source, we have just seen, of both their hopes and doubts as peer tutors) and to experience instead the authority co-learners invest in each other as they forge a common language to solve the problems writers face.

Tutors need, that is, to develop confidence in their autonomous activity as co-learners, without the sanction of faculty leaning over their shoulder and telling them and their tutees when something is learned and when not. For most new tutors, the terms "peer" and "tutor" come together in meaningful ways as tutors learn to work with their tutees, when together they jointly control their purposes, set the agenda, and evaluate the results of their learning—as autonomous co-learners outside official academic channels. It is this autonomous activity that creates the social space for peer tutoring and makes writing centers an extension of the social solidarity and collaborative practices in student culture.

To return to Kail's remark about how peer tutors teach us how to train them, I must admit that often new tutors want me to teach them how to teach. They expect me to tell them what to do, to tell them what messages to send to their tutees, and to give them the methods to deliver these messages. But these questions are part of the old script, the script new tutors bring with them from their experience in the academic hierarchy of passing down knowledge. The initial stage of tutor training must address these expectations but indirectly, by structuring activities in which new tutors can gain experience co-learning. The point of tutor training at this stage is to resocialize tutors as collaborative learners within student culture. For this reason, I agree with Bruffee that tutor training must avoid producing "little teachers." It's important to see, though, that the problem is not just the half-truth that a little knowledge can be a dangerous thing. The problem is that knowledge is a powerful thing that aligns people with particular communities. To emphasize expertise in the initial stages of tutor training treats tutors as apprentices who are learning to join the community of professional writing teachers. I would argue that expertise in teaching writing is not so much dangerous as it is premature because it takes peer tutors out of student culture, the social medium of co-learning.

For me, tutor training is a matter of timing and community allegiance. The apprentice model of tutor training invokes a kind of knowledge—the theory and practice of teaching writing—that pulls tutors toward the professional community that generates and authorizes such knowledge. Instead of imparting the professional expertise of the community of writing teachers, tutor trainers need to tap and organize the native expertise of co-learning that is latent in the student's own community of undergraduates. What I'm arguing is that we need to resist the temptation to professionalize peer tutors by treating them as apprentices and by designing training courses as introductions to the field of teaching writing. We need to treat peer tutors as students, not as paraprofessionals or preprofessionals, and to recognize that their community is not necessarily ours.

Through their tutoring experience, students may well gravitate toward the community of professional writing teachers, become interested in composition studies, and perhaps go on to graduate school and careers as writing teachers. Most of us involved in peer tutoring programs have seen this happen. In fact, tutors are in general so bright and articulate it is tempting to look at writing centers as recruiting grounds, not just for English or writing majors but for colleagues. My point here is simply that if experienced peer tutors do gravitate toward our profession, this should grow out of their own experience as co-learners in the semi-autonomous territory of writing centers.

Tutor trainers need to nurture the development of experienced tutors as much as that of new tutors, and advanced tutor training courses or practicums can help tutors deepen their awareness of the collaborative process of learning to write. Advanced training courses might well include composition theory and pedagogy, but this study should take place in a developmental sequence of the tutors' interests and purposes—the result of their experience tutoring and not a prerequisite to it. My worry is that the conception of tutoring as an apprenticeship treats students as extensions of our profession and can reinforce their dependence on faculty authority. To emphasize expertise at the expense of an experiential knowledge of co-learning risks short circuiting the dynamics of collaboration in student culture—the communities of readers and writers that are always in the process of formation when peers work together in writing centers.

WORKS CITED

Bruffee, Kenneth A. "Training and Using Peer Tutors." *College English* 40 (1978): 432-49.

Garrett, Marvin. "Towards a Delicate Balance: The Importance of Role-Playing and Peer Criticism in Peer Tutor Training." *Tutoring Writing*. Ed. Muriel Harris. Glenview: Scott, 1981. 94-100.

Hawkins, Nathaniel. "An Introduction to the History and Theory of Peer Tutoring in Writing." *A Guide to Writing Programs: Writing Centers, Peer Tutoring, Writing Across the Curriculum*. Ed. Tori Haring-Smith. Glenview: Scott, 1984. 7-18.

Kail, Harvey. "Collaborative Learning in Context." *College English* 45 (1983): 592-99.

North, Stephen. "Training Tutors to Talk about Writing." *College Composition and Communication* 33 (1982): 434-41.

Progression

JENNIFER C. MALONEY

At the beginning of my peer tutoring class, I was assigned to go into the writing center to experience a consulting session from the writer's point of view. I flipped through a stack of papers from the previous semester and picked out one of my B+ efforts to bring to the consulting session. I sashayed into the writing center one sunny fall afternoon and met with Maggie, who told me after reading my paper that I needed to expand on my ideas and go into more detail to clarify my thesis. She said that overall my paper was generally well-written. There weren't any problems with structure—it was really good, as a matter of fact. That was a nice little boost to my ego. When the session was over, I decided to tell her about my "secret mission"— that I was in the consulting class and had come in as part of an assignment.

"Oh," she said. "I wish you hadn't told me that. Now I'm nervous that I was being evaluated."

Surfing along on my wave of confidence, I told her not to worry and that she had done just fine. My (minimal) experience in the writing center so far had been rather positive, and basically painless.

I quickly learned that not every writer's experience was as painless as mine had been. It was my first day as a consultant-in-training at the writing center. That morning a student named Denise came in with a paper that was due the next night. She had already received some feedback from her professor. There were various little messages scrawled in the margins, written in that barely decipherable script that seems to be a prerequisite if you're a doctor or a college professor. Denise had been instructed to expand on her ideas and go into more detail to clarify her thesis, just as Maggie had instructed me to do with my paper. Nancy, the consultant I was training with, put forth an admirable effort. She used listing techniques to help Denise generate more ideas. She reinforced her, telling her what good ideas she had. However, I noticed that Denise was becoming increasingly frustrated when her questions such as "What do you think about this, Nancy? Is this right? Do you think this is right?" were answered with, "It's not important what I think, Denise. It's important what *you* think. How do *you* feel about this?" Even though it was early in the semester, I had already learned one of the writing center's sacred commandments: the writers' ideas and work must be their own.

It was obvious that Denise wasn't very happy about this notion as she began to pack up her notes and tears began to fill her eyes.

"You're not helping me. You're not helping me," she sniffed.

I felt terrible for Denise because she desperately wanted someone else's opinion other than her own. She wasn't confident about what she had to say. I felt terrible for Nancy, too, because she was trying so hard to get Denise to develop her own thoughts and have confidence in them. Instead of losing her patience, Nancy comforted Denise and gently explained that she couldn't do the work for her. Denise blurted out that she knew this, but that the assignment was very difficult for her since she was starting college later in life and had been away from school for so long. She had already raised her family. She was more comfortable doing math, where you're only dealing with numbers. Her professor demanded so much from her. He could read her paper and, by changing one word, make a profound impact. She knew that he wouldn't like this paper and that her work was wrong.

I was amazed that my first time observing a real consulting session had been so dramatic. I was also amazed by Nancy's ability to calm Denise and persuade her into staying a while longer to work some more. They worked together until Denise looked at the clock and said that she was going to be late for her next class. She apologized profusely to both Nancy and me.

"This is just so hard for me. I hope you understand," she said as she left.

I received my strongest dose of reality a few weeks later. At this point it's probably relevant to explain that I am not the most outgoing person in the world—not in the sense that I'm rude (I hope), but more in the sense that I'm shy and reserved. Writing is my favorite form of expression. I do not relish the spotlight in any way whatsoever; in fact I feel uncomfortable in it. I don't like knowing that all eyes are upon me, and I get very distracted when I know my performance is being evaluated. How I ever made it through public speaking class is really quite beyond me.

Nancy and I were participating in the assigned role play one Monday morning. I had been up late studying for a midterm the night before and was tired and irritable. I read through the assignment and the draft. I saw what should be corrected, but since my mouth and brain weren't working together that morning. I couldn't seem to articulate it to Nancy. The pressure of knowing I was being evaluated further hampered me in the situation.

I interrupted the role play and told Nancy that I couldn't think of ways to explain what was going on in the draft. She offered a few suggestions and asked me if I wanted to continue. Not wanting to be perceived as a quitter even in the sleep-deprived state I was in, I took the ball and ran the wrong way with it (I get taken back to playing basketball in my fourth grade gym class and making a picture-perfect lay-up—for the other team). Instead of trying to get Nancy, in her role as the writer, to recognize and see what should have been done, I began telling her, "Okay. Here and here you're doing this. But what you really should be doing is that. I think it would be much better if you took this approach."

Nancy stopped me before I realized what I was doing. I was violating that writing center commandment, "The writers' ideas and work must be their own." I felt like I had botched the entire role play at that point and became very discouraged and aggravated with myself. We stopped and talked about my difficulties. Nancy was very supportive. She kept reminding me that this was only the second time we had done role play and that this was the purpose of it—to get things wrong so that the next time I could get them right.

This was the most valuable experience of my training program. I gained a better understanding of how it can feel for a writer to come in to the writing center. I felt awkward, nervous, frustrated, vulnerable, and intimidated. I was worrying, like Denise, about what was wrong and what was right. My confidence had been shattered. I felt nervous, like Maggie, about being evaluated. I also realized the importance of being, like Nancy, a supportive, conscientious consultant.

On a final note, my role plays with Nancy improved with every session. While practice may not make perfect, it definitely helped in my case.

Peer Tutoring and the "Conversation of Mankind"

KENNETH A. BRUFFEE

The beginnings of peer tutoring lie in practice, not in theory. A decade or so ago, faculty and administrators in a few institutions around the country became aware that, increasingly, students entering college had difficulty doing as well in academic studies as their abilities suggested they should be able to do. Some of these students were in many ways poorly prepared academically. Many more of them, however, had on paper excellent secondary preparation. The common denominator among the poorly prepared and the apparently well prepared seemed to be that, for cultural reasons we may not yet fully understand, all these students had difficulty adapting to the traditional or "normal" conventions of the college classroom.

One symptom of the difficulty was that many of these students refused help when it was offered. Mainly, colleges offered ancillary programs staffed by professionals. Students avoided them in droves. Many solutions to this problem were suggested and tried, from mandated programs to sink-or-swim. One idea that seemed at the time among the most exotic and unlikely (that is, in the jargon of the Sixties, among the most "radical") turned out to work rather well. Some of us had guessed that students were refusing the help we were providing because it seemed to them merely an extension of the work, the expectations, and above all the social structure of traditional classroom learning. And it was traditional classroom learning that seemed to have left these students unprepared in the first place. What they needed, we had guessed, was help of a sort that was not an extension but an alternative to the traditional classroom.

To provide that alternative, we turned to peer tutoring. Through peer tutoring, we reasoned, teachers could reach students by organizing them to teach each other. Peer tutoring was a type of collaborative learning. It did not seem to change what people learned but, rather, the social context in which they learned it. Peer tutoring made learning a two-way street, since students' work tended to improve when they got help from peer tutors and tutors learned from the students they helped and from the activity of tutoring itself. Peer tutoring harnessed the powerful educative force of peer influence that had been—and largely still is—ignored and hence wasted by traditional forms of education.[1]

These are some of the insights we garnered through the practical experience of organizing peer tutoring to meet student needs. More recently, we have begun to learn that much of this practical experience and the insights it yielded have a conceptual rationale, a theoretical dimension, that had escaped us earlier as we muddled through, trying to solve practical problems in practical ways. The better we understand this conceptual rationale, however, the more it leads us to suspect that peer tutoring (and collaborative learning in general) has the potential to challenge the theory and practice of traditional classroom learning itself.

This essay will sketch what seems to me to be the most persuasive conceptual rationale for peer tutoring and will suggest what appear to be some of the larger implications of that rationale. The essay will begin by discussing the view of thought and knowledge that seems to underlie peer tutoring. Then it will suggest what this view implies about how peer tutoring works. Finally, the essay will suggest what this concept of knowledge may suggest for studying and teaching the humanities.

Conversation and the Origin of Thought

In an important essay on the place of literature in education published some twenty years ago, Michael Oakeshott argues that what distinguishes human beings from other animals is our ability to participate in unending conversation. "As civilized human beings," Oakeshott says,

> we are the inheritors, neither of an inquiry about ourselves and the world, nor of an accumulating body of information, but of a conversation, begun in the primeval forests and extended and made more articulate in the course of centuries. It is a conversation which goes on both in public and within each of ourselves....Education, properly speaking, is an initiation into the skill and partnership of this conversation in which we learn to recognize the voices, to distinguish the proper occasions of utterance, and in which we acquire the intellectual and moral habits appropriate to conversation. And it is this conversation which, in the end, gives place and character to every human activity and utterance.[2]

Arguing that the human conversation takes place within us as well as among us and that conversation as it takes place within us is what we call reflective thought, Oakeshott makes the assumption that conversation and reflective thought are related in two ways: organically and formally. That is, as the work of Lev Vygotsky and others has shown,[3] reflective thought is public or social conversation internalized. We first experience and learn "the skill and partnership of this conversation" in the external arena of direct social exchange with other people. Only then do we learn to displace that "skill and partnership" by playing silently, in imagination, the parts of all the participants in the conversation ourselves. As Clifford Geertz has put it, "thinking as an overt, public act, involving the purposeful manipulation of objective materials, is probably fundamentals to human beings; and thinking as a covert, private act, and without recourse to such materials, a derived, though not unuseful, capability."[4]

Since what we experience as reflective thought is organically related to social conversation, the two are also related functionally. That is, because thought originates in conversation, thought and conversation tend to work largely in the same way. Of course, in thought some of the limitations of conversation are absent. Logistics, for example, are no problem at all; I don't have to go anywhere or make an appointment to get together with myself for a talk. I don't even need to dial the phone, although I do sometimes need a trip to the coffeemaker. And in thought there are no differences among the participants in preparation, interest, native ability, or spoken vernacular. On the other hand, in thought some of the less fortunate limitations of conversation may hang on. Limitations imposed by my ethnocentrism, inexperience, personal anxiety, economic interest, and paradigmatic inflexibility can constrain my thinking just as they can constrain my conversation. If my talk is narrow, superficial, biased, and confined to cliches, my thinking is likely to be so, too. Still, it remains the case that many of the social forms and conventions of conversation, most of its language conventions and rhetorical structures, its impetus and goals, its excitement and drive, its potentially vast range and flexibility, and the issues it addresses are the sources of the forms and conventions, structures, impetus, range and flexibility, and the issues of reflective thought.

The formal and organic relationship I have been drawing here between conversation and thought illuminates, therefore, the source of the quality, depth, terms, character, and issues of thought. The assumptions underlying this argument differ considerably, however, from the assumptions we ordinarily make about the nature of thought. We ordinarily assume that thought is some sort of "essential attribute" of the human mind. The view that conversation and thought are fundamentally related assumes instead that thought is a social artifact. As Stanley Fish has put it, the thoughts we "can think and the mental operations [we] can perform have their source in some or other interpretive community."[5] Reflective thinking is something we learn to do, and we learn to do it from and with other people. We learn to think reflectively as a result of learning to talk, and the ways we can think reflectively as adults depend on the ways we have learned to talk as we grew up. The range, complexity, and subtlety of our thought, its power, the practical and conceptual uses we can put it to, as well as the very issues we can address result in large measure (native aptitude, the gift of our genes, aside) directly from the degree to which we have been initiated into what Oakeshott calls the potential "skill and partnership" of human conversation in its public and social form.

To the extent that thought is internalized conversation, then, any effort to understand how we think requires us to understand the nature of conversation; and any effort to understand conversation requires us to understand the nature of community life that generates and maintains conversation. Furthermore, any effort to understand and cultivate in ourselves a particular kind of thinking requires us to understand and cultivate the community life that generates and maintains the conversation from which a particular kind of thinking originates. The first steps to learning to think better are to learn to converse better and to learn to create and maintain the sort of social contexts, the sorts of community life, that foster the kinds of conversations we value.

These relationships have broad applicability and implications far beyond those that may be immediately apparent. For example, Thomas Kuhn has argued that to understand scientific thought and knowledge, we must understand the nature of scientific communities.[6] Richard Rorty, carrying Kuhn's view and terminology further, argues that to understand any kind of knowledge, we must understand what Rorty calls the social justification of belief; that is, we must understand how knowledge is generated and maintained by communities of knowledgeable peers.[7] Stanley Fish completes the argument by positing that these "interpretive communities" are the source not only of our thought and the "meanings" we produce through the use and manipulation of symbolic structures, chiefly language; interpretive communities may also be in large measure the source of what we regard as our very selves.[8]

Conversation, Writing, and Peer Tutoring

The line of argument I have been pursuing has important implications for educators, especially those of us who teach composition. If thought is internalized public and social talk, then writing is internalized talk made public and social again. If thought is internalized conversations, then writing is internalized conversation re-externalized.[9]

Like thought, therefore, writing is temporally and functionally related to conversation. Writing is in fact a technologically displaced form of conversation. When we write, having already internalized the "skill and partnership" of conversation, we displace it once more onto the written page. But because thought is already one step away from conversation, the position of writing relative to conversation is more complex than even that of thought. Writing is at once both two steps away from conversation and a return to conversation. By writing, we re-immerse conversation in its social medium. Writing is two steps removed from conversation because, for example, my ability to write this essay depends on my ability to talk through with myself the issues I address here. And my ability to talk through an issue with myself derives largely from my ability to converse directly with other people in an immediate social situation.

The point is not that every time I write, what I say must necessarily be something I have talked over with other people first, although I may well often do just that. What I say can originate in thought. But since thought is conversation as I have learned to internalize it, the point is that writing always has its roots deep in the acquired ability to carry on the social symbolic exchange we call conversation. The inference writing tutors and teachers should make from this line of reasoning is that our task must involve engaging students in conversation at as many points in the writing process as possible and that we should contrive to ensure that that conversation is similar in as many ways as possible to the way we would like them eventually to write.

Peer Tutoring as Social Context

This practical inference returns us to peer tutoring. If we consider thought as internalized conversation and writing as re-externalized conversation, peer tutoring plays an important role in education for at least two reasons—both resulting from the fact that peer tutoring is a form of collaborative learning. First, peer tutoring provides a social context in which students can experience and practice the kinds of conversation that academics most value. The kind of conversation peer tutors engage in with their tutees can be emotionally involved, intellectually and substantively focused, and personally disinterested. There could be no better source of this than the sort of displaced conversation (i.e., writing) that academics value. Peer tutoring, like collaborative learning in general, makes students—both tutors and tutees—aware that writing is a social artifact, like the thought that produces it. However displaced writing may seem in time and space from the rest of a writer's community of readers and other writers, writing continues to be an act of conversational exchange.

Peer Tutoring as a Context for "Normal Discourse"

The second reason is somewhat more complex. Peer tutoring, again like collaborative learning in general, plays an important role in education because it provides a particular kind of social context for conversation, a particular kind of community: that of status equals, or peers. This means that students learn the "skill and partnership" of re-externalized conversation not only in a community that fosters the kind of conversation academics most value, but also in a community like the one most students must eventually write for in everyday life—in business, government, and the professions.

It is worthwhile digressing a moment to establish this last point. Ordinarily people write to inform and convince other people within the writer's own community, people whose status and assumptions approximate the writer's own.[10] That is, the sort of writing most people do most frequently in their everyday working lives is what Rorty calls "normal discourse." Normal discourse, a term of Rorty's coinage based on Kuhn's term "normal science," applies to conversation within a community of knowledgeable peers. A community of knowledgeable peers is a group of people who accept, and whose work is guided by, the same paradigms and the same code of values and assumptions. In normal discourse, as Rorty puts it, everyone agrees on the "set of conventions about what counts as a relevant contribution, what counts as a question, what counts as having a good argument for that answer or a good criticism of it." The product of normal discourse is "the sort of statement that can be agreed to be true by all participants whom the other participants count as 'rational.'"[11]

The essay I am writing here is an example of normal discourse in this sense. I am writing to members of my own community of knowledgeable peers. My readers and I (I suppose) are guided in our work by the same set of conventions about what counts as a relevant contribution, what counts as a question, what counts as an answer, what counts as a good argument in support of that answer or a good criticism of it. I judge my essay finished when I think it conforms to that set of conventions and values. And it is within that set of conventions and values that my readers will evaluate the essay, both in terms of its quality and in terms of whether or not it makes sense. Normal discourse is pointed, explanatory, and argumentative. Its purpose is to justify belief to the satisfaction of other people within the author's community of knowledgeable peers. Much of what we teach today—or should be teaching—in composition and speech courses is the normal discourse of most academic, professional, and business communities. The "rhetoric" taught in our composition textbooks comprises—or should comprise—the conventions of normal discourse of those communities.[12]

Teaching normal discourse in its written form is thus central to a college curriculum because the one thing college teachers in most fields commonly want students to acquire, and what teachers in most fields consistently reward students for, is the ability to carry on in speech and writing the normal discourse of the field in question. Normal discourse is what William Perry calls the fertile "wedding" of "bull" and "cow," of facts and their relevances: discourse on the established contexts of knowledge in a field that makes effective reference to facts and ideas as defined within those contexts. In a student who can consummate this wedding, Perry says, "we recognize a colleague."[13] This is so because to be a conversant with the normal discourse in a field of study or endeavor is exactly what we mean by being knowledgeable—that is, knowledge*able*—in that field. Not to have mastered the normal discourse of a discipline, no matter how many "facts" or data one may know, is not to be knowledgeable in that discipline. Mastery of a "knowledge community's" normal discourse is the basic qualification for acceptance into that community.

The kind of writing we hope to teach students in college, therefore, is not only the kind of writing most appropriate to work in fields of business, government, and the professions; it is also writing most appropriate to gaining competence in most academic fields that students study in college. And what both kinds of writing have in common is that they are written within and addressed to a community of status equals: peers. They are both normal discourse.

This point having, I hope, been established, the second reason peer tutoring is important in education becomes clear. As a form of collaborative learning, peer tutoring is important because it provides the kind of social context in which normal discourse occurs: a community of knowledgeable peers. This is the main goal of peer tutoring.

Objections to Peer Tutoring

But to say this only raises another question: How can student peers, not themselves members of the knowledge communities they hope to enter, help other students enter those communities? This question is of course a variation of the question most often raised about all kinds of collaborative learning: isn't it the blind leading the blind?

One answer to this question is that while neither peer tutors nor their tutees may alone be masters of the normal discourse of a given knowledge community, by working together—pooling their resources—they are very likely to be able to master it if their conversation is structured indirectly by the task or problem that a member of that community (the teacher) provides.[14] The conversation between peer tutor and tutee, in composition or for that matter any other subject, is structured by the demands of the assignment and by the formal conventions of academic discourse and of standard written English. The tutee brings to the conversation knowledge of the subject to be written about and knowledge of the assignment. The tutor brings to the conversation knowledge of the conventions of discourse and knowledge of standard written English. If the tutee does not bring to the conversation knowledge of the subject and the assignment, the peer tutor's most important contribution is to begin at the beginning: help the tutee acquire the relevant knowledge of the subject and the assignment.

What peer tutor and tutee do together is not write or edit, or least of all proofread. What they do together is converse. They converse about the subject and about the assignment. They converse about, in an academic context, their own relationship and the relationships between student and teacher. Most of all they converse about and pursuant to writing.

Peer Tutoring and the Humanities

The place of conversation in learning, especially in the humanities, is the largest context in which we must see peer tutoring. To say that conversation has a place in learning should not of course seem peculiar to those of us who count ourselves humanists, a category that includes many if not most writing teachers. Most of us count "class discussion" one of the most effective ways of teaching. The truth, however, is that we tend to honor discussion more in the breach than in the observance. The person who does most of the "discussing" in most discussion classes is usually the teacher.

Our discussion classes have this fateful tendency to turn into monologues because underlying our enthusiasm for discussion is a fundamental distrust of it. The graduate training most of us have enjoyed—or endured—has taught us that collaboration and community activity is inappropriate and foreign to work in humanistic disciplines. Humanistic study, we have been led to believe, is a solitary life, and the vitality of the humanities lies in the talents and endeavors of each of us as individuals.[15] What we call discussion is more often than not an adversarial activity pitting individual against individual in an effort to assert what one literary critic has called "will to power over the text," if not over each other. If we look at what we do instead of what we say, we discover that we think of knowledge as something we acquire and wield relative to each other, not something we generate and maintain in company with and in dependency upon each other.

Two Models of Knowledge

Only recently have humanists of note, such as Stanley Fish in literary criticism and Richard Rorty in philosophy, begun to take effective steps toward exploring the force and implications of knowledge communities in the humanistic disciplines and toward redefining the nature of our knowledge as a social artifact. Much of this recent work follows a trail blazed a decade ago by Thomas Kuhn. The historical irony of this course of events lies in the fact that Kuhn developed his notion about the nature of scientific knowledge after first examining the way knowledge is generated and maintained in the humanities and social sciences. For us as humanists to discover in Kuhn and his followers the conceptual rationale of collaborative learning in general and peer tutoring in particular is to see our own chickens come home to roost.

Kuhn's position that even in the "hard" sciences knowledge is a social artifact emerged from his attempt to deal with the increasing indeterminacy of knowledge of all kinds in the twentieth century.[16] To say that knowledge is indeterminate is to say that there is no fixed and certain point of reference against which we can measure truth. If there is no such referent, then knowledge must be a made thing, an artifact. Kuhn argued that to call knowledge a social artifact is not to say that knowledge is merely relative, that knowledge is what any one of us says it is. Knowledge is generated by communities of knowledgeable peers. Rorty, following Kuhn, argues that communities of knowledgeable peers make knowledge by a process of socially justifying belief. Peer tutoring, as one kind of collaborative learning, models this process.

Here then is a second and more general answer to the objection most frequently raised to collaborative learning of any type: that it is a case of the blind leading the blind. It is of course exactly the blind leading the blind if we insist that knowledge is information impressed upon the individual mind by some outside source. But if we accept the premise that knowledge is an artifact created by a community of knowledgeable peers and that learning is a social process not an individual one, then learning is not assimilating information and improving our mental eyesight. Learning is an activity in which people work collaboratively to create knowledge among themselves by socially justifying belief. We create knowledge or justify belief collaboratively by concealing each other's biases and presuppositions; by negotiating collectively toward new paradigms of perception, thought, feeling, and expression; and by joining larger, more experienced communities of knowledgeable peers through assenting to those communities' interests, values, language, and paradigms of perception and thought.

The Extension of Peer Tutoring

By accepting this concept of knowledge and learning even tentatively, it is possible to see peer tutoring as one basic model of the way that even the most sophisticated scientific knowledge is created and maintained. Knowledge is the product of human beings in a state of continual negotiation or conversation. Education is not a process of assimilating "the truth" but, as Rorty has put it, a process of learning to "take a hand in what is going on" by joining "the conversation of mankind." Peer tutoring is an arena in which students can enter into that conversation.

Because it gives students access to this "conversation of mankind," peer tutoring and especially the principles of collaborative learning that underlie it have an important role to play in studying and teaching the humanities. Peer tutoring is one way of introducing students to the process by which communities of knowledgeable peers create referential connections between symbolic structures and reality, that is, create knowledge, and by doing so maintain community growth and coherence. To study humanistic texts adequately, whether they be student themes or Shakespeare, is to study entire pedagogical attitudes and classroom practices. Such are the implications of integrating our understanding of social symbolic relationships into our teaching—not just into *what* we teach but also into *how* we teach. So long as we think of knowledge as a reflection and synthesis of information about the objective world, teaching *King Lear* seems to involve providing a correct text and rehearsing students in correct interpretations of it. But if we think of knowledge as socially justified belief, teaching *King Lear* involves creating context where students undergo a sort of cultural change in which they loosen ties to the knowledge community they currently belong to and join another. These two communities can be seen as having quite different sets of values, mores, and goals, and above all quite different languages. To speak in one of a person asking another to "undo this button" might be merely to tell a mercantile tale, or a prurient one, while in the other such a request could be both a gesture of profound human dignity and a metaphor of the dissolution of a world.

Similarly, so long as we think of learning as reflecting and synthesizing information about the objective world, teaching expository writing means providing examples, analysis, and exercises in the rhetorical modes—description, narration, comparison-contrast—or in the "basic skills" of writing and rehearsing students in the proper use. But if we think of learning as a social process, the process of socially justifying belief, teaching expository writing is a social symbolic process, not just part of it. Thus, to study and teach the humanities is to study and teach the social origin, nature, reference, and function of symbolic structures.

Humanistic study defined in this way requires, in turn, a reexamination of our premises as humanists and as teachers in light of the view that knowledge is a social artifact. Since to date very little work of this sort has been done, one can only guess what might come of it. But when we bring to mind for a moment a sampling of current theoretical thought in and allied to a single field of the humanities, for example, literary criticism, we are likely to find mostly bipolar forms: text and reader, text and writer, symbol and referent, signifier and signified. On the one hand, a critique of humanistic studies might involve examining how these theories would differ from their currently accepted form if they included the third term missing from most of them. How, for instance, would psychoanalytically oriented study of metaphor differ if it acknowledged that psychotherapy is fundamentally a kind of social relationship based on the mutual creation or recreation of symbolic structures by therapist and patient? How would semiotics differ if it acknowledged that connecting "code" and phenomenon are the complex social symbolic relations among the people who make up a semiotic community? How would rhetorical theory look if we assumed that writer and reader were partners in a common, community-based enterprise, partners rather than adversaries?

And having reexamined humanistic study in this way, we could suppose on the other hand that a critique of humanistic teaching might suggest changes in our demonstrating to students that they know something only when they can explain it in writing to the satisfaction of the community of their knowledgeable peers. To do this, in turn, seems to require us to engage students in collaborative work that does not just reinforce the values and skills they begin with but that promotes a sort of resocialization.[17] Peer tutoring is collaborative work of just this sort.

The Last Frontier of Collaborative Learning

The argument I have been making here assumes, of course, that peer tutors are well trained in a coherent course of study. The effectiveness of peer tutoring requires more than merely selecting "good students" and, giving them little or no guidance, throwing them together with their peers. To do that is to perpetuate, perhaps even aggravate, the many possible negative effects of peer group influence: conformity, anti-intellectualism, intimidation, and the leveling of quality. To avoid these pitfalls and marshal the powerful educational resource of peer group influence requires an effective peer tutor training course based on collaborative learning, one that maintains a demanding academic environment and makes tutoring a genuine part of the tutors' own educational development.

Given this one reservation, it remains to be said only that peer tutoring is not, after all, something new under the sun. However we may explore its conceptual ramifications, the fact is that people have always learned from their peers and doggedly persist in doing so, whether we professional teachers and educators take a hand in it or not. Thomas Wolfe's *Look Homeward, Angel* records how in grammar school Eugene learned to write (in this case, form words on a page) from his "comrade," learning from a peer what "all instruction failed" to teach him. In business and industry, furthermore, and in professions such as medicine, law, engineering, and architecture, where to work is to learn or fail, collaboration is the norm. All that is new in peer tutoring is the systematic application of collaborative principles to that last bastion of hierarchy and individualism, institutionalized education.

FOOTNOTES

1. The educative value of peer group influence is discussed in Nevitt Sanford, ed., *The American College* (New York: Wiley, 1962), and Theodore M. Newcomb and Everett K. Wilson, eds., *College Peer Groups* (Chicago: Aldine, 1966).
2. Michael Oakeshott, "The Voice of Poetry in the Conversation of Mankind," in *Rationalism in Politics* (New York: Basic Books, 1962), 199.
3. For example, L.S. Vygotsky, *Mind in Society* (Cambridge, Mass.: Harvard University Press, 1978).
4. Clifford Geertz, "The Growth of Culture and the Evolution of Mind," in *The Interpretation of Cultures* (New York: Basic Books, 1973), 76-77. See also in the same volume "The Impact of the Concept of Culture on the Concept of Man" and "Ideology as a Cultural System," Parts IV and V.
5. Stanley Fish, *Is There a Text in This Class? The Authority of Interpretive Communities* (Cambridge, Mass.: Harvard University Press, 1980), 14. Fish develops his argument fully in Part 2, pages 303-71.
6. Thomas Kuhn, *The Structure of Scientific Revolutions,* 2nd ed., International Encyclopedia of Unified Science, vol. 2, no. 2 (Chicago: University of Chicago Press, 1970).
7. Richard Rorty, *Philosophy and the Mirror of Nature* (Princeton, N.J.: Princeton University Press, 1979). Some of the larger educational implications of Rorty's argument are explored in Kenneth A. Bruffee, "Liberal Education and the Social Justification of Belief," *Liberal Education* (Summer 1982): 8-20.
8. Fish, 14.

9. A case for this position is argued in Kenneth A. Bruffee, "Writing and Reading as Collaborative or Social Acts: The Argument from Kuhn and Vygotsky," in *The Writer's Mind* (Urbana, Ill.: NCTE, 1983).

10. Some writing in business, government, and the professions may of course be like the writing that students do in school for teachers, that is, for the sake of practice and evaluation. Certainly some writing in everday working life is done purely as performance, for instance, to please superiors in the corporate or department hierarchy. So it may be true that learning to write to someone who is not a member of one's own status and knowledge community, that is, to a teacher, has some practical everyday value; but the value of writing of this type is hardly proportionate to the amount of time students normally spend on it.

11. Rorty, 320.

12. A textbook that acknowledges the normal discourse of academic disciplines and offers ways of learning it in a context of collaborative learning is Elaine Maimon, Gerald L. Belcher, Gail W. Hearn, Barbara F. Nodine, and Finbarr W. O'Connor, *Writing in the Arts and Sciences* (Cambridge, Mass.: Wintrhop, 1981; distributed by Little, Brown). Another is Kenneth A. Bruffee, *A Short Course in Writing* (Cambridge, Mass.: Winthrop, 1980; distributed by Little, Brown).

13. William G. Perry, Jr., "Examsmanship and the Liberal Arts," in *Examining in Harvard College: A Collection of Essays by Members of the Harvard Faculty* (Cambridge, Mass.: Harvard University Press, 1963); as reprinted in Bruffee, Short Course, 221.

14. For examples and an explanation of this process see Kenneth A. Bruffee, Short Course, and "CLTV: Collaborative Learning Television," *Educational Communication and Technology Journal* 30 (Spring 1982): 31ff.

15. The individualistic bias of our current interpretation of the humanistic tradition is discussed further in Kenneth A. Bruffee, "The Structure of Knowledge and the Future of Liberal Education," *Liberal Education* (Fall 1981): 181-85.

16. The history of the growing indeterminacy of knowledge and its relevance to the humanities is traced briefly in Bruffee, "The Structure of Knowledge," 177-81.

17. Some possible curricular implications of the concept of knowledge as socially justified belief are explored in Bruffee, "Liberal Education and the Social Justification of Belief," *Liberal Education* (Summer 1982): 8-20.

Rehabilitating the Writing Center Junkie

JEANNINE A. BROADWELL

When I first began tutoring in the Learning Center at the State University of New York at Plattsburgh, I figured that if I could give a writer enough of myself, we could accomplish anything...and everything. Their potential for improvement was boundless. Where do these illusions come from? Students often arrive, paper in hand, envisioning some distant perfection. And we have been and often are them—students—victims of the same untraceable social false advertising. Instructors (people who should know better) also frequently expect that tutoring will perfect their students' writing. It is this expectation of fixing *everything* that impedes the setting of goals in tutoring sessions. Unlimited aspirations require unlimited time. It took over a year of working with writers, much of the time still trying to give them too much, for me to realize what was wrong.

Just two weeks into my tutor training course, my friend Randy asked for help. "On what?" I asked. "Everything," she said, "This paper's got to be perfect." Our very first session quickly transformed my fantasies into nightmares. At that point, I had learned little more than that tutors should ask writers questions to stimulate thought instead of telling them what to fix.

I went over to her house at 6 p.m., and we sat down with her paper. The first mistake we made was trying to go line-by-line. We hadn't really gotten into specifics in my class yet, so I didn't realize we were asking for trouble. We tried to work on individual lines and entire paragraphs at the same time. Problems of spelling, punctuation, grammar, passive voice, unclear sentences, unsubstantiated assertions, and flawed ideas rose up before us. And it became impossible to continue trying to fix everything at once. Within half an hour the number of problems in the paper had overwhelmed and paralyzed us.

After that, we practically had to whip ourselves to keep going. Since I insisted on using the questioning method we were learning in class, I had a blinding headache from trying to think of a question for everything I could find wrong. Randy suffered countless lethargic fits of propping her forehead on her hand and her elbow on the table and moaning, "Ohhhhhh, I don't knoooow." We both thought she was a completely hopeless writer with hundreds of insurmountable problems, even though she wasn't—our unchecked sprawling had only succeeded in muddying everything.

At half-past midnight, I absolutely had to leave. I had postponed my own work until I no longer had time to do it. The fact that we hadn't even touched the last two pages of her paper frustrated both of us. We felt as if we had opened the door to a messy closet, and been buried in the avalanche of its contents. Whenever we recovered enough strength to try to clean up the debris, the stuff wouldn't fit back in—it was more than we could pick up in an hour. Really, opening and shutting a closet door is a lot like tutoring: if it takes more than an hour, there's something wrong.

Somewhere during that first appointment, Randy had become addicted to tutoring. She could not understand how she had managed without it all these years. She also couldn't write another word without seeking some sort of guidance. Randy had insisted that we meet again the next day. And, although I couldn't stand the idea of spending another six hours trapped in a room with her, I agreed purely out of a sense of obligation: I saw no other way for her to become "functional" by the end of the semester.

I also felt helpless. I decided that the questioning method we learned in class was defective. It never occurred to me to wait until the end of the semester before I worked with my first victim. I was actually like a pre-med student trying to diagnose and cure my best friend, using only the first chapter of my *Concepts In Biology* text.

Looking back, I know Randy's addiction actually started during the first fifteen minutes, when we failed to set reasonable goals. From that point on, we were only wasting our time. We applied so many different strategies and rules to her paper that she ended up remembering none of them. Randy learned nothing that evening except that she desperately needed a tutor— unfortunately, this one thing wasn't even true.

It probably wouldn't surprise you to hear that, at the same time, I also had this problem working with my brother. One Saturday afternoon, he asked me if I would look over his paper. I asked him to sit down for a minute, but it was actually about an hour and a half before we reached the end of his paper. Afterward, he snatched it back, glared at me, and shuffled away. He hated writing and I hated helping him. He recently told me that he had "just wanted a few ideas or suggestions, not a complete overhaul. I didn't want to put up with all that," he said. "It made me feel like writing it the first time was a complete and utter waste of time." He also said he had felt like neither he nor his writing were good enough.

Although my inexperience caused these problems, it allowed me the opportunity to learn from my mistakes. Because I didn't know any better, I stumbled upon a problem it turned out many of my fellow tutors had also encountered. Whenever a writer I worked with became dependent, it was because we both saw tutoring as a quick fix instead of a step in their learning process. Tutors who expect to fix all of their writers' problems actually force them to give up responsibility for their writing. Dependence occurs because they expect the tutor will transform their writing. This line of thinking automatically renders students helpless: if everything they write must be perfect, every word must be approved by the tutor.

I now know that bringing a paper to a tutor is not like bringing a car to a mechanic. Good tutors do not "fix" papers. Good tutors help students become better writers—no, not perfect writers—there's no such thing as a perfect writer or a perfect paper. Those who expect perfection will be disappointed to hear this. They might wonder what good tutoring is at all, then—since they need to end up with a perfect paper. Tutors need to remember that, though they can't get to everything, the paper will inevitably be better than if the writer hadn't come for help at all. We must each decide for ourselves where the line is between too much help and not enough.

The expectation that seeing a tutor will fix all of a paper's problems disempowers the writer and lends itself to a line-by-line approach. By trying to work on everything at once, the writer doesn't get any control over any one thing. Going over a paper sentence-by-sentence results in tutors doing the writers' work for them. And, if you try to do everything, you will end up doing nothing. As I found with both Randy and my brother, this approach obscured our vision of the paper. We couldn't see that there were patterns of error—we saw, instead, five or six problems per line spread out over hundreds of lines, which added up to thousands of problems.

When I asked my brother what would have changed our session into a positive one, he said, "Students and tutors both have to be focused on one or two things. Otherwise, you concentrate on the big things and the little things so it seems like much more. It's overwhelming when no one's focused. I also didn't like to feel pressured like I had to be tutored." The first step in solving my writer-dependence problem was to reject the myths of unlimited time, unlimited goals, and the perfect paper. Then, after considering the impact these myths and ineffective strategies had on the students, I arrived at a conclusion that both tutors and writers can live with.

To prevent tutoring addiction, time limits are essential. In a one-on-one setting, appointments should last no longer than an hour. In walk-in where there is often a waiting line, the amount of time spent actually working on the paper should be limited to roughly 15 minutes. The time limits themselves are not the only thing that makes this solution effective—their consequences are equally important. When tutors and writers both know from the start that time is limited, they are much more likely to set specific priorities and stick with them.

Generally speaking, if a writer comes to a session without goals, making sure the paper contains well developed, well thought-out ideas should be most important, then substantiation using specific personal examples. Finally, in the event of an otherwise beautiful paper, writer and tutor can worry about grammar or punctuation or spelling. In an appointment situation, tutors should read the students' work and then help them decide what to work on. In walk-in, after reading papers, tutors should help writers identify their *most important* concern. Sessions in which writers continue without questions or goals are the most likely to lead to dependence. Vague requests for help tempt us most to skim the surface or analyze line-by-line.

When students come to the sessions with predetermined goals, those goals should come first—whenever practical. For instance, if writers are worried about comma splices and their ideas are well thought out and supported, by all means work on comma splices. However, when tutors find more fundamental concerns, they should explain those concerns and their impact first, giving students an opportunity to adjust their priorities accordingly.

If at the end not enough time remains to work on comma splices, students could also take a hand-out home or make another appointment. Conceptual problems are usually more significant than mechanical ones. For example, a few weeks ago my Shakespeare professor returned a paper to me in which I had made several logical errors, but had used commas and semi-colons beautifully. His comments did not read: "Your paper doesn't make a lot of sense, but your punctuation was beautiful—I'll give you the A anyway."

Furthermore, in either walk-in or appointment situations, fifteen minutes is plenty of time to tackle one particular problem or concept. Even just a bit more time often leads students to believe that they need the tutor beside them in order to make progress, instead of understand that tutoring should make them able to tackle even more by themselves. My poor brother was worried about proper semi-colon use. In five minutes, I should have been able to explain that they are used to join two related independent clauses that could ordinarily stand alone. In the next five minutes, I could have helped him find a couple of places where he used semi-colons in his paper and determine whether or not they were used correctly. Finally, in the last five minutes, he would have been able to do a few practice sentences or correct misuses in his own paper. After fifteen minutes, he would have been able to handle semi-colones on his own with confidence. In an hour he could have conquered four different groups of problems.

However, we need to remember that these time guidelines are just that—guidelines. Rigid agendas don't allow writers or tutors to be human, and occasionally exert too much pressure. I would never recommend that tutors should end sessions in the middle of their explanation (or writers' questions) simply because sixty minutes had elapsed. Fifteen and sixty are not magic numbers and do not, by themselves, prevent writer dependence. Even within these guidelines, tutors and writers must remember to set goals and priorities. They need to focus. Time limits simply help us make a habit of practicing these strategies.

Finally, I need to mention that I am encouraged by discovering I've made these mistakes. The idea of *not* discovering them is what would horrify me. We all benefit from learning to recognize and prevent writer dependence. We can take comfort in realizing that sometimes it's wrong to try as hard as we are often expected to, and we should no longer feel guilty that hectic schedules and waiting lines limit the time we can devote to our students.

The Voyage Out

Peter Elbow

EDITOR'S NOTE: In this chapter from his book Writing with Power, *Peter Elbow describes what he calls "the loop writing process." In the first half of the loop, "the voyage out," the writer generates a wealth of material without censoring or critiquing it—this is the creative part of the writing process. In the second half of the loop, "the voyage back," the writer assesses what's been generated, deciding what to keep and continue working with—this is the critical part of the writing process. The loop or voyage can be repeated until the writer is satisfied with the results. Elbow's suggestions for "the voyage out" form a rich and sometimes surprising list of ideas for getting started.*

For the voyage out I suggest thirteen procedures for loop writing: directed freewriting. I will explain and discuss them before going on to describe the voyage home. You won't need all of them for any one piece of writing. Usually a few are enough. But if you practice them all you will have them all available and know which will be most suitable for any given writing task you face.

1. *First thoughts.* This is a good one to start with. Do it even before you have done any reading, research, planning, or new thinking about your topic. Just put down as fast as you can all the thoughts and feelings you happen to have about the topic. *You will discover much more material than you expected.* And not just feelings and memories either: there are probably solid facts and ideas you forgot you had.

Writing down first thoughts is more or less what you did during the first half of the direct writing process, and for some topics you will turn up enough material with first thoughts for your whole piece of writing. If so, go on to revising. Your ideas won't be as numerous or interesting as they would have been if you used some of the techniques I describe below, but you will have saved a lot of time and effort.

If it seems to you that you don't have any first thoughts, you are mistaken. It is because you aren't listening or accepting them. *That is, I'm not calling for good thoughts or true thoughts*—just first thoughts. If you have trouble, adopt the frame of mind of a scientist and simply record the reactions and thoughts that pass through consciousness as you struggle with the topic. More often you will have too many rather than too few first thoughts. Take the ones that appeal most.

If you are writing some kind of analysis or description—perhaps an evaluation of a person or a program, a write-up of a case, an abstract of a long article—first thoughts will often consist of certain details or incidents simply jumping out from your memory. You may not know why. They may seem senseless or random but they are not. These first tiny details and quick impressions often hold the key to important insights that you would miss if you proceeded straight to careful analytic thinking.

If you are having a particularly hard time making up your mind between two or three opinions—perhaps you are writing a report on two competing proposals, an essay on conflicting theories, a piece of personal writing to help you decide whether to break up with someone—first thoughts are particularly valuable. "What do you think you should do? Give an instant answer." "Which plan do you suspect you'll endorse in the end? First thoughts." Because these are naked hunches that lack any clear justification or support, you often feel shy about taking them seriously, much less writing them down. But you should. It's not that you can trust these hunches to be right (though surprisingly often they are: your instantaneous-computer-mind has taken everything into account and cranked out a judicious answer). But the slower, careful thinking you need for *deciding* if your hunch is right will go much better because you wrote it down blatantly: "Jung's account feels better than Freud's. Jung's feels... while Freud's feels...." Of course your hunch may be wrong but if so, it turns out that writing it down bluntly somehow helps you to abandon it more easily than if you leave it lurking in the back of your mind.

Spend at least fifteen minutes of nonstop writing on first thoughts even if the process seems a waste of time. Take longer of course if the material seems good. But don't spend any time at this early stage trying to get your thoughts correctly ordered or reconciled with each other. Just get them all down as quickly as you can.

2. *Prejudices.* This, too, is a good one to start with—even before reading, thinking, or researching your topic. What are your biases in the area of your topic. With the example of the Jung/Freud first thoughts above, I was obviously illustrating prejudices too. What kind of explanation of the French Revolution would be most *satisfying* to you? Do you suspect that monarchy is an inherently unjust form of government? That royalty was really the root cause of the revolution? Do you feel that mobs always do the wrong thing? Or that "the people" are always right in the end? That intellectuals are trouble-makers? If you are writing to persuade someone or a committee to adopt a certain policy, write out your naked prejudices and preferences before you do any careful thinking. It will help you see the difference between your biases and your genuine arguments—something you need to see if you want to persuade effectively.

If it isn't clear to you what your prejudices or preferences are, do first thoughts and then—in a somewhat detached and clinical spirit—look through what you've written to see what point of view or assumptions or biases are revealed there. But then jump with both feet into that point of view and write in as prejudiced a way as you can. You aren't trying to think carefully, you're trying to let your own prejudices run rampant without any censorship so you can see more clearly what they are. If it is hard to stop censoring, pretend to be *someone else* who is an extremist. Write his views.

Even if your topic seems more a matter of facts than of opinion—perhaps you are writing an environmental impact statement—it is still helpful to write prejudices. Prejudice and point of view are even more slippery in issues of fact. Perhaps you can't find a prejudice in yourself to exaggerate if you are writing, for example, about the effects of widening a road on the adjoining area of the county. But even if you do lack overt prejudices, you still have a whole web of assumptions and preconceptions of which you are probably unaware but which you can learn about if you write as though you *were* someone who is very prejudiced on the issue—perhaps someone who lives on the road and feels strongly against the widening. By taking a point of view as different as possible from your own, and really trying to enter into it as seriously as you can, you will begin to notice your own unconscious assumptions as they begin to be violated. You do best of all, perhaps, if you take two or three different points of view—one of them your own "objective" view—and write an argument among them. (See Number 4, *Dialogues,* below.)

Writing down your prejudices also helps you generate new ideas and insights. It's only by being obsessed with an idea, taking it as far as you can and seeing it everywhere, that you will notice all the arguments and evidence that support it. Copernicus wouldn't have found the evidence for the heliocentric model of the planets if he hadn't been obsessed with the importance of the sun and given some scope to his obsession. In addition, when you give more scope to your prejudice you will be led to notice more ideas that run *counter* to it that you wouldn't otherwise have seen. That is, you will start to pay attention to what an opponent would say. This helps you think of better arguments for your own point of view.

3. *Instant Version.* It would be a miracle to turn out a final version of any extensive writing task in half an hour. But it's worth while pretending to pull off this miracle. Simply deny the need for research, thinking, planning and turn out a kind of sketch of your final piece—an instant projected version. You'll have to pretend you know things you don't know, act as though you have made up your mind where you're uncertain, make up facts and ideas, and leave out large chunks (perhaps symbolizing these omissions with little boxes). But by doing so you can *will* yourself into producing a quickly written final version.

Some people are paralyzed by the process of extensive research for a major report or paper. The more research you do, the more impossible it is to start writing. You already have so much material—whether it is in your head or in your notes—that you can't find a place to start, you can't find a beginning to grab hold of in that tangled ball of string. You can write more notes but you can't start. Besides, you never feel you have finished your research: there are a couple more books or articles to get a hold of; they sound promising; better not write anything yet because they probably have some very important material that will change the whole picture. This is the path to panicked 3 A.M. writing the night before the due date. (Or the night after.) Writing first thoughts or prejudices or an instant version keeps you from falling into this research paralysis. *Have the sense to realize that it's easier to write* now when you know less. You can use subsequent research to check your thinking and to revise your writing to any level of sophistication that you wish.

If you do write first thoughts or prejudices or an instant version—and especially if you use a couple of these techniques—you will be able to get much more out of any reading and research you have to do for your paper. The more boring or difficult the research, the more helpful these early pieces of writing. They will make dull research interesting because you will already be an "authority" on the topic: you will already have lots of thoughts and a point of view. You will find yourself interested and alert as you read to see when the other authorities are smart enough to agree with your prejudices and when they get off track. When they come up with data or thinking that is new to you, it will be interesting and energizing. In short, your mind will already have a "set" or receptive net which will help you absorb all this otherwise dull information. You won't be in that demoralizingly passive position of doing research with your mouth hanging open and trying to take in everything. You'll remember more with fewer notes.

You will also discover, by the way, how close you often come to valid conclusions and sound arguments before you have consulted the data and arguments of others. You end up feeling much more powerful. It gets you out of that helpless position where you feel you cannot write anything unless you find out what all the "authorities" have said—a frame of mind that seduces you into one of the major forms of poor writing: writing that merely summarizes what "they" say. First thoughts, prejudices, and instant versions catapult you into a position of initiative and control so that you use reading and research to check and revise your thinking actively, not passively just to find something to think.

Even if your research is purely quantitative, these early-writing procedures will help a lot. Perhaps you are writing about levels of pollution of various chemicals in Puget Sound; or about government expenditures for various kinds of armaments and "defense." Write an instant version by making up your own numbers (based either on intuition or fantasy) and reaching your own conclusions. Afterward you'll do a much better job of seeing, remembering, and understanding the real numbers when you turn to the dull research.

These three early-writing procedures have another benefit that is especially important when the paper is difficult for you. Even experienced and professional writers often waste a lot of energy with old and sometimes unconscious fears of "This one's too hard, I won't be able to think of anything to say this time, I'll be a failure." After you have written first thoughts or prejudices or an instant version, these old feelings can't trouble you so much because you don't, in a sense, have to "write a paper," you just have to "revise a paper": change some numbers, add some sections, reverse some conclusions, perhaps even adjust the whole organization. That's all. Even though you may start with a short, sketchy, disorganized paper consisting entirely of fantasy thoughts and information, it is still a sort of paper. And more often than not, there are strong parts that you will keep in your final version. You have already performed the essential inner miracle that makes all writing mysterious and difficult: you have created something out of nothing.

4. *Dialogues.* If you discover that instead of having one clear prejudice you have two or three conflicting feelings, you are in a perfect position to write a dialogue. Give each of the feelings a voice and start them talking to each other. Keep your pencil moving and stand out of the way and these voices will have a lot to say that is important for your piece. You will probably discover somewhere along the way *who* these people are: perhaps one is your head and the other is your heart or guts; perhaps one is your mother who always saw things in terms of individuals, and the other is your father who always saw things in terms of their public consequences. Perhaps one voice is someone especially wise or perceptive who once gave you a glimpse of how things could be. It will probably help your dialogue writing to give these voices their right names and actually be these people as you write in each voice. But don't get side-tracked into wondering what these people would actually say: just keep them talking. If the effort to be these people slows down your writing, go back to the nameless dialogue you started with.

But I'm not recommending that you always do dialogues before you have engaged in research or thought about your topic. They are also especially valuable afterward. They help you to digest and understand all that thinking, research, and early writing and help you to come up with conclusions. After you have read about Louis XVI and Voltaire, get them talking and arguing with each other about the causes of the French Revolution. Let others join the conversation: a peasant, a courtier, one or two of the authors you have read on the topic, yourself, whoever might have something to say. Or get that homeowner who objects to having the road widened talking to a land developer—but not just off the tops of their heads this time: pretend they know all this specific data you've turned up in your research on environmental impact and watch them help you interpret it as they argue.

The main principle of dialogue writing is that you don't have to know ahead of time what a person is going to say. Just pick the speakers, get them talking, and see what they do say. They will often surprise you by saying things you've never thought of. For though you may know everything that two old friends of yours might say on some topic if you just wrote solitary monologues for each of them, you don't know all they will say if you start them interacting with each other. Arguments are especially fertile ground for new insights.

It's sometimes helpful to pick people whose opinions are not completely obvious to you. If, for example, you have the feeling that you already know everything Louis XVI will say about the French Revolution, don't pick him, pick some courtier whose opinions will be related but slightly unpredictable. But don't worry about this issue: even if you think you already know what

Louis XVI or your mother will say, they will come up with new and surprising things under the circumstances of a real dialogue. Think of a dialogue as an invitation to the unexpected and spontaneous.

Part of the power of dialogues comes from using the language of speech and talking and getting away from "essay language" which is usually more cumbersome and artificial and farther away from your felt perceptions. Therefore, make sure you talk on paper. It is important to sit inside each person's head in turn and actually write down the words that come out of that person's mouth. This means you'll probably write down lots of little words and phrases that occur in speech which don't contain much substantive meaning—phrases like "Well, um, maybe," or "You have a point there," or "I don't know, let me think about that," and so on. These are the phrases that occur when a person is in the middle of a conversation but isn't quite sure for a moment exactly what he things. That's exactly the position you should be in as you write your dialogue. Unless you write down what the people *say*, you won't actually get yourself into their heads and get the benefit of their thinking and points of view. Their "speech" is what they are, and since you need them to get the benefit of their thinking, you need their speech. Besides it's more fun just to let a real conversation unfold than to look for ideas or arguments. (And it helps all your writing to keep it in contact with the rhythms and textures of speech.)

Dialogues are especially useful if you have trouble writing analytically (which means you probably have trouble writing essays and reports). Writing a dialogue produces reasoning, but produces it spontaneously out of your feelings and perceptions. Get two people arguing with each other on paper—or give your opponent a voice so he can argue with you on paper—and you will naturally produce arguments: assertions, supporting reasons, and evidence. Since you are producing them in the heat of battle with your opponent interrupting you and perhaps changing arguments in midstream, they may be disordered or flawed, but you will nevertheless already have written most of the ingredients you need for an intelligent and muscular train of reasoning.*

5. *Narrative Thinking.* If your topic is confusing to you—if for example you find your mind shifting from one thought to another or from one point of view to another without any sense of which thought or point of view makes more sense—then simply write *the story of your thinking*. "I thought this, then I thought that," and so on. This process can help untangle bad snarls in your mind. It is especially useful if you are having trouble writing about something very complicated. If, for example, you are trying to analyze a tangled movie plot or a confusing legal case, move into the strict narrative mode

---

*Part of the reason why inexperienced essay writers benefit so little from the corrections of teachers on their essays is because the teacher is usually trying to correct *flaws* in an argument, while the student hasn't yet learned simply to engage in sustained argument by himself on paper. The student experiences the feedback as a double-bind: "You ask me to *engage* in sustained, abstract solitary reasoning—something that is difficult for me—and when I do it you punish my behavior."

and tell what happened and how you reacted; for example, "She described what happened to her and why she deserved to be repaid and I thought she was right, but when he answered I agreed with him, but then I began to change my mind again when I thought of....." Needless to say you may not want your final version in this narrative mode—it's very slow—but this early narrative writing can help you finally see the issue clearly enough so you can write something very tight and to the point. In particular it often helps you notice unconscious assumptions that have trapped you.

6. *Stories.* The best way to write a letter of recommendation or a job analysis or an evaluation of a person or project is to start by letting stories and incidents come to mind and jotting them down very briefly: good stories and bad ones, typical stories and unusual ones, funny stores and, best of all, stories that somehow stick in your mind for reasons you cannot pin down. This will spare you from that awful dullness so characteristic of evaluations and reports: empty generalizations and dead lists of qualities or adjectives. Each story will have a lively insight for you and most of those insights—especially the ones that grow out of the perplexing stories—will be far more useful than what you come up with when you just try to *think* about the person or the project or the job. In addition you can include some scraps of these stories in your final version to make it more clear and alive. Letters of recommendation are most useful if they include examples of actual incidents.

As you think through your reading about the French Revolution, what stories or incidents come to mind? Some will be obviously important and illustrative. But stand out of the way and let others simply occur to you. They won't all be from your reading. Perhaps the plight of the royalty or the peasantry reminds you of situations you were in. Perhaps the behavior of the urban poor reminds you of something you once did. Write these associations down. Try, in addition, to think of stories and incidents related to theoretical or structural elements in the topic. For example, what stories strike you about *causes:* occasions when one thing caused another but it seemed different from what you usually think of as a cause; perplexing arguments you've had about whether or not you caused something; cases where something had no cause or too many causes?

Write down these stories and events briefly and in a thumbnail way. You are trying to record as many as you can as quickly as you can. If there is a long and complex story, run through it in your head and write down a summary version in a long paragraph. You can use strings of phrases instead of whole sentences, but do include details. The effectiveness of this loop writing procedure stems from dredging up lots of rich concrete detail from your memory. You want to get your mind working on the narrative and experiential level, and away from saying, "What are my *thoughts* about the causes of the French Revolution?" The previous loop writing procedures will give you thoughts. Now you want your mind asking, "What are my *memories* and *experiences* that somehow relate to the French Revolution?" There is plenty of precious knowledge locked away in your narrative and experiential memory that you can't get to by thinking. Many wise people do their best thinking by telling stories.

Learn to trust yourself. Learn that the stories and events that intrigue you in connection with your topic will end up useful to you later. Practice this technique so you can end up with at least three or four pages containing at least fifteen or twenty stories or events briefly told. Sometimes the material you come up with is so obviously important that you know you should devote more time to get it all.

7. *Scenes.* Stop the flow of time and take still photographs. Focus on individual moments. What places, moments, sounds, or moods come to mind in connection with the French Revolution? Not only from your reading, but also from your own experience. Assume that they will be important if they come to mind, especially if they stick in mind.

If you are trying to decide on a career or choose between two people or life situations, jot down as many scenes as you can think of from your past when things were going well or you were functioning well. Then note just as many bad ones. Afterwards read through these scenes and you will be able to reach some really trustworthy judgments about your skills and strengths and what you need to function at your best; and your weaknesses and what you should try to avoid.*

It is particularly valuable to use scenes if you are writing some kind of analysis of a novel, story, poem, or movie. What moments, sights, and sounds stick in your mind from the work? This will give you insights about where some of the centers of gravity are. What structure emerges when you look at all these snapshots together? Add scenes from the rest of your experience that come to mind. These will lead you to important insights about the work under analysis and about your own preconceptions and point of view.

8. *Portraits.* Think about your topic and see what people come to mind. Give thumbnail portraits of them: again not necessarily with full syntax; just phrases will do. Tell the qualities or characteristics of these people that stick in mind, such as their physical appearance, odd movements or posture or gait, intriguing qualities, things they said or did. Some portraits will have obvious relevance to your analysis. But see who else comes to mind as you muse about your topic: people from other areas of your experience who pop up in your train of reflection. Have faith that there is something useful in the fact that your third grade teacher comes to mind as you think about the causes of the French Revolution. Tell what particular things you remember about this teacher and later on you will probably reap an insight.

If you are trying to evaluate an organization or analyze a novel, portraits will often lead you immediately to your best insights. If you are trying to make a hard personal decision, portraits of important people in your life will help you see what matters most to you and separate it from what's merely attractive or tempting.

9. *Vary the audience.* Write about your topic to someone very different from the real audience of your paper. If your audience is sophisticated, try

---

*I first learned this useful tactic from Gail Martin.

writing to someone very unsophisticated, perhaps to a young child. If the audience is someone you don't know, write to a close friend. If the audience has a definite point of view about the topic, write to someone with the opposite view. If you are having trouble writing a letter of recommendation for a friend who is applying for a job, put aside for a while the question of what you want to say to the employer and do a freewriting letter to your friend telling him bluntly everything you feel about him.

If you have difficulty varying the audience, try actually visualizing these alternate audiences you are writing to; address them by name periodically in your writing as though you were actually talking to them. If you are one of the many people who tend in general to forget about their audience and write to sort-of-nobody-in-particular, your writing probably tends to be dead. Practice visualizing your audience as you write—your real audience and some of these alternate audiences.

The act of writing to a different audience doesn't just clarify your thinking. It also leads you to new insights. If you have to write a job description for a very bureaucratic audience, but you start by writing it to your children or your parents or to a close friend who has no connection with your workplace, you will find yourself noticing important aspects of the job you are trying to analyze that you never would have noticed if you just wrote to the official audience. Write about the causes of the French Revolution as though you were Mao Tse-tung giving advice to revolutionaries or as though you were Kissinger writing a memo to the rest of the government about how to prevent revolution. You will have new insights.

10. *Vary the writer.* As you vary the audience, you often naturally vary the writer. Each device has its own power to generate new insights. Write as though you were someone whose view on the topic is very different from your own. Or write as though you lived in a different culture. If you are analyzing a particular policy, pretend to be someone affected by it. If you are writing about a particular person—perhaps an essay about a historical character or an evaluation of a client or colleague—it is enormously fruitful to be that person and write a *self*-portrait or *self*-analysis. Again you will learn things you didn't know. If you are writing about a novel or poem or movie, *be* one of the people in it and see what he or she has to say. Or be the author and give your understanding of your own creation.

11. *Vary the time.* Write as though you were living in the past or the future. Write, for example, about the French Revolution as though you were living at the time or as though it hadn't happened yet but you had an intuition of its possibility. Write as though the *topic* were in a different time: if you are writing about civil disobedience or the relationship between the sexes, write about the topic in the distant past or future. Similarly, try writing to an *audience* in the past or the future.

Varying the audience and the writer and the time is particularly fruitful if you can't think of anything to say about your topic, or if everything you think of seems ordinary and obvious and uninteresting.

12. *Errors*. Write down things that are almost true or trying to be true; things that you are tempted to think or that others think but you know are false; dangerous mistakes. "People only take care of things they own." "John is essentially lazy." "Revolutions are always part of progress." Writing these down lessens the static in your head. The process corrals your thinking bit by bit into a narrower and narrower space so that a sprawling, confusing issue slowly becomes clearer and more manageable.

13. *Lies*. Write down quickly all the odd or crazy things you can come up with. For example: "The French Revolution wasn't started by the Wobblies in Seattle, or by Lenin, or by Marx, or by the Marx brothers. It wasn't part of the women's movement. It didn't last forty days and nights, it isn't in the Bible, they didn't just get the enemy drunk and slide them into the sea." If you let the nonsense roll effortlessly for ten or fifteen minutes—spelling out some of the individual fantasies at more length, too—you can discover some ideas that will help your thinking even if they are not true. (And they may be true. Could the French Revolution have been part of the women's movement?)

Writing down as many lies as you can as quickly as you can gives you glimpses of your unconscious mind. You will discover some important preoccupations and assumptions that relate to the topic. Many, of course, will be irrelevant, but if you are more aware of them you can think better about the topic. In addition, even if you cannot draw any conclusions from reading back over the nonsense you have written, the process of writing it all down serves to clear some of the fog in your mind that was confusing or slowing down your thinking. You often end up with renewed energy.

The Marathon Session
That Wasn't a Real Session

JAMES M. TILT, JR.

I sat in the Writing Center listening to students talking in the cubicle next door. Nicole, the consultant on duty, was busy with her own work. Nobody had made an appointment during my shift and there seemed to be very little traffic in the halls, so I prepared myself for boredom. Then a writer walked through the door.

He was a man who looked to be in his mid-thirties. I guessed that he was a continuing education student. He floated in on a sea of energy which washed me out of my catatonic state. Speaking quickly and loudly, he explained that he had a paper he wanted us to look at. Nicole directed him to a seat and asked to see the draft. He hurriedly explained that he had not finished and had only a sloppy hand-written copy. Nicole offered to take a look but he refused, saying he wanted to make a better copy before she saw it. Assuming, as I did, that he was going home to produce a typed copy, Nicole offered to make an appointment for him. But he was not ready to leave—he said that he'd just sit down and make a more legible copy for us to go over. Nicole directed him to the corner of the room where he could have a little more privacy.

During the remainder of Nicole's shift, he kept at his copying, pausing every once in awhile to ask questions about the writing center, such as what the difference was between a consultant and a consultant-in-training. He blessed us for our skills as writers. Nicole and I exchanged confused glances; this session, which wasn't quite a session, was beginning to feel weird. When Nicole's shift ended and Janet came in to take over, our guest was still in the same spot.

I discreetly briefed Janet about him, and for a moment I had the feeling that we should offer him coffee and danish, or perhaps a bed. As Janet and I went through our role-playing exercise and some small talk, he remained where he was, working diligently. Now it was almost time for me to leave, and Janet casually mentioned that she could talk to him about his work as soon as he was ready. He announced that he had finished copying the old draft awhile ago, and was now working on some new ideas for the paper.

By the time I left, he had been in the center for almost two hours. Although we hadn't done a thing, he was obviously making good progress on his paper. Maybe all he needed was the right place to sit down and write.

Though its primary purpose is to help writers with papers, the Writing Center has a good atmosphere for solo work on papers as well. The center is usually quieter than the library and much less crowded and intimidating.

Perhaps just knowing that this is a center for writing is enough to inspire someone to write. Also, a writer does not feel uneasy about making a mistake here because he knows if he does or if he gets stuck he has a consultant to depend on. In short, the Writing Center can provide the comfortable support that a writer needs to begin writing and to forget about the insurmountable task of building the perfect paper.

The Cognition of Discovery: Defining a Rhetorical Problem

Linda Flower and John R. Hayes

Metaphors give shape to mysteries, and traditionally we have used the metaphor of *discovery* to describe the writer's creative process. Its broad meaning has sheltered many intellectual styles ranging from classical invention to modern heuristics such as tagmemics to self-exploratory modes such as Pre-Writing. Furthermore, *discovery* carries an implicit suggestion that, somewhere in the mind's recesses or in data outside the mind, there is something waiting to be discovered, and that writing is a way to bring that something out. However, if we try to use this metaphor to teach or analyze the creative process itself, we discover its limitations.[1]

First of all, because *discovery* emphasizes the rather glamorous experience of "Eureka, now I see it," it obscures the fact that writers don't find meanings, they make them. A writer in the act of discovery is hard at work searching memory, forming concepts, and forging a new structure of ideas, while at the same time trying to juggle all the constraints imposed by his or her purpose, audience, and language itself.[2] Discovery, the event, and its product, new insights, are only the end result of a complicated intellectual process. And it is this process we need to understand more fully.

There is a second, practical reason for teachers to probe this metaphor. The notion of discovery is surrounded by a mythology which, like the popular myth of romantic inspiration, can lead writers to self-defeating writing strategies. The myth of discovery implies a method, and this method is based on the premise that hidden stores of insight and ready-made ideas exist, buried in the mind of the writer, waiting only to be "discovered." Or they are to be found in books and data if only the enterprising researcher knows where to look. What does one do when a ready-made answer can't be found in external sources? The myth says, "look to your own experience." But what happens when a writer on this internal voyage of discovery still can't "find" something to say because his or her "ideas" as such are not actually formed? What is there to "discover" if only confused experience and conflicting perceptions are stored in a writer's memory? The mythology of discovery doesn't warn the writer that he or she must often build or create new concepts out of the raw material of experience; nor does it tell the writer how to do it. And yet, this act of *creating* ideas, not finding them, is at the heart of significant writing.

When an attempt at this literal discovery fails, as it often must, it leads inexperienced writers to an unnecessary defeat. Fluent writers are affected by the myth of discovery in another way. As Nancy Sommers has shown, many seem to equate the successful discovery of something to say (i.e., the "flow" of stored ideas) with successful writing, whether that flow is appropriate to the rhetorical situation or not.[3] The myth of discovery, as many of us see it in students, leads the poor writer to give up too soon and the fluent writer to be satisfied with too little.

Discovery, then, is a perplexing notion. On the one hand, it metaphorically describes an intellectual process we want to teach. On the other hand, the metaphor and mythology of discovery itself often distort our vision of that process. This paper attempts to probe the cognition of discovery, the process itself, by studying the way writers initiate and guide themselves through the act of making meaning.

Our approach has been to study writing as a problem-solving, cognitive process. From a psychological point of view, people have a "problem" whenever they are at some point "A" and wish to be at another point "B"; for example, when they have a new insight into *Hamlet*, but have yet to write the paper that will explain it. Their problem-solving process is the thinking process they use to get to point "B," the completed paper. That process might involve many intellectual skills including open, exploratory procedures, such as free writing and day dreaming. But it is important to remember that this process is not a creative accident.

In this study we wanted to explore the problem-solving or discovery process that produces new insights and new ideas. So we started with what many feel to be the most crucial part of that process—the act of finding or defining the problem to be "solved." As Ann Berthoff says, "A shortcoming of most of our students [is] they do not easily recognize particular problems [that need to be solved] because they do not have a method for, that is, a means of formulating critical questions."[4]

This shortcoming turns out to be critical because people only solve the problem they give themselves to solve. The act of formulating questions is sometimes called "problem-finding," but it is more accurate to say that writers build or represent such a problem to themselves, rather than "find" it. A rhetorical problem in particular is never merely a given: it is an elaborate construction which the writer creates in the act of composing. We wanted to see how writers actually go about building this inner, private representation.

There are a number of reasons why this act of constructing an image of one's rhetorical problem is worth study. First, it helps explain why writing, like other creative thinking, can be so utterly unpredictable. Even though a teacher gives 20 students the same assignment, *the writers themselves create the problem they solve*. The reader is not the writer's only "fiction." Furthermore, the act of problem-finding is a critical part of general creativity in both the arts and sciences. Because people only solve the problems they give themselves, the act of representing the problem has a dramatic impact on performance. James Britton saw this with bewildered or unmotivated children, with their strange notions of what the teacher wanted, as did Sondra Perl working with adult basic writers. People simply rewrite an assignment or a situation to make it commensurate with their own skills, habits, or fears.[5] Although writing texts generally ignore this part of the writing process,[6] our work suggests that it may be one of the most critical steps the average writer takes.

The first part of this paper, then, will describe our method for studying the cognitive process by which people represent the rhetorical problem. Then we will present a model of the rhetorical problem itself, that is, a description of the major elements writers could consider in building such an image. Finally, we will use this model of the possible as a basis for comparing what good and poor writers actually do.

Studying Cognitive Processes

The research question we posed for ourselves was this: if discovery is an act of making meaning, not finding it, in response to a *self-defined problem* or goal, how does this problem get defined? Specifically, we wanted to answer three questions:

1. What aspects of a rhetorical problem do people actively represent to themselves? For example, do writers actually spend much time analyzing their audience, and if so, how do they do it?
2. If writers do spend time developing a full representation of their problem, does it help them generate new ideas?
3. And finally, are there any significant differences in the way good and poor writers go about this task?

In order to describe the problem definition process itself, we collected thinking-aloud protocols from both expert and novice writers. A protocol is a detailed record of a subject's behavior. Our protocols include a transcript of a tape recording made by writers instructed to verbalize their thinking process as they write, as well as all written material the writer produced. A typical protocol from a one-hour session will include four to five pages of notes and writing and 15 pages of typed transcript. The novice writers were college students who had gone to the Communication Skills Center for general writing problems such as coherence and organization. The expert writers were teachers of writing and rhetoric who had received year-long NEH fellowships to study writing. Each writer was given the following problem: "write about your job for the readers of *Seventeen* magazine, 13-14 year-old girls," and was asked to compose out loud into a tape recorder as he or she worked. They were told to verbalize everything that went through their minds, including stray thoughts and crazy ideas, but not to try to analyze their thought process, just to express it.

A Model of the Rhetorical Problem

From these protocols, we pulled together a composite picture or model of the rhetorical problem itself. This composite is shown in Figure 1, with examples drawn from our writers' protocols. It is based on what the group of writers did and shows the basic elements of a writing problem which a given writer *could* actively consider in the process of composing, *if* he or she chose to. For example, the writer in the following excerpt is actively creating an image of himself or his *persona,* an image of what effect he might have on his reader, and on initial representation of a meaning or idea he might choose to develop, as the words in brackets indicate.

> Ah, in fact, that might be a useful thing to focus on, how a professor differs from... How a teacher differs from a professor, [meaning], and I see myself as a teacher, [*persona*], that might help them, my audience, to reconsider their notion of what an English teacher does. [effect on audience]

The Rhetorical Problem	
Elements of the Problem	Examples
THE RHETORICAL SITUATION	
Exignecy or Assignment	"Write for Seventeen magazine; this is impossible."
Audience	"Someone like myself, but adjusted for twenty years"
THE WRITER'S OWN GOALS involving the	
Reader	"I'll change their notion of English teachers..."
Persona or Self	"I'll look like an idiot if I say..."
Meaning	"So if I compare those two attitudes..."
Text	"First we'll want an introduction."

Figure 1. Elements of the rhetorical problem writers represent to themselves in composing.

Taken as a whole, the *rhetorical problem* breaks into two major units. The first is the rhetorical *situation.* This situation, which is the writer's given, includes the audience and assignment. The second unit is the set of *goals* the writer himself creates. The four dominant kinds of goals we observed involved affecting the *reader,* creating a *persona* or voice, building a *meaning,* and producing a formal *text.* As you see, these turned out to closely parallel the four terms of the communication triangle: reader, writer, world, word. This parallel between communication theory and our study is a happy one, since protocol analysis lets us describe what writers actually do as they write, not just what we, as theorists, think they should do. And, as we will see, one of the major differences between good and poor writers will be how many aspects of this total rhetorical problem they actually consider and how thoroughly they represent any aspect of it to themselves.

This model of the rhetorical problem reflects the elements writers actively consider as they write. It accounts for the conscious representation going on as writers compose. But is that enough? Protocols yield a wealth of information available in no other way, but they are limited to those aspects of the problem the writer is able in some way to articulate. But in understanding a writer's process we can't ignore that rich body of inarticulate information Polanyi would call our "tacit knowledge." We think that much of the information people have about rhetorical problems exists in the form of *stored problem representations*. Writers do no doubt have many such representations for familiar or conventional problems, such as writing a thank-you letter. Such a representation would contain not only a conventional definition of the situation, audience, and the writer's purpose, but might include quite detailed information about solutions, even down to appropriate tone and phrases. Experienced writers are likely to have stored representations of even quite complex rhetorical problems (e.g., writing a book review for readers of *The Daily Tribune*) if they have confronted them often before.

Naturally, if a writer has a stored representation that is fully adequate for the current situation, we wouldn't expect him to spend time building a new one. Achieving that kind of mental efficiency is what learning is all about. However, many writing problems, such as the one we gave our subjects, are unique and require a writer to build a *unique representation*. In such situations, we would expect a good writer to explore the problem afresh and to give conscious time and attention to building a unique representation. Therefore, in capturing the conscious representation of these unique problems, we feel we are likely to capture the critical part of the process. As it turned out, one of the most telling differences between our good and poor writers was the degree to which they created a unique, fully-developed representation of this unique rhetorical problem.

Our model or composite picture of the writer's rhetorical problem specifies two kinds of information writers represent to themselves: information about the rhetorical situation and information about the writer's own purpose and goals. We will discuss these two aspects of the rhetorical problem in order.

Representing a Rhetorical Situation

A *rhetorical situation* is the name we assign to the givens with which a writer must work, namely, the audience and assignment. Lloyd Bitzer's description of this situation as an exigency (e.g., assignment), an audience, and a set of constraints is a good description of what our subjects actually considered or represented to themselves.[7] (However, unlike Bitzer, we see this external situation as only part of a larger entity we call the rhetorical problem.)

The writer's initial analysis of the assignment and audience was usually brief. Most writers—both novice and expert—plunged quickly into generating ideas, but often returned to reconsider these givens later. For the novice writer, however, this re-examination of the *situation* often took the form of simply rereading the assignment, maybe two or three times, as if searching for a clue in it. A more intense form of this strategy was also observed by Perl, whose basic writers would read the assignment over and over until some key word struck an associative chord and reminded them of a topic on which they had something to say.[8] Although the novice writers in our study were actually analyzing the situation, they never moved beyond the sketchy, conventional representation of audience and assignment with which they started.

The good writers, by contrast, used their re-examination of the situation to add to their image of the audience or assignment. For example, this writer initially defined the audience as "someone like myself when I read—well, not like myself but adjusted for, well, twenty years later." Later in the protocol her image of the reader became significantly different:

> I feel a certain constraint knowing as I do the rather saccharine editorial policy. Perhaps I'm mistaken, but the last time I had my hair cut or something, I read it and they still seemed to be mostly looking at women as consumers of fashion and as consumers of men and really not as capable or interested in or likely to be drawn to an occupation like mine which is rather low paying and unglamorous and, ah, far from chic clothes.

As you can see, this writer is creating a sophisticated, complex image of a reader—half alter-ego, half fashion consumer—which she will have to deal with in the act of writing. No doubt it will be harder to write for such an audience than for a simple stereotype, but the final result is going to be more effective if she has indeed represented her audience accurately. We can imagine similar differences in two students' representations of an assignment such as "analyze *Hamlet*." Let us assume that both writers have roughly equal bodies of knowledge stored in memory. One writer might draw on that knowledge to give herself detailed instructions, e.g., "analyze this play'; that means I should try to break it down into some kind of parts. Perhaps I could analyze the plot, or the issues in the play, or its theatrical conventions." This student is drawing on the experience and semantic knowledge which both students possess to create a highly developed image of how to analyze something (e.g., break it into parts) and how to analyze this play in particular (e.g., find the critical issues). Meanwhile, another writer might blithely represent the problem as "Write another theme and talk about *Hamlet* this time, in time for Tuesday's class. That probably means about two pages."

Representing One's Purpose and Goals

An audience and exigency can jolt a writer into action, but the force which drives composing is the writer's own set of goals, purposes, or intentions. A major part of defining the rhetorical problem then is representing one's own goals. As we might predict from the way writers progressively fill in their image of the audience, writers also build a progressive representation of their goals as they write.

We can break these goals into four groups. The first is focused on the effect the writer wants to have on the *reader*. These can range from quite ambitious global plans, such as "I'll change their image of English teachers," down to decisions about local effects, such as "make this sound plausible," or "make this seem immediate to their experience." At times the intention of the writer is to have a direct personal effect on the reader as a person. For example, one writer structured her paper in order to make her reader "remain in a state of suspension [about jobs] and remain in an attentive posture toward her own history, abilities, and sources of satisfaction." She wanted to make the reader "feel autonomous and optimistic and effective." At other times the goal is a more general one of making the reader simply see something or comprehend accurately a train of thought (e.g., "I've got to attract the attention of the reader," or "There needs to be a transition between those two ideas to be clear").

One of the hallmarks of the good writers was the time they spent thinking about how they wanted to affect a reader. They were clearly representing their rhetorical problem as a complex speech act. The poor writers, by contrast, often seemed tied to their topic. This difference matters because, in our study, one of the most powerful strategies we saw for producing new ideas throughout the composing process was planning what one wanted to do to or for one's reader.

A second kind of purpose writers represent to themselves involves the relationship they wish to establish with the reader. This relationship can also be described as the *persona*, projected self, or voice the writer wishes to create. This part of the problem representation is the least likely to appear in a protocol because writers are probably likely to draw on a stored representation of their *persona* even for unique problems. Furthermore, decisions about one's *persona* are often expressed by changes in word choice and tone, not by direct statements. Nevertheless, this is a part of a writer's goals or purpose which he or she must define in some way. In one writer this issue was directly broached three times. At the beginning of composing, she saw her role as that of a free-lance writer writing to a formula. But unfortunately

> my sense is that it's a formula which I'm not sure I know, so I suppose what I have to do is invent what the formula might be, and then try to include events or occurrences or attitude or experiences in my own job that could be conveyed in formula. So let's see… .

Clearly, her sense of her role as formula writer affects how she will go about writing this paper. But later this same writer revised her relationship with the reader and in so doing radically changed the rhetorical problem. She accused herself of taking the hypocritical voice of adulthood and set a new goal:

> I feel enormously doubtful of my capacity to relate very effectively to the audience that is specified and in that case, I mean, all I can do is, is just, you know, present myself, present my concepts and my message or my utterance in a kind of simple and straightforward and unpretentious way, I hope.

A third goal writers develop involves the writer's attempt to build a coherent network of ideas, to create *meaning*. All writers start, we assume, with a stored goal that probably says something like, "Explore what you know about this topic and write it down; that is, generate and express relevant ideas." We see evidence of this goal when writers test or evaluate what they've just said to see if it is related to or consistent with other ideas. Many of our writers never appeared to develop goals much more sophisticated than this generate-and-express goal, which, in its most basic form, could produce simply an interior monologue. However, some writers defined their meaning-making problem in more complex and demanding ways, telling themselves to focus on an important difference, to pursue an idea because it seemed challenging, or to step back and decide "more generally, how do I want to characterize my job." Perhaps the difference here is one of degree. At one end of a spectrum, writers are merely trying to express a network of ideas already formed and available in memory; at the other, writers are consciously attempting to probe for analogues and contradictions, to form new concepts, and perhaps even to restructure their old knowledge of the subject.

Finally, a fourth goal which writers represent involves the formal or conventional features of a written text. Early in composing, writers appear to make many basic decisions about their genre and set up goals such as "write an introduction first." Most college students no doubt have a great deal of information in their stored representation of the problem "write a short essay." However, once into the text, writers often expand their image of possibilities by considering unique features the text might include. For example, writers tell themselves to "fictionalize it," to "use a direct question," "try a rhetorical question," or "try to add a little example or little story here to flesh it out." In doing so, they set up goals based primarily on their knowledge of the conventions of writing and the features of texts. This may be one way in which extensive reading affects a person's ability to write: a well-read person simply has a much larger and richer set of images of what a text can look like. Goals such as these often have plans for reaching the goal built right into them. For example, when one of the expert writers decided to use a problem/solution format for the paper, he was immediately able to tap a pocket of stored plans for creating such a format. The convention itself specified just what to include. Furthermore, once he set up this familiar format as a goal, he saw what to do with a whole body of previously unorganized ideas.

Differences among Writers

This six-part model of the rhetorical problem attempts to describe the major kinds of givens and goals writers could represent to themselves as they compose. As a model for comparison it allowed us to see patterns in what our good and poor writers actually did. The differences, which were striking, were these:

1. Good writers respond to *all* aspects of the rhetorical problem. As they compose they build a unique representation not only of their audience and assignment, but also of their goals involving the audience, their own *persona,* and the text. By contrast, the problem representations of the poor writers were concerned primarily with the features and conventions of a written text, such as number of pages or magazine format. For example, Figure 2 shows a vivid contrast between an expert and novice when we compare the way two writers represented their rhetorical problem in the first 60 lines of a protocol. The numbers are based on categorizing phrases and sentences within the protocol.

	Analysis of rhetorical situation: Audience and Assignment:	Analysis of goals				Total
		Audience	Self	Text	Meaning	
Novice	7	0	0	3	7	17
Expert	18	11	1	3	9	42

Figure 2. Number of times writer explicitly represented each aspect of the rhetorical problem in first 60 lines of protocol

As you can see, the expert made reference to his audience or assignment 18 times in the first seven to eight minutes of composing, whereas the novice considered the rhetorical situation less than half that often. The most striking difference, of course, is in their tendency to represent or create goals for dealing with the audience. Finally, the column marked "Total" shows our expert writer simply spending more time than the novice in thinking about and commenting on the rhetorical problem, as opposed to spending that time generating text.

2. In building their problem representation, good writers create a particularly rich network of goals for affecting their reader. Furthermore, these goals, based on affecting a reader, also helped the writer generate new ideas. In an earlier study we discovered that our experienced writers (a different group this time) generated up to 60 per cent of their new ideas in response to the larger rhetorical problem (that is, in response to the assignment, their audience, or their own goals). Only 30 per cent were in response to the topic alone. For example, a writer would say, "I'll want an introduction that pulls you in," instead of merely reciting facts about the topic, such as "As an engineer the first thing to do is ..." In the poor writers the results were almost reversed: 70 per cent of their new ideas were statements about the topic alone

without concern for the larger rhetorical problem.[9] All of this suggests that setting up goals to affect a reader is not only a reasonable act, but a powerful strategy for generating new ideas and exploring even a topic as personal as "my job."

As you might easily predict, plans for affecting a reader also give the final paper a more effective rhetorical focus. For example, one of the novice writers, whose only goals for affecting the audience were to "explain [his] job simply so it would appeal to a broad range of intellect," ended up writing a detailed technical analysis of steam turbulence in an electrical generator. The topic was of considerable importance to him as a future research engineer, but hardly well focused for the readers of *Seventeen*.

3. Good writers represent the problem not only in more breadth, but in depth. As they write, they continue to develop their image of the reader, the situation, and their own goals with increasing detail and specificity. We saw this in the writer who came back to revise and elaborate her image of her fashion-consuming reader. By contrast, poor writers often remain throughout the entire composing period with the flat, undeveloped, conventional representation of the problem with which they started.

The main conclusion of our study is this: good writers are simply solving a different problem than poor writers. Given the fluency we can expect from native speakers, this raises an important question. Would the performance of poor writers change if they too had a richer sense of what they were trying to do as they wrote, or if they had more of the goals for affecting the reader which were so stimulating to the good writers? People only solve the problems they represent to themselves. Our guess is that the poor writers we studied possess verbal and rhetorical skills which they fail to use because of their underdeveloped image of their rhetorical problem. Because they have narrowed a rhetorical act to a paper-writing problem, their representation of the problem doesn't call on abilities they may well have.

This study has, we think, two important implications, one for teaching and one for research. First, if we can describe how a person represents his or her own problem in the act of writing, we will be describing a part of what makes a writer "creative." A recent, long-range study of the development of creative skill in fine art showed some striking parallels between successful artists and our expert writers. This seven-year study, entitled *The Creative Vision: A Longitudinal Study of Problem-Finding in Art,* concluded that the critical ability which distinguished the successful artists was not technical skill, but what the authors call *problem-finding*—the ability to envision, pose, formulate, or create a new problematic situation.[10] Furthermore, in this experimental study of artists at work, the three behaviors which distinguished the successful artists were the breadth and depth of their exploration of the problem and their delay in reaching closure on the finished product. In this experiment the artists were given a studio equipped with materials and a collection of objects they might draw. The successful artists, like our expert writers, explored more of the materials before them and explored them in more depth, fingering, moving, touching, rearranging, and playing with alternatives, versus moving quickly to a rather conventional arrangement and sketch. Once drawing was begun, the artists' willingness to explore and reformulate the problem continued, often until the drawing was nearly completed. Similarly, our successful writers continued to develop and alter their representation of the problem throughout the writing process. This important study of creativity in fine art suggested that problem-finding is a talent, a cognitive skill which can lead to creativity. The parallels between these two studies suggest that problem-finding in both literature and art is related not only to success, but in some less well defined way to "creativity" itself.

Other studies in the psychology of creativity make this link between creative thinking and problem-solving processes more explicit.[11] Many "creative" breakthroughs in science and the arts are not the result of finding a better technical solution to an old problem (e.g., the disease-producing influence of evil spirits), but of seeing a new problem (e.g., the existence of germs). In many cases, the solution procedure is relatively straightforward once one has defined the problem. For example, Virginia Woolf's *The Waves* or Van Gogh's impressionistic landscapes are less a technical feat than an act of imagining a new problem or set of goals for the artist.

We feel there are implications for exciting research in this area. This study has attempted to develop a model of the rhetorical problem as a guide to further research, and to describe three major differences between good and poor writers. But there is much we could learn about how people define their rhetorical problems as they write and why they make some of the choices they do.

The second implication we see in our own study is that the ability to explore a rhetorical problem is eminently teachable. Unlike a metaphoric "discovery," problem-finding is not a totally mysterious or magical act. Writers discover what they want to do by insistently, energetically exploring the entire problem before them and building for themselves a unique image of the problem they want to solve. A part of creative thinking is just plain thinking.

Exploring a topic alone isn't enough. As Donald Murray put it, "writers wait for signals" which tell them it is time to write, which "give a sense of closure, a way of handling a diffuse and overwhelming subject."[12] Many of the "signals" Murray described, such as having found a point of view, a voice, or a genre, parallel our description of the goals and plans we saw good writers making. If we can teach students to explore and define their own problems, even within the constraints of an assignment, we can help them to create inspiration instead of wait for it.

FOOTNOTES

[1]This research was partially supported by a grant from the National Institute of Education, Department of Health, Education, and Welfare, Grant NIE G780195.

[2]Linda Flower and John R. Hayes, "The Dynamic of Composing: Making Plans and Juggling Constraints," in *Cognitive Processes in Writing,* ed. Lee Gregg and Erwin Steinberg (Hillsdale, NJ: Lawrence Erlbaum, in press); Linda Flower and John R. Hayes, "Problem Solving Strategies and the Writing Process," *College English,* 39 (Dec. 1977), 449-461.

[3]Nancy I. Sommers, "Revision Strategies of Student Writers and Experienced Writers," MLA Convention, New York, 28 Dec. 1978.

[4]Ann E. Berthoff, "Towards a Pedagogy of Knowing," *Freshman English News,* 7 (Spring 1978), 4.

[5]James Britton et al., *The Development of Writing Abilities (11-18)* (London: Macmillan, 1975); Sondra Perl, "Five Writers Writing: Case Studies of the Composing Process of Unskilled College Writers," Diss. New York University, 1978.

[6]Richard L. Larson, "The Rhetorical Act of Planning a Piece of Discourse." Beaver College Conference on Evaluation of Writing, Glenside, PA, October 1978.

[7]Lloyd Bitzer, "The Rhetorical Situation," *Philosophy and Rhetoric,* 1 (Jan. 1968), 1-14.

[8]Perl, "Five Writers Writing."

[9]Linda Flower and John R. Hayes, "Process-Based Evaluation of Writing: Changing the Performance, Not the Product," American Educational Research Association Convention, San Francisco, 9 April 1979.

[10]Jacob W. Getzels and Mihaly Csikszentmilhalyi, *The Creative Vision: A Longitudinal Study of Problem Finding in Art* (New York: John Wiley and Sons, 1976).

[11]John R. Hayes, *Cognitive Psychology: Thinking and Creating* (Homewood, LD: Dorsey Press, 1978); M. Wertheimer, Productive Thinking (New York: Harper and Row, 1945).

[12]Donald M. Murray, "Write Before Writing," *College Composition and Communications,* 29 (Dec. 1978), 375-381.

An Experience to Remember
ELIZABETH FOOTE

By the time I had had my fourth observation day in the writing center, I was discouraged. No one had come in for help with a paper. I was beginning to think that I would never see a consultant in action and I would have to live by role-playing alone. You can imagine my excitement when Karen walked through the door with a paper in hand. Finally, a chance to test out some of the theories we had discussed in class.

Kelly and I introduced ourselves to Karen and we all sat down at the table. Karen said she wanted us to read over her paper and "Be brutal." The assignment was for the student to study a piece of artwork and write a formal analysis of it. The professor wanted a three-page essay with a clear introduction and strong conclusion. No problem, I thought, a nice short essay to start off my first session, piece of cake. Wrong! The session was anything but a piece of cake.

When Kelly and I finished reading the paper, I didn't have a clue of where to begin. I was totally overwhelmed. First of all, Karen had misinterpreted the assignment. She had written a three-page, extremely detailed description of a painting. It wasn't anything close to an analysis. The introduction didn't relate to the paper. It was just a few sentences of random information. The entire paper lacked focus and organization. The information was in a random order as if Karen had written things down as they came into her head. The paper was due the next day and I didn't think there was any way we were going to be able to help this writer. I looked at Kelly and wondered if she felt as hopeless and I did.

If Kelly was nervous, she didn't show it at all. She began by asking Karen what the thesis of the paper was. Karen didn't know what a thesis was. It took us about 15 minutes of asking questions before we could figure out what Karen wanted to focus the paper on. Once we had established the focus, Kelly explained what a formal analysis should be.

Karen had a problem with taking a stand and voicing an opinion in her paper. She thought she had to write her professor's point of view, which was different from her own. She avoided that by writing a description instead. Once Karen understood the difference between an analysis and a description, she was able to write a clear thesis statement.

By this time, I was feeling better. I no longer had the desire to run from the writing center and never return. I felt like we were making progress and I thought the hard part was over. Now all we had to do was help Karen reorganize her paper. Most of what had had written just needed to be reordered and expanded a bit to include an analysis. Kelly had told me earlier that her strong point was organization. I figured we'd be done in no time. Wrong again, Liz! I soon discovered why Karen's paper was so unfocused and unorganized.

Karen lacked concentration. While we were discussing what information should be included in a certain paragraph, she would ask questions about another part of the paper. This went on for another half-hour. Kelly and I did our best to keep Karen focused. Finally, after what seemed like an eternity, we were ready to talk about the conclusion, when Karen announced she had to leave.

I gave Kelly a look of surprise. We had come so far and now Karen had to leave, just as we were approaching the end. Actually, I was relieved that after an hour and a half the session was finally over, but I still felt like things were not finished. Kelly quickly tried to give Karen some helpful hints about writing a conclusion, as Karen was gathering her things. Karen thanked us for our help and breezed out the door.

My first session certainly was not typical. It left both Kelly and me feeling very frustrated; however, it was a learning experience. I learned that not every session is going to be easy and end like a fairy tale so that everyone lives happily ever after. Although I was overwhelmed at first, by the time the session was over I realized that it wasn't completely impossible. If a session like this happens again, I know I'll be able to handle it.

Northern Realities, Northern Literacies: The Writing Center in the "Contact Zone"

JENNIFER BRICE

Recently, I tutored a Koyukon Athabaskan man in his early thirties who'd been assigned to write a five-page essay about a significant event in his life. I'll call him Phillip. His paper, an account of a snow machine trip between two remote Alaska villages, ran to an unruly twelve pages. The teacher had given it a B-, and Phillip wished to rewrite for a higher grade. So we met in the writing center at the University of Alaska Fairbanks, where 15 percent of the student body is Alaska Native, like Phillip, and 70 percent is white, like me.

Here, roughly one in ten writing center sessions takes place between a non-Native graduate student tutor and an Alaska Native undergraduate tutee. I've borrowed the term "contact zone" to describe these interactions, freighted as they are with three centuries of exploitation, colonization, and repression of both Alaska Native languages and cultures. Mary Louise Pratt has described a contact zone as a "social space where cultures meet, clash, grapple with each other, often in contexts of highly asymmetrical relations of power." This definition means that virtually every writing center is a contact zone of sorts because of the perceived hierarchy of knowledge about what constitutes good writing. In a multicultural writing center such as the one at the University of Alaska, however, the importance of communicating clearly across lines of culture as well as hierarchy cannot be overstated. Clear writing is almost always preceded by clear communication about writing. As tutors, we need to pay attention to what we don't say as well as what we do, and to how we say whatever we wish to say. Culture loads our gestures in ways we may not be aware of, but we can try to learn.

After thirty years in the Far North, I sometimes feel discouraged about how much I don't know about my own home. Alaska's vastness alone defies comprehension: it covers a territory of 378 million acres and stretches 1,400 miles from north to south. In the introduction to his 1914 memoir, *Ten Thousand Miles by Dog Sled*, Archdeacon Hudson Stuck writes that "Alaska is not one country but many countries . . . And what is true of one part of it is often grotesquely untrue of other parts." The same can be said of Alaska's diverse Native population. At the AUF Writing Center, we frequently see Inupiak and Yupik Eskimos as well as Athabaskan Indians from the northern, western and interior regions of the state, respectively. It would be a mistake to assume, however, that an Athabaskan Indian has more in common with another Athabaskan than with a Yupik or even a white student. The term "Athabaskan" refers not to a tribe but to a cluster of communicative patterns and cultural traditions rooted in Athabaskan life and languages, more than twenty of which are still in circulation today. The heterogeneity of northern cultures and northern literacies means that improving communication in the contact zone is not as simple as, say, memorizing the sixteen Yupik words for snow. Susan Blalock, director of the UAF Writing Center, teaches tutors to cultivate a sense of respect for difference: "While learning about particular cultures is very important, only the experience of 'otherness' will make us sufficiently attentive to the way students react to their assignments and to the tutors."

One big difference between Phillip and myself is that I cannot imagine traveling by snow machine across several hundred miles of frozen tundra and rivers, trusting in the hospitality of strangers for a hot meal and a bed every other night or so. His paper was organized chronologically, beginning not with the journey itself, but with Phillip's idea of it, conceived years earlier during an airplane flight over the same terrain. The second section dealt with the purchase of a snow machine, choice of a partner, and other preparations. The journey comprised the third section, and the fourth was given over to thanking by name the friends and family members who fed, housed and entertained the travelers. The construction of a four-part narrative conformed to that of most Alaska Native folk tales. While many of these oral narratives have been recorded, translated and published in recent years, they haven't attracted a widespread readership, even in Alaska. European folk tales, in contrast, tend to have only three parts: a beginning, middle and ending. Readers such as myself who were weaned on Hans Christian Anderson might find, on first reading, that a typical Alaska Native folk tale—or an essay such as Phillip's—begins too early or ends too late.

In places, Phillip's control over his material was strong, as when he described in harrowing detail the disorientation and fear brought on by a sudden snowstorm, and when he conveyed the laughter and goodwill of late-night storytelling sessions in the homes of people who, hours earlier, had been complete strangers. On the whole, however, the essay seemed sprawling, disjointed, peppered with usage errors, and, most seriously, lacking a central point or revelation. The crafting of a strong thesis statement is perhaps the greatest bugbear for all freshman writing students, but especially for Alaska Natives. Prohibitions against predicting the future, which is tantamount to bragging, characterize the social discourse of many northern cultures. "Unqualified assertions of personal ability and/or intent offend socially, and are considered egocentric and inept to the point of rudeness," write anthropologists Patricia Kwatchka and Charlie Basham. Synonymous with assertions of personal ability and/or intent to prove a particular point, the thesis statement poses a Catch-22 for Alaska Native students: to write one is to disregard the teachings of their culture; not to write one is to disregard the teachings of their professors. Here is one area in which the writing center tutor may follow Mary Lou Pratt's advice, acting as a mediator or guide, outlining not only the expectations of the dominant culture but the ways in which such expectations may differ among members of the minority. In Phillip's case, I explained that his teacher probably expected a pithy sentence or two, somewhere near the beginning of the essay, hinting at the trials and lessons ahead. He was reluctant to compose such a statement, but I felt I had done my job.

Is the first-year graduate student who just traded Los Angeles for Fairbanks likely to be aware of cultural prohibitions against predicting the future of bragging? I doubt it, but she or he can learn. During the week-long tutor training every fall, new tutors and teaching assistants in the UAF English department visit the Rural Student Services center on campus. There, Native students show slides and talk about subsistence hunting and fishing, and what it's like to attend a one-room school in a village of several hundred people at most. The graduate students sample Native delicacies such as Eskimo ice cream (made with Crisco) or muktuk (slabs of whale blubber). During this experience, the lines of culture may become clearer while the lines of hierarchy get erased or even reversed. As writing center director Blalock points out, "The new tutors' first experience with Native students at this university is to learn from them rather than teach them."

It is one thing to recognize difference, another to communicate across the gulf that difference creates. In "Arts of the Contact Zone," Pratt identifies the need for ground rules "that go beyond politeness but maintain mutual respect." What follows are a few of the established ground rules at the UAF writing center for tutoring across lines of culture and hierarchy. In some cases, the policies may be applicable to multicultural writing centers in general; in others, they may be specific to the northern contact zone. I've divided the ground rules into five categories: 1) create a "safe house"; 2) learn before you teach; 3) listen; 4) be polite; 5) negotiate.

1) Create a "safe house."

Situated in a different building from the English Department on the UAF campus, the Rural Student Services (RSS) center fits Pratt's definition of a "safe house," or a "social and intellectual [space] where groups can constitute themselves as horizontal, homogeneous, sovereign communities with high degrees of trust, shared understandings, temporary protection from legacies of oppression." In contrast to the hushed environs of the main writing center, the RSS lounge is a vast common room with couches, a coffee machine, computers and adjoining counselors' offices. Here, amid the noisy current of conversations, ringing telephones and playing children, is an outpost of the writing center. The Connection has existed since 1991 in the form of a desk staffed by a single tutor for two hours every weekday afternoon. Because The Connection sits on the Native students' turf, so to speak, tutorials here tend to be more relaxed, spontaneous and informal than most sessions in the main writing center. Writing center statistics reveal that the number of appointments at RSS has risen steadily in the past four years, and anecdotal evidence points to greater numbers of rural students using both The Connection and the main writing center. (The evidence is anecdotal because, in the past, requests for information have contained questions only about students' linguistic background, not cultural background.)

Not every university that caters to students of many cultures has the equivalent of a Rural Student Services center, nor is it always practical in places that do to establish an outpost of the writing center there. Other ways to create a sympathetic atmosphere might include decorating the walls with paintings by artists from other cultures, or posting notices in several languages. Offering all students coffee or popcorn makes them feel less like humble penitents and more like honored guests.

2) Learn before you teach.

As I mentioned earlier, constraints against predicting the future, speaking well of oneself, and speaking ill of another are prevalent among many Native Alaskans. Hypothesis is typically valued above assertion, indirection above forthrightness. For these reasons, direct questioning may be met with silence from members of a culture unaccustomed to our western, Socratic teaching tradition. Researchers observe that many cultural prohibitions among Alaska Natives transcend mere convention: if the rules for interpersonal communication are upheld, a delicate balance between humans and the natural world is maintained.

If we tutors set ourselves the task of learning before teaching, we can let our learning inform our tutoring sessions. For instance, as a writing technique, indirection is not highly valued by the dominant culture in America; as a tutoring technique, it's highly underrated. We could do worse than to remember that indirect criticism—that is, criticism leveled at a thing rather than a person—is less threatening or invasive than direct criticism. For instance, instead of saying "You seem to have trouble with sentence boundaries," we could say, "Comma splices tend to happen when a writer gets swept up in the enthusiasm of good ideas."

3) Listen.

Remember the stereotype of the silent Native and garrulous white? Studies have documented that Athabaskans pause roughly half again as long as whites between statements. Non-native people tend to be uncomfortable with what they perceive as over-long silences, so they rush to fill in the gaps, usually just about the time the Native with whom they are conversing opens his or her mouth to speak. Ann LeFavor, a graduate student tutor in the writing center, once chided a colleague who worked with her in an alcohol treatment facility for being overly talkative around Alaska Natives. "Henry," she told him, laughing, "You're just too white." The punch line is that Henry is black.

When she works with Alaska Natives in the writing center, LeFavor says she finds herself doing a lot more listening, a lot of exploring, a lot of validation: "It works better if they verbalize [what they need help with]. You have to wait a lot longer than you think. If they're not going to tell you anything, they'll let you know that, too."

4) Be polite.

Sounds easy, right? But politeness varies among cultures. What constitutes good manners among English teachers at a national conference is not, and should not be, the same as what constitutes good manners in the contact zone. Linguists Ron and Suzanne Scollon have isolated two forms of politeness: the first, "solidarity politeness" emphasizes what two speakers have in common and assumes little social or power difference between them; the second, "deference" politeness, is based on the premise that all communication is difficult and problematical. Deference politeness respects autonomy and self-determination and avoids, at all costs, imposition. Deference politeness does not presume to know what another person wants, thinks or needs. The Scollons' point is that instead of trying to draw out a quiet Alaska Native student, teachers should answer reticence with reticence.

5) Negotiate.

Here is where the adept tutor can array the materials of the dominant culture and allow the student to select and invent from what is available, acting as a guide in a process that Pratt describes as "transculturation." Phillip and I worked from the bottom up—from lower- to higher-order concerns—instead of the reverse. I was impressed with his use of Athabaskan words in parentheses when the English equivalents struck him as inadequate, and I told him so. We made quick work of mechanical errors, but when we touched on structure and content, Phillip's attitude subtly changed. He became an advocate for sections that I recommended condensing or cutting altogether.

When I observed in passing that the journey was at the heart of the essay, he interrupted me, saying his true subject was the people he met along the way. Instead of identifying individual qualities of perseverance or strength, which might be interpreted as bragging, he wished to celebrate the hospitality of an extended community. Aha! I thought: here's his thesis. I suggested he frontload some of this information, which, in the essay's present form, appeared near the end. While reluctant to reveal at the beginning of his essay the lessons he'd learned by the end of his journey, Phillip was willing to compromise. He crafted a sentence expressing curiosity about relatives he'd never met, and whom he expected to visit along the way.

As I read about Alaska Native culture and communication as background for this article, it occurred to me that much of what I learned could be put into action in the writing center. For instance, what if we tutors were to incorporate some of the prohibitions of which Phillip seemed mindful into our writing center philosophy? What if we avoided speaking too highly of ourselves, putting others down, and predicting the future? (After all, one of the luxuries of being the tutor rather than the instructor is not having to concern ourself overly with the grade a paper is likely to receive.) In the student-oriented writing center, we measure our success largely on the basis of attendance, especially return attendance. Therefore we like to make students feel welcome before, during and after their sessions, often following them to the door to say, "Good-bye. Come again soon." In my case, no amount of research into other cultures can erase the habits of a lifetime. Believing that Phillip and I had established some rapport during our half-hour together, I was stricken when he walked out of the writing center without a backward glance. Then I remembered: to promise to return might have seemed tantamount to tempting fate. After some thought, I decided I could live with this explanation.

WORKS CITED

Basham, Charlie, and Patricia Kwatchka. In Blalock, 16.

Blalock, Susan. "Negotiating Authority through One-to-One Collaboration in the Multicultural Writing Center." *Writing in Multicultural Settings.* Eds. Carol Severino, Juan C. Guerra, and Johnella E. Butler. New York: MLA, 1997. 79-93.

LeFavor, Ann. Telephone interview. 3 March 1995.

McHenry, Sue. Personal interview. 10 March 1995.

Pratt, Mary Louise. "Arts of the Contact Zone." *MLA Profession* 91. 33-40.

Scollon, Ron, and Suzanne B.K. Scollon. "Interethnic Communication: How to Recognize Negative Stereotypes and Improve Communication Between Ethnic Groups." Fairbanks: Alaska Native Language Center, 1980.

Stuck, Hudson. *Ten Thousand Miles by Dog Sled.* NY: Scribner, 1914.

I Am Eager To Begin

LYNETTE GAJTKA

When the Writing Practicum class began, I assumed it was going to be a laborious review of previously learned material. I don't consider myself an expert on the English language, but I wasn't looking forward to having the rules of grammar/syntax drilled into my head again. For some reason, I associated correcting papers with correcting grammar. Even though I knew that I put a lot of work into my own papers, I pictured the Writing Center as focusing on more "basic" things. I figured it was a pretty cut-and-dry procedure: "Hi, how are you... Do this, do that... o.k... Come again..."

It wasn't until my first session that I realized what a challenge working in the Writing Center can be. Unfortunately, I think many students share my original attitude about the Writing Center: that it is a place where you go through some brief formalities in order to receive some quick painless help and hopefully an easy A paper. Just as I did not want to be bombarded with the basics of how the Writing Center was run, neither do the students who go there. Luckily for them, they don't need to know why and how the Writing Center is effective, as long as they experience results. But for me, I quickly realized I had the pressure of learning how to produce results for these students.

After I began to observe in the Writing Center, I became overwhelmed with doubt about my ability to run a consulting session. I worried I would focus too much on positive aspects of a paper (no matter how few they might be), and be scared to criticize or acknowledge faults. My fear of being critical stemmed from my being self-conscious about offending someone, because I see writing as a reflection of oneself.

Most papers, no matter how well written, have a variety of things that can be improved. I noticed that different tutors focused on different aspects of a paper when analyzing or correcting it. I did not think I would be able to focus on a paper in order to find its strengths and weaknesses. Without focus, my session would have no theme; it would be unorganized and unproductive. Knowing that there is only a half hour to find and make most corrections also added to my anxiety, especially considering that I might have only one shot, because some people do not plan to return to the Writing Center. I was weighed down by the pressure of feeling that I had to turn papers into A material before they left the room. I wasn't sure I had what it takes to deal with the responsibilities of becoming a tutor.

There was one role-playing session in which I was faced with some of the challenges I hoped to avoid. I had gone through the basic formalities, the introduction, and now I began to feel uncomfortable. I was distracted as I read the paper, so it was difficult to determine what to discuss about it. When I finished reading the paper I wasn't sure what approach to take. I noticed several details that needed improvement, but I knew that I could not cover them all. At this point I checked the assignment again to confirm one of my doubts: the paper did not adhere to the assignment. The writer needed to use quotes more explicitly and make clearer connections between personal experience and the point of view of the article she had quoted. Because I knew that the paper was not due for a few days, I decided to try to work with this concept. I saw this to be a central problem with the paper and I anticipated that the writer would correct some of the other errors in the process of making this particular revision.

My challenge was to try to make the writer realize she had not fulfilled the task, without blatantly telling her. I began informing her that I liked the paper, that she seemed to have a reasonable structure, and that she had some good descriptions. Now I had to help her to see why she had chosen to use those descriptions. I chose to use a chart. The writer was comparing and contrasting two coaches, so we listed the qualities of coach one and coach two on the chart. Now, I began to inquire about this comparison and contrast. She informed me that one coach was an example of the quote she had given at the beginning of her essay, and the other coach contradicted the quote. At this point she had made the connection with the assignment. I explained to her that she needed to make this much more clear to the reader, because the reader needed to know what her purpose was for describing these two coaches. I also stressed the fact that the reader had no background knowledge of the article referred to, so the writer needed to make sure that the quotes she was using were clearly connected to her feelings about the coaches. She suggested some changes she could make, I listened and made appropriate comments, and then she made an appointment to come back. I was ecstatic—the focus of my revision was a success.

Originally, I oversimplified the task of being a tutor. Then I was faced with the responsibilities and challenges of peer tutoring. When I began the previously described role playing, I was overwhelmed with doubts about my ability to succeed as a peer tutor. At the end I overcame my anxieties. Granted, I may not have created an A paper, but that was not my responsibility; it was the writer's responsibility. I now know I have potential as a peer tutor; now my challenge is to convince my peers to work to their greatest potential, and to appreciate the Writing Center as much as I have learned to. I am eager to begin...

Revision Strategies of Student Writers and Experienced Adult Writers

Nancy Sommers

Although various aspects of the writing process have been studied extensively of late, research on revision has been notably absent. The reason for this, I suspect, is that current models of the writing process have directed attention away from revision. With few exceptions, these models are linear; they separate the writing process into discrete stages. Two representative models are Gordon Rohman's suggestion that the composing process moves from prewriting to writing to rewriting and James Britton's model of the writing process as a series of stages described in metaphors of linear growth, conception—incubation—production.[1] What is striking about these theories of writing is that *they model themselves on speech*: Rohman defines the writer in a way that cannot distinguish him from a speaker ("A writer is a man who... puts [his] experience into words in his own mind"—p. 15); and Britton bases his theory of writing on what he calls (following Jakobson) the "expressiveness" of speech.[2] Moreover, Britton's study itself follows the "linear model" of the relation of thought and language in speech proposed by Vygotsky, a relationship embodied in the linear movement "from the motive which engenders a thought to the shaping of the thought, *first* in inner speech, *then* in meanings of words, and *finally* in words" (quoted in Britton, p. 40). What this movement fails to take into account is its linear structure—"first... Then... finally"—is the recursive shaping of thought by language; what it fails to take into account is *revision*. In these linear conceptions of the writing process revision is understood as a separate stage at the end of the process—a stage that comes after the completion of a first or second draft and one that is temporally distinct from the prewriting and writing stages of the process.[3]

The linear model bases itself on speech in two specific ways. First of all, it is based on traditional rhetorical models, models that were created to serve the spoken art of oratory. In whatever ways the parts of classical rhetoric are described, they offer "stages" of composition that are repeated in contemporary models of the writing process. Edward Corbett, for instance, describes the "five parts of a discourse"—*inventio, dispositio, elocutio, memoria, pronuntiatio*—and, disregarding the last two parts since "after rhetoric came to be concerned mainly with written discourse, there was no further need to deal with them,"[4] he produces a model very close to Britton's conception [*inventio*], incubation [*dispositio*], production [*elocutio*]. Other rhetorics also follow this procedure, and they do so not simply because of historical accident. Rather, the process represented in the linear model is based on the irreversibility of speech. Speech, Roland Barthes says, "is irreversible":

"A word cannot be retracted, except precisely by saying that one retracts it. To cross out here is to add: if I want to erase what I have just said, I cannot do it without showing the eraser itself (I must say: *'or rather...'* *'I expressed myself badly...'*); paradoxically, it is ephemeral speech which is indelible, not monumental writing. All that one can do in the case of a spoken utterance is to tack on another utterance."[5]

What is impossible in speech is revision: like the example Barthes gives, revision in speech is an afterthought. In the same way, each stage of the linear model must be exclusive (distinct from the other stages) or else it becomes trivial and counterproductive to refer to these junctures as "stages."

By staging revision after enunciation, the linear models reduce revision in writing, as in speech, to no more than an afterthought. In this way such models make the study of revision impossible. Revision, in Rohman's model, is simply the repetition of writing; or to pursue Britton's organic metaphor, revision is simply the further growth of what is already there, the "preconceived" product. The absence of research on revision, then, is a function of a theory of writing which makes revision both superfluous and redundant, a theory which does not distinguish between writing and speech.

What the linear models do produce is a parody of writing. Isolating revision and then disregarding it plays havoc with the experiences composition teachers have of the actual writing and rewriting of experienced writers. Why should the linear model be preferred? Why should revision be forgotten, superfluous? Why do teachers offer the linear model and students accept it? One reason, Barthes suggests, is that "there is a fundamental tie between teaching and speech," while "writing begins at the point where speech becomes *impossible*."[6] The spoken word cannot be revised. The possibility of revision distinguishes the written text from speech. In fact, according to Barthes, this is the essential difference between writing and speaking. When we must revise, when the very idea is subject to recursive shaping by language, then speech becomes inadequate. This is a matter to which I will return, but first we should examine, theoretically, a detailed exploration of what student writers as distinguished from experienced adult writers *do* when they write and rewrite their work. Dissatisfied with both the linear model of writing and the lack of attention to the process of revision, I conducted a series of studies over the past three years which examined the revision processes of student writers and experienced writers to see what role revision played in their writing processes. In the course of my work the revision process was redefined *as a sequence of changes in a composition—changes which are initiated by cues and occur continually throughout the writing of a work.*

Methodology

I used a case study approach. The student writers were twenty freshmen at Boston University and the University of Oklahoma with SAT verbal scores ranging from 450-600 in their first semester of composition. The twenty experienced adult writers from Boston and Oklahoma City included journalists, editors, and academics. To refer to the two groups, I use the terms *student writers* and *experienced writers* because the principal difference between these two groups is the amount of experience they have had in writing.

Each writer wrote three essays, expressive, explanatory, and persuasive, and rewrote each essay twice, producing nine written products in draft and final form. Each writer was interviewed three times after the final revision of each essay. And each writer suggested revisions for a composition written by an anonymous author. Thus extensive written and spoken documents were obtained from each writer.

The essays were analyzed by counting and categorizing the changes made. Four revision operations were identified: deletion, substitution, addition, and reordering. And four levels of changes were identified: word, phrase, sentence, theme (the extended statement of one idea). A coding system was developed for identifying the frequency of revision by level and operation. In addition, transcripts of the interviews in which the writers interpreted their revisions were used to develop what was called a *scale of concerns* for each writer. This scale enabled me to codify what were the writer's primary concerns, secondary concerns, tertiary concerns, and whether the writers used the same scale of concerns when revising the second or third drafts as they used in revising the first draft.

Revision Strategies of Student Writers

Most of the students I studied did not use the terms *revision* or *rewriting*. In fact, they did not seem comfortable using the word *revision* and explained that revision was not a word they used, but the word their teachers used. Instead, most of the students had developed various functional terms to describe the type of changes they made. The following are samples of these definitions:

Scratch Out and Do Over Again: "I say scratch out and do over, and that means what it says. Scratching out and cutting out. I read what I have written and I cross out a word and put another word in; a more decent word or a better word. Then if there is somewhere to use a sentence that I have crossed out, I will put it there."

Reviewing: "Reviewing means just using better words and eliminating words that are not needed. I go over and change words around."

Reviewing: "I just review every word and make sure that everything is worded right. I see if I am rambling; I see if I can put a better word in or leave one out. Usually when I read what I have written, I say to myself, 'that word is so bland or so trite,' and then I go and get my thesaurus."

Redoing: "Redoing means cleaning up the paper and crossing out. It is looking at something and saying, no that has to go, or no, that is not right."

Marking Out: "I don't use the word rewriting because I only write one draft and the changes that I make are made on top of the draft. The changes that I make are usually just marking out words and putting different ones in."

Slashing and Throwing Out: "I throw things out and say they are not good. I like to write like Fitzgerald did by inspiration, and if I feel inspired then I don't need to slash and throw much out."

The predominant concern in these definitions is vocabulary. The students understand the revision process as a rewording activity. They do so because they perceive words as the unit of written discourse. That is, they concentrate on particular words apart from their role in the text. Thus one student quoted above thinks in terms of dictionaries, and, following the eighteenth century theory of words parodied in *Gulliver's Travels,* he imagines a load of things carried about to be exchanged. Lexical changes are the major revision activities of the students because economy is their goal. They are governed, like the linear model itself, by the Law of Occam's razor that prohibits logically needless repetition: redundancy and superfluity. Nothing governs speech more than such superfluities; speech constantly repeats itself precisely because spoken words, as Barthes writes, are expendable in the cause of communication. The aim of revision according to the students' own description is therefore to clean up speech; the redundancy of speech is unnnecessary in writing, their logic suggests, because writing, unlike speech, can be reread. Thus one student said, "Redoing means cleaning up the paper and crossing out." The remarkable contradiction of cleaning by marking might, indeed, stand for student revision as I have encountered it.

The students place a symbolic importance on their selection and rejection of words as the determiners of success or failure for their compositions. When revising, they primarily ask themselves: can I find a better word or phrase? A more impressive, not so cliched, or less hum-drum word? Am I repeating the same word or phrase too often? They approach the revision process with what could be labeled as a "thesaurus philosophy of writing"; the students consider the thesaurus a harvest of lexical substitutions and believe that most problems in their essays can be solved by rewording. What is revealed in the students' use of the thesaurus is a governing attitude toward their writing: that the meaning to be communicated is already there, already finished, already produced, ready to be communicated, and all that is necessary is a better word "rightly worded." One student defined revision as "redoing"; "redoing" meant "just using better words and eliminating words that are not needed." For the students, writing is translating: the thought to the page, the language of speech to the more formal language of prose, the word to its synonym. Whatever is translated, an original text already exists for students, one which need not be discovered or acted upon, but simply communicated.[7]

The students list repetition as one of the elements they most worry about. This cue signals to them that they need to eliminate the repetition either by substituting or deleting words or phrases. Repetition occurs, in large part, because student writing imitates—transcribes—speech: attention to repetitious words is a manner of cleaning speech. Without a sense of the developmental possibilities of revision (and writing in general) students seek, on the authority of many textbooks, simply to clean up their language and prepare to type. What is curious, however, is that students are aware of lexical repetition, but not conceptual repetition. They only notice the repetition if they can "hear" it; they do not diagnose lexical repetition as symptomatic of problems on a deeper level. By rewording their sentences to avoid the lexical repetition, the students solve the immediate problem, but blind themselves to problems on a textual level; although they are using different words, they are sometimes merely restating the same idea with different words. Such blindness, as I discovered with student writers, is the inability to "see" revision as a process: the inability to "re-view" their work again, as it were, with different eyes, and to start over.

The revision strategies described above are consistent with the students' understanding of the revision process as requiring lexical changes but not semantic changes. For the students, the extent to which they revise is a function of their level of inspiration. In fact, they use the word *inspiration* to describe the ease or difficulty with which their essay is written, and the extent to which the essay needs to be revised. If students feel inspired, if the writing comes easily, and if they don't get stuck on individual words or phrases, then they say that they cannot see any reason to revise. Because students do not see revision as an activity in which they modify and develop perspectives and ideas, they feel that if they know what they want to say, then there is little reason for making revisions.

The only modification of ideas in the students' essays occurred when they tried out two or three introductory paragraphs. This results, in part, because the students have been taught in another version of the linear model of composing to use a thesis statement as a controlling device in their introductory paragraphs. Since they write their introductions and their thesis statements even before they have really discovered what they want to say, their early close attention to the thesis statement, and more generally the linear model, function to restrict and circumscribe not only the development of their ideas, but also their ability to change the direction of these ideas.

Too often as composition teachers we conclude that students do not willingly revise. The evidence from my research suggests that it is not that students are unwilling to revise, but rather that they do what they have been taught to do in a consistently narrow and predictable way. On every occasion when I asked students why they hadn't made any more changes, they essentially replied, "I knew something larger was wrong, but I didn't think it would help to move words around." The students have strategies for handling words and phrases and their strategies helped them on a word or sentence level. What they lack, however, is a set of strategies to help them identify the "something larger" that they sensed was wrong and work from there. The *s*tudents do not have strategies for handling the whole essay. They lack procedures or heuristics to help them reorder lines of reasoning or ask questions about their purposes and readers. The students view their compositions in a linear way as a series of parts. Even such potentially useful concepts as "unity" or "form" are reduced to the rule that a composition, if it is to have form, must have an introduction, a body, and a conclusion, or the sum total of the necessary parts.

The students decide to stop revising when they decide that they have not violated any of the rules for revising. These rules, such as "Never begin a sentence with a conjunction" or "Never end a sentence with a preposition," are lexically cued and rigidly applied. In general, students will subordinate the demands of the specific problems of their text to the demands of the rules. Changes are made in compliance with abstract rules about the product, rules that quite often do not apply to the specific problems in the text. These revision strategies are teacher-based, directed towards a teacher-reader who expects compliance with rules—with pre-existing "conceptions"—and who will only examine parts of the composition (writing comments about those parts in the margins of their essays) and will cite any violations of rules in those parts. At best the students see their writing altogether passively through the eyes of former teachers or their surrogates, the textbooks, and are bound to the rules which they have been taught.

Revision Strategies of Experienced Writers

One aim of my research has been to contrast how student writers define revision with how a group of experienced writers define their revision processes. Here is a sampling of the definitions from the experienced writers:

> *Rewriting:* "It is a matter of looking at the kernel of what I have written, the content, and then thinking about it, responding to it, making decisions, and actually restructuring it."
>
> *Rewriting:* "I rewrite as I write. It is hard to tell what is a first draft because it is not determined by time. In one draft, I might cross out three pages, write two, cross out a fourth, rewrite it, and call it a draft. I am constantly writing and rewriting. I can only conceptualize so much in my first draft—only so much information can be held in my head at one time; my rewriting efforts are a reflection of how much information I can encompass at one time. There are levels and agenda which I have to attend to in each draft."
>
> *Rewriting:* "Rewriting means on one level, finding the argument, and on another level, language changes to make the argument more effective. Most of the time I feel as if I can go on rewriting forever. There is always one part of a piece that I could keep working on. It is always difficult to know at what point to abandon a piece of writing. I like this idea that a piece of writing is never finished, just abandoned."

Rewriting: "My first draft is usually very scattered. In rewriting, I find the line of argument. After the argument is resolved, I am much more interested in word choice and phrasing."

Revising: "My cardinal rule in revising is never to fall in love with what I have written in a first or second draft. An idea, sentence, or even a phrase that looks catchy, I don't trust. Part of this idea is to wait a while. I am much more in love with something after I have written it than I am a day or two later. It is much easier to change anything with time."

Revising: "It means taking apart what I have written and putting it back together again. I ask major theoretical questions of my ideas, respond to those questions, and think of proportion and structure, and try to find a controlling metaphor. I find out which ideas can be developed and which should be dropped. I am constantly chiseling and changing as I revise."

The experienced writers describe their primary objective when revising as finding the form or shape of their argument. Although the metaphors vary, the experienced writers often use structural expressions such as "finding a framework," "a pattern," or "a design" for their argument. When questioned about this emphasis, the experienced writers responded that since their first drafts are usually scattered attempts to define their territory, their objective in the second draft is to begin observing general patterns of development and deciding what should be included and what excluded. One writer explained, "I have learned from experience that I need to keep writing a first draft until I figure out what I want to say. Then in a second draft, I begin to see the structure of an argument and how all the various sub-arguments which are buried beneath the surface of all those sentences are related." What is described here is a process in which the writer is both agent and vehicle. "Writing," says Barthes, unlike speech, "develops like a seed, not a line,"[8] and like a seed it confuses beginning and end, conception and production. Thus, the experienced writers say their drafts are "not determined by time," that rewriting is a "constant process," that they feel as if (they) "can go on forever." Revising confuses the beginning and end, the agent and vehicle; it confuses, *in order to find,* the line of argument.

After a concern for form, the experienced writers have a second objective: a concern for their readership. In this way, "production" precedes "conception." The experienced writers imagine a reader (reading their product) whose existence and whose expectations influence their revision process. They have abstracted the standards of a reader and this reader seems to be partially a reflection of themselves and functions as a critical and productive collaborator—a collaborator who has yet to love their work. The anticipation of a reader's judgment causes a feeling of dissonance when the writer recognizes incongruities between intention and execution, and requires these writers to make revisions on all levels. Such a reader gives them just what the students lacked: new eyes to "re-view" their work. The experienced writers believe that they have learned the causes and conditions, the product, which will influence their reader, and their revision strategies are geared towards creating these causes and conditions. They demonstrate a complex understanding of which examples, sentences, or phrases should be included or excluded. For example, one experienced writer decided to delete public examples and add private examples when writing about the energy crisis because "private examples would be less controversial and thus more persuasive." Another writer revised his transitional sentences because "some kinds of transitions are more easily recognized as transitions than others." These examples represent the type of strategic attempts these experienced writers use to manipulate the conventions of discourse in order to communicate to their reader.

But these revision strategies are a process of more than communication; they are part of the process of *discovering meaning* altogether. Here we can see the importance of dissonance; at the heart of revision is the process by which writers recognize and resolve the dissonance they sense in their writing. Ferdinand de Saussure has argued that meaning is differential or "diacritical," based on differences between terms rather than "essential" or inherent qualities of terms. "Phonemes," he said, "are characterized not, as one might think, by their own positive quality but simply by the fact that they are distinct."[9] In fact, Saussure bases his entire *Course in General Linguistics* on these differences, and such differences are dissonant; like musical dissonances which gain their significance from their relationship to the "key" of the composition which itself is determined by the whole language, specific language (parole) gains its meaning from the system of language (langue) of which it is a manifestation and part. The musical composition—a "composition" of parts—creates its "key" as in an over-all structure which determines the value (meaning) of its parts. The analogy with music is readily seen in the compositions of experienced writers: both sorts of composition are based precisely on those structures experienced writers seek in their writing. It is this complicated relationship between the parts and the whole in the work of experienced writers which destroys the linear model; writing cannot develop "like a line" because each addition or deletion is a reordering of the whole. Explicating Saussure, Jonathan Culler asserts that "meaning depends on difference of meaning."[10] But student writers constantly struggle to bring their essays into congruence with a predefined meaning. The experienced writers do the opposite: they seek to discover (to create) meaning in the engagement with their writing, in revision. They seek to emphasize and exploit the lack of clarity, the differences of meaning, the dissonance, that writing as opposed to speech allows in the possibility of revision. Writing has spatial and temporal features not apparent in speech—words are recorded in space and fixed in time—which is why writing is susceptible to reordering and later addition. Such features make possible the dissonance that both provokes revision and promises, from itself, new meaning.

For the experienced writers the heaviest concentration of changes is on the sentence level, and the changes are predominantly by addition and deletion. But, unlike the students, experienced writers make changes on all levels and use all revision operations. Moreover, the operations the students fail to use—reordering and addition—seem to require a theory of the revision process as a totality—a theory which, in fact, encompasses the *whole* of the composition. Unlike the students, the experienced writers possess a nonlinear theory in which a sense of the whole writing both precedes and grows out of an examination of the parts. As we saw, one writer said he needed "a first draft to figure out what to say," and "a second draft to see the structure of an argument buried beneath the surface." Such a "theory" is both theoretical and strategical; once again, strategy and theory are conflated in ways that are literally impossible for the linear model. Writing appears to be more like a seed than a line.

Two elements of the experienced writers' theory of the revision process are the adoption of a holistic perspective and the perception that revision is a recursive process. The writers ask: what does my essay as a *whole* need for form, balance, rhythm, or communication. Details are added, dropped, substituted, or reordered according to their sense of what the essay needs for emphasis and proportion. This sense, however, is constantly in flux as ideas are developed and modified; it is constantly "re-viewed" in relation to the parts. As their ideas change, revision becomes an attempt to make their writing consonant with that changing vision.

The experienced writers see their revision process as a recursive process—a process with significant recurring activities—with different levels of attention and different agenda for each cycle. During the first revision cycle their attention is primarily directed towards narrowing the topic and delimiting their ideas. At this point, they are not as concerned as they are later about vocabulary and style. The experienced writers explained that they get closer to their meaning by not limiting themselves too early to lexical concerns. As one writer commented to explain her revision process, a comment inspired by the summer 1977 New York power failure: "I feel like Con Edison cutting off certain states to keep the generators going. In first and second drafts, I try to cut off as much as I can of my editing generator, and in a third draft, I try to cut off some of my idea generators, so I can make sure that I actually finish the essay." Although the experienced writers describe their revision process as a series of different levels or cycles, it is inaccurate to assume that they have only one objective for each cycle and that each cycle can be defined by a different objective. The same objectives and sub-processes are present in each cycle, but in different proportions. Even though these experienced writers place the predominant weight upon finding the form of their argument during the first cycle, other concerns exist as well. Conversely, during the later cycles, when the experienced writers' primary attention is focused upon stylistic concerns, they are still attuned, although in a reduced way, to the form of the argument. Since writers are limited in what they can attend to during each cycle (understandings are temporal), revision strategies help balance competing demands on attention. Thus, writers can concentrate on more than one objective at a time by developing strategies to sort out and organize their different concerns in successive cycles of revision.

It is a sense of writing as discovery—a repeated process of beginning over again, starting out new—that the students failed to have. I have used the notion of dissonance because such dissonance, the incongruities between intention and execution, governs both writing and meaning. Students do not see the incongruities. They need to rely on their own internalized sense of good writing and to see their writing with their "own" eyes. Seeing in revision—seeing beyond hearing—is at the root of the word *revision* and the process itself; current dicta on revising blind our students to what is actually involved in revision. In fact, they blind them to what constitutes good writing altogether. Good writing disturbs: it creates dissonance. Students need to seek the dissonance of discovery, utilizing in their writing, as the experienced writers do, the very difference between writing and speech—the possibility of revision.

FOOTNOTES

[1] D. Gordon Rohman and Albert O. Wiecke, "Pre-writing: The Construction and Application of Models for Concept Formation in Writing," Cooperative Research Project No. 2174, U.S. Office of Education, Department of Health, Education, and Welfare; James Britton, Anthony Burgess, Nancy Martin, Alex McLeod, Harold Rosen, *The Development of Writing Abilities* (11-18) (London: Macmillan Education, 1975).

[2] Britton is following Roman Jakobson, "Linguistics and Poetics," in T. A. Sebeok, *Style in Language* (Cambridge, Mass: MIT Press, 1960).

[3] For an extended discussion of this issue see Nancy Sommers, "The Need for Theory in Composition Research," *College Composition and Communication,* 30 (February, 1979), 46-49.

[4] *Classical Rehtoric for the Modern Student* (New York: Oxford University Press, 1965), p. 27.

[5] Roland Barthes, "Writers, Intellectuals, Teachers," in *Image-Music-Text,* trans. Stephen Heath (New York: Hill and Wang, 1977), pp. 190-191.

[6] "Writers, Intellectuals, Teachers," p. 190.

[7] Nancy Sommers and Ronald Schleifer, "Means and Ends: Some Assumptions of Student Writers," *Composition and Teaching,* 11 (in press).

The Twenty-Minute Solution: Mapping in the Writing Center

JOY A. FARMER

In 1979 when I established Newberry College's first writing center, I was about as lonely as the Maytag repairman, at least for the first couple of months. Eventually, students discovered that real help was to be found in that ground-floor room, and they began to trickle in. Before too long, the trickle had become a steady enough flow to keep three tutors busy, but never did we find ourselves so deluged that we had to set a time limit on our sessions with students. Today, of course, in writing centers across the country, the situation has changed so drastically that the twenty-minute tutorial has become standard in many centers. I can satisfactorily address most students' writing problems in that length of time; however, I have found two types of problems to be particularly resistant. The first is the sentence-sense problem. A student with this difficulty writes such tangled construction as, "For those who find parallel parking difficult, a test most people wish to avoid, is about the only way you can park in the urban areas," or "Being a commuting student has disadvantages that only apply to the commuting student such as the experience of college life." Explaining logical syntax to these authors may take hours or even days. The other type of problem that does not readily lend itself to the twenty-minute solution is the essay-sense problem. Students lacking essay sense do not know what a thesis is or where it comes from. They are equally baffled by topic sentences, and they have no idea how to go about effectively organizing and developing ideas for their body paragraphs.

The pedagogical method that has revolutionized my work with the second group of students is a technique I call "mapping." This rhetorical strategy is at least as old as Aristotle and is immediately recognizable to many writers as the mental process they themselves go through before they commit their ideas to paper or computer screen. Dr. Thomas Cooley of Berry College is the first composition teacher whom I have observed apply the technique on a large scale: his suggestions in his *Rhetoric Handout for English 101* are the basis of the entire composition program at Berry and of a forthcoming textbook. I adopted mapping in my own classroom in the fall of 1987; students responded to it by writing better developed, more analytical essays with sounder organization and clearer theses than their predecessors had written. At the same time, I began to use mapping in my writing center tutorials with similar results: students who came in with no notion of where to begin an essay left with an approach to writing that worked and a new confidence in their ability to succeed in their composition classes.

The mapping I model has nothing to do with the circles and diagrams called mapping in most textbooks. Nor is mapping related to outlining since outlining technically cannot take place until a text exists. If the reader does not believe me, she might remember what she did in high school when required to submit an outline several weeks before her senior research paper was due. She wrote that paper first; then she outlined it; then she felt guilty (probably to this day) because her teacher had insisted that outlines precede texts. In fact, a thing must exist before it can be outlined: to outline a hand, one first needs a hand. For this reason, many students find outlining to be more useful as a reading and study strategy than as a writing strategy. Mapping, on the other hand, recognizes that the writer's problem is to invent a text in response to a writing assignment; the completed map is the result of that invention process.

In mapping, the student's first step is to formulate a simple, straightforward assertion prompted by the essay assignment. My task as a writing center tutor is to help the student make this assertion by presenting him or her with several practice options requiring a response: Do you have a positive or negative view of lawyers? Should computer literacy by required of all college students? How does a person make a good first impression in an interview? What childhood game taught you an important lesson about yourself, other people, or life in general? Most students catch on immediately: "I have a negative view of lawyers," they reply; "computer literacy should be required of all college students"; "there are four things a potential employee can do to make a good first impression in an interview"; "the childhood game that taught me an important truth about myself is *Monopoly*." The next step is to have the student formulate a statement that answers a question based on the topic she has been assigned. Once she has done so, the student is elated to discover that she has just written the first sentence of her essay—an accomplishment that usually suffices to overcome writer and thinker's block.

Because color is a useful visual cue to help a student focus on concept similarities, I keep a set of highlighters or crayons on hand for the third step, which entails working from the statement of the main idea to the major and minor support material in the ensuing map sections. First, I encourage the student to identify and highlight the portion of the central statement that clearly needs further elaboration through definition or analysis. In the four examples just cited, the student might use a yellow marker to highlight "negative view of lawyers," "computer literacy should be required," "four things a potential employee can do to make a good first impression in an interview," or "taught me an important truth about myself is *Monopoly*." She then brings the same phrase down to the next line, highlights it again in yellow, and uses the equal sign to link it to material that either defines the idea or explains it.

To illustrate, the student might write, "negative view of lawyers=the way television and the movies portray members of the legal profession." At this point, I tell the student that the equal sign can mean either "is" or "because," depending on whether the problem demands a definitional or a cause-and-effect approach. In the preceding example, the equals sign obviously indicates cause-and-effect: "I have a negative view of lawyers *because of* the way television and the movies portray members of the legal profession." Then I encourage the student to see that she has just generated, not one, but two new ideas that need further elaboration—the way lawyers are depicted on television and the way they are depicted in films. Immediately we highlight television in blue and movies in green and on the next line isolate the phrase, "the way television portrays lawyers." After highlighting this phrase in blue, we follow it with the equal sign and leave a big space. On the line following the space, we write and highlight in green, "the way films portray lawyers," again following the phrase with the equal sign. By this time, the student has usually caught on to the extent that she recognizes that the equal sign now means "is." For instance, if her complete equation reads, "the way films portray lawyers=*The Philadelphia Story*," it will mean something like, "A film portraying lawyers in an unflattering light *is The Philadelphia Story*." Bringing *The Philadelphia Story* down to the next line and linking the title to "dishonest lawyers, heartless lawyers, and ignorant lawyers" via the equal sign will prompt the student to generate specific film support relevant to "dishonest lawyers=," "vicious lawyers=," and "ignorant lawyers=."

The process I have just described takes about fifteen minutes to demonstrate to the average student, twenty at the most. When the student is at a point where she must decide how best to develop a topic area, I leave her to her own devices for a while. Only when she has fully and relevantly developed one section of her map do I sit down again to help her with her next section. We return to her "yellow" idea, "negative view of lawyers," bring it down to a new line, highlight it once more in yellow, and follow it with an equal sign and a different reason, perhaps the student's own experience with an unsympathetic or incompetent attorney. We highlight this idea in pink and isolate it on the next line, and the student proceeds as she did earlier. When the student has returned to her yellow idea at least three times and created at least three clear-cut, fully illustrated divisions in support of her original statement, she is ready for the next step in mapping, writing her analytical thesis.

Helping a student in the writing center to discover her thesis after she has struggled to produce her first map is the most satisfying part of the whole process. Quite simply, I encourage her to look back at the map material she has highlighted in yellow (italicized below):

- *Negative view of lawyers*=the way television and the movies portray members of the legal profession
- *Negative view of lawyers*=my recent experience with an attorney
- *Negative view of lawyers*=two news-magazine stories that appeared this week

Once the student has expressed these equations in one, two, or three sentences, she will have her thesis. Moreover, when she combines this thesis statement with the first sentence she wrote—that is, her statement of her main idea—she will have crafted a serviceable introduction. To continue with the example begun above, the introduction might read as follows:

> I have a negative view of lawyers. This opinion has been shaped by the way I see lawyers portrayed on television and in the movies, by my recent experience with my attorney during a D.U.I. Conviction, and by two articles on lawyers that I just read in *Time* and *Newsweek*.

But the introduction, complete with analytical thesis, is not the only item the student has handy once she has finished her map. She also has her entire well-developed and logically structured essay sitting before her. All she has to do is transform the major map divisions into body paragraphs by adding connective material. (She will need the tutor's guidance here since a major map division may need to be broken down into two or more paragraphs. For example, the first and last divisions in the map described above call for at least two paragraphs each.) Even her topic sentences are virtually written. Like the analytical thesis, these come from the yellow areas of the map. To write topic sentences, the student need strive only for variety of expression and attach an appropriate transition. A possible topic sentence for the student's first body paragraph of her essay on lawyers is, "First, I do not admire lawyers because I often see them depicted as white-collar criminals by the entertainment media." As with the introduction, the key word here is *serviceable*. After students master the basics in the writing center, their classroom teachers can address matters of style.

Often when students grasp how relatively easy it is to construct a competent essay from a well-thought-out map, I have to deal with their unrestrained glee: in one memorable moment, a sinewy soccer player tried to hoist me onto his shoulders. They have not yet voiced a complaint that I thought I might here: mapping is too much work because it is like writing the whole essay twice. Rather, they share the unhappy experience of having attempted to write papers from rough drafts, and they realize that any essay that goes through two version is written twice; furthermore, they understand that if the writer has no method, neither version will amount to much. Mapping, on the other hand, insures that the first "draft," which is the map itself, will form a solid foundation for the actual paper—a fact that cheers my writing center students immensely. They also do not seem bothered that mapping could become somewhat formulaic or worry that it might stifle their creativity. On the contrary, students are grateful to be presented with an approach to composition that works every time. Indeed, many have landed in the writing center because twelve years of English have taught them no practicable expository method and because their problems are, therefore, not being effectively addressed in the regular composition classes.

A peculiar thing happens, though, once students master mapping. They become more creative; their examples and illustrations become more vivid and involved; their rhetorical strategies become more complex and varied. Furthermore, mapping facilitates their graduation from the tri-thesis, five-paragraph theme to more sophisticated essays. For instance, several quarters ago, an advanced mapmaker with whom I was working was struggling with a concept analysis on morality. As her statement of the central idea, she wrote, "Several characteristics are common to every moral person."

Then, she wrote, "characteristics=as a child, a moral person *has observed moral behavior being modeled* and *has been required to behave morally*." Recognizing that she had generated two thesis ideas (as shown by single and double underlining in her paper and italics and underlined italics here), she treated each to independent development by citing several instances from her own experience.

She began her next topic area with "characteristics=moral people can distinguish between right and wrong," followed by , "distinguish between right and wrong=make obvious choices." After isolating, "make obvious choices" and pondering the phrase for a few minutes, she recalled and located a *Newsweek* article profiling a young gang member who thought that a personal insult was reason enough to murder a rival gang member. According to the article, the killer genuinely believed that he had made the ethically correct decision. "So much for the clearly immoral person with a warped sense of values," I prompted. "But what about the finer distinctions that ordinary, law-abiding people have to make?" She responded by writing, "characteristics=the moral person can distinguish between good and better," followed by "distinguish between good and better=make difficult distinctions." Eventually, she decided to illustrate this idea by discussing an interview she had read in Bill Moyers' A *World of Ideas*. In this interview, ethicist Michael Josephson discusses the propriety and the necessity of choosing between the good and the better or the bad and the worse and of sometimes sacrificing one ethical principle for another (21).

By then, the student had enough material for a four-part thesis and five body paragraphs, but she chose to continue with, "characteristics=the moral person acts on his or her knowledge of right and wrong." First, she considered the behavior of Mr. Adams in Shirley Jackson's "The Lottery." In speaking out against the ritual, Mr. Adams shows that he knows the difference between right and wrong; however, he is not a moral man because he is "in the front of the crowd of villagers" (219) when the stoning of Tessie Hutchinson begins. As a contrast to Mr. Adams, the student chose Harper Lee's Atticus Finch, who consistently elects to do the right thing. By the time the student had explored Finch's defense of Tom Robinson and his protection of Boo Radley, she had expanded her last topic area to three paragraphs. She was also able to work toward a powerful conclusion since Atticus must sacrifice a moral principle and tell a lie if he wishes to keep Boo out of the public eye. In other words, mapping had led the second student to respond to her topic by crafting a multi-layered, informed definition based on material that went beyond personal experience, an approach she said would not have occurred to her if she had not been using the map tool. The resulting essay was anything but a formulaic, five-paragraph theme.

When I have asked for candid evaluations of mapping from writing center students like this one and from others just learning the technique, I get the same answer: mapping, they reply, encourages originality, first by freeing them from having to worry about essay form so they can concentrate on content, and second by stimulating them to come up with clever material to fill the blank sections of the map. The map, they further agree, challenges them to grapple with ideas on a higher intellectual level than they have ever thought before. With equal enthusiasm, students praise the system of colorcoding and isolating ideas that need further elaboration because they claim that this system reminds them of the need to invent pertinent detail.

The improvement in the grades students receive on their papers most certainly explains their enthusiastic endorsements: the freshman I described in the example dealing with lawyers saw her grade jump from an *F* to a *C* after she learned mapping at mid-term; the veteran map-maker, who came for help after her first *D*, finished with an *A*. That this technique enables students to improve their class standing is hardly a surprise. We English teachers give the highest marks to papers that do the best job of marrying form and relevance to expressiveness and originality—the very skill that mapping cultivates.

Mapping, then, is the rhetorical method that has helped me effectively tutor the writing center student who has no essay sense. Mapping is simple to demonstrate; it lends itself nicely to a twenty-minute session; it need not tie a tutor down with a single student even during that twenty-minute time slot since a crucial part of the process involves leaving the student alone to develop her own supportive material—an important advantage at periods of peak demand. Furthermore, mapping gives the student something to hold on to as she begins to deal independently with all types of writing assignments, from the backyard topics of state Regents' exams and some freshman composition classes to the literary topics of introductory analysis to the research assignments of advanced courses. I have even known a student who, unable to afford an attorney, used mapping to prepare his case in a child custody hearing, which he won in a state that traditionally awards legal guardianship of minor children to their mothers. Finally, mapping sends a student forth with the conviction that the writing center is a useful place, for there she has mastered a new skill. This conviction is guaranteed to endure until she returns with a sentence like the following and asks the tutor for help understanding the illogic of the thing: "People who do not go to bars and still have lifestyles generally have big appetites, critic capabilities, and lots of clothes," or "Hunting is a sport that takes all morning and afternoon to try and kill an animal, yet my son's favoritism is to the activity of downtown shopping because clothes are much cheaper than the malls." I don't know what the first sentence explains, but the second obviously accounts for why we see so few people wearing malls these days! I check my watch, note the line forming at the computer check-in, and sigh nostalgically for the leisurely afternoons in the writing centers of fifteen years ago. Depending on one's perspective, it's going to be either a very short or a very long twenty minutes.

WORKS CITED

Josephson, Michael. Interview with Bill Moyers. *A World of Ideas.* Ed. Betty Sue
    Flowers. New York: Doubleday, 1989. 14-27.
Jackson, Shirley. "The Lottery." *The Lottery.* New York: Avon Books, 1949. 211-219.

Introduction to Errors and Expectations
Mina P. Shaughnessy

EDITOR'S NOTE: In this book addressed to teachers of basic writing, Mina Shaughnessy explains and then builds on the theory of error analysis, drawing illustrations and examples from her experience at City University of New York during the early years of open admissions.

Background

Toward the end of the sixties and largely in response to the protests of that decade, many four-year colleges began admitting students who were not by traditional standards ready for college. The numbers of such students varied from college to college as did the commitment to the task of teaching them. In some, the numbers were token; in others, where comprehensive policies of admissions were adopted, the number threatened to "tip" freshman classes in favor of the less prepared students. For such colleges, this venture into mass education usually began abruptly, amidst the misgivings of administrators, who had to guess in the dark about the sorts of programs they ought to plan for the students they had never met, and the reluctancies of teachers, some of whom had already decided that the new students were ineducable.

It was in such an atmosphere that the boldest and earliest of these attempts to build a comprehensive system of higher education began: in the spring of 1970, the City University of New York adopted an admissions policy that guaranteed to every city resident with a high-school diploma a place in one of its eighteen tuition-free colleges (ten senior colleges and eight two-year colleges), thereby opening its doors not only to a larger population of students than it had ever had before (enrollment was to jump from 174,000 in 1969 to 266,000 in 1975) but to a wider range of students than any college had probably ever admitted or thought of admitting to its campus—academic winners and losers from the best and worst high schools in the country, the children of the lettered and the illiterate, the blue-collared, the white-collared, and the unemployed, some who could barely afford the subway fare to school and a few who came in the new cars their parents had given them as a reward for staying in New York to go to college; in short, the sons and daughters of New Yorkers, reflecting that city's intense, troubled version of America.

One of the first tasks these students faced when they arrived at college was to write a placement essay and take a reading test. Judged by the results of these tests, the young men and women who were to be known as open admissions students fell into one of three groups: (1) those who met the traditional requirements for college work, who appeared from their tests and their school performance to be competent readers and writers with enough background in the subjects they would be studying in college to be able to begin at the traditional starting points; (2) those who had survived their secondary schooling but not thrived on it, whose reading was seldom voluntary and whose writing reflected a flat competence, by no means error-free but limited more seriously by its utter predictability—its bare vocabulary, safe syntax, and platitudinous tone, the writing of students who had learned to get by but who seemed to have found no fun nor challenge in academic tasks; (3) those who had been left so far behind the others in their formal education that they appeared to have little chance of catching up, students whose difficulties with the written language seemed of a different order from those of the other groups, as if they had come, you might say, from a different country, or at least through different schools, where even very modest standards of high-school literacy had not been met.

Of these groups, the first was clearly the group whom college teachers knew best. They were the students for whom college courses and tests had been designed and about whom studies had been made. The second group, however, was also known to them; its students resembled the academic stragglers of another era, those who had tended to end up in "bonehead English" perhaps but at least some of whom had been known to take hold at a later point in their development and go on to complete their academic work creditably. The third group contained the true outsiders. Natives, for the most part, of New York, graduates of the same public school system as the other students, they were nonetheless strangers in academia, unacquainted with the rules and rituals of college life, unprepared for the sorts of tasks their teachers were about to assign them. Most of them had grown up in one of New York's ethnic or racial enclaves. Many had spoken other languages or dialects at home and never successfully reconciled the worlds of home and school, a fact which by now had worked its way deep into their feelings about school and about themselves as students.

They were in college now for one reason: that their lives might be better than their parents', that the lives of their children might be better than theirs so far had been. Just how college was to accomplish these changes was not at all clear, but the faith that education was the one available route to change empowered large numbers of students who had already endured twelve years of compulsory schooling to choose to go to college when the doors of City University suddenly swung open.

Not surprisingly, the essays these students wrote during their first weeks of class stunned the teachers who read them. Nothing, it seemed, short of a miracle was going to turn such students into writers. Not uncommonly, teachers announced to their supervisors (or even their students) after only a week of class that everyone was probably going to fail. These were students, they insisted, whose problems at this stage were irremediable. To make matters worse, there were no studies nor guides, nor even suitable textbooks to turn to. Here were teachers trained to analyze the belletristic achievements of the centuries marooned in basic writing classrooms with adult student writers who appeared by college standards to be illiterate. Seldom had an educational venture begun so inauspiciously, the teachers unready in mind and heart to face their students, the students weighted by the disadvantages of poor training yet expected to "catch up" with the front-runners in a semester or two of low-intensity instruction.

Five years have passed since that first class of open admissions students entered City University. Some of those "ineducable" students have by now been graduated; some have dropped out; some have transferred to other types of programs after having found their vocational directions; and still others remain in college, delayed because of outside jobs that eat into their college time and because of the extra time they spent at the outset developing their skills as readers and writers. The teachers who five years ago questioned the educability of these students now know of their capabilities and have themselves undergone many shifts in attitude and methodology since their first encounters with the new students.

Despite such advances, the territory I am calling basic writing (and that others might call remedial or developmental writing) is still very much of a frontier, unmapped, except for a scattering of impressionistic articles and a few blazed trails that individual teachers propose through their texts. And like the settlers of other frontiers, the teachers who by choice or assignment are heading to this pedagogical West are certain to be carrying many things they will not be needing, that will clog their journey as they get further on. So too they will discover the need of other things they do not have and will need to fabricate by mother wit out of whatever is at hand.

This book is intended to be a guide for that kind of teacher, and it is certain to have the shortcomings of other frontier maps, with doubtless a few rivers in the wrong place and some trials that end nowhere. Still, it is also certain to prepare the inexperienced teacher for some of the difficulties he is likely to encounter and even provide him with a better inventory of necessary supplies than he is likely to draw up on his own.[1]

The book is mainly an attempt to be precise about the types of difficulties to be found in basic writing (BW) papers at the outset, and beyond that, to demonstrate how the sources of those difficulties can be explained without recourse to such pedagogically empty terms as "handicapped" or "disadvantaged." I have divided this territory of difficulty into familiar teaching categories, which serve as headings for the main sections of the book: Handwriting and Punctuation, Syntax, Common Errors, Spelling, Vocabulary, and Beyond the Sentence. In each of these sections, I have tried to do three things: first, to give examples of the range of problems that occur under each category of difficulty; second, to reason about the causes of these problems; and third, to suggest ways in which a teacher might approach them.

The examples have been drawn largely from placement essays, some 4,000 of them, that were written by incoming freshmen at City College of the City University of New York over the years 1970 through 1974. To the criticism that samples written under testing situations do not represent the true compe-tence of writers, I can only answer that where writers are as unskilled as the student writers we are considering, the conditions of writing seem to matter less than they do for more advanced writers. Thus the initial essays of this group proved to be highly accurate guides to placement. Indeed, it was not unusual to find students at this level doing better on their test essays than on outside assignments.

The reader will quickly—perhaps even impatiently—note that I have tended to use more examples of individual difficulties than he needs in order to identify the sort of problem I am discussing. I have done this in part to sug-gest that the problem I am naming occurs in a variety of contexts but also because I see a value to being immersed in examples. It deepens one's sense of pattern and thereby develops the ability to make swift assessments and classi-fications of writing difficulties. Should the reader feel no need for this immersion, however, he will be able to follow my line of analysis without heeding all the examples.

In reasoning about the causes of the various difficulties BW students have as writers, I have drawn from three resources: my students and the explana-tions they have given me, directly and indirectly, of their difficulties with written English; my colleagues, who have shared their insights with me over the years in many different settings, both formal and informal; and my own experience as someone who writes and therefore understands the pressures and peculiarities of that behavior.

From these resources, I have reached the persuasion that underlies this book—namely, that BW students write the way they do, not because they are slow or non-verbal, indifferent to or incapable of academic excellence, but because they are beginners and must, like all beginners, learn by making mis-takes. These they make aplenty and for such a variety of reasons that the inexperienced teacher is almost certain to see nothing but a chaos of error when he first encounters their papers. Yet a closer look will reveal very little that is random or "illogical" in what they have written. And the keys to their development as writers often lie hidden in the very features of their writing that English teachers have been trained to brush aside with a marginal code letter or a scribbled injunction to "Proofread!" Such strategies ram at the doors of their incompetence while the keys that would open them lie in view. This is not to say that learning to write as a young adult does not involve hard work, for certainly it does, but only that the work must be informed by an understanding not only of what is missing or awry but of why this is so. In each chapter, I will therefore be trying to tease out the reasons that lie behind the problems I have illustrated.

My suggestions for helping students overcome these problems are of sev-eral sorts. Sometimes I offer actual lessons; sometimes I recommend a method or strategy, such as sentence-combining or free writing, that is already (or ought to be) part of a teacher's technology; and at others, I merely urge a fresh perspective on an old problem. The teacher therefore who is searching for a tightly and fully structured writing program will not find it here. This book is concerned with the orientations and perceptions of teachers in relation to a specific population of student writers. It assumes that programs are not the answers to the learning problems of students but that teachers are and that, indeed, good teachers create good programs, that the best programs are developed *in situ*, in response to the needs of individual student populations and as reflections of the particular histories and resources of individual colleges. Thus, while I have sketched out a course plan in my final chapter which arranges the pieces of my analysis into teaching order, I do not expect anyone to accept it as a prototype. It is, let us say, a tried way of beginning a writing apprenticeship.

The course plan also serves to suggest the proportion of time that would be given in class to the goal of achieving correct form. Without this indication, the reader is certain to conclude that the "basic" of basic writing is not how to write but how to be right, for five of the book's eight chapters are devoted to the errors students make. This attention to error is certain to raise questions—both pedagogical and political—in the minds of many teachers. Why, some will ask, do English teachers need to be told so much about errors? Isn't their concern with error already a kind of malignancy? Ought we not to dwell instead upon the options writers have rather than the constraints they must work under if they are to be read without prejudice?

There is a short answer to these questions—namely that the proportion of time I spend analyzing errors does not reflect the proportion of time a teacher should spend teaching students how to avoid them. But since teachers' preconceptions about errors are frequently at the center of their misconceptions about BW students, I have no choice but to dwell on errors. The long answer to these questions leads us into more controversial territory. Yet it is important, before this exploration of student writing begins, that I explain more fully why error figures so importantly in this book.

Some views on error

For the BW student, academic writing is a trap, not a way of saying something to someone. The spoken language, looping back and forth between speakers, offering chances for groping and backing up and even hiding, leaving room for the language of hands and faces, of pitch and pauses, is generous and inviting. Next to this rich orchestration, writing is but a line that moves haltingly across the page, exposing as it goes all that the writer doesn't know, then passing into the hands of a stranger who reads it with a lawyer's eyes, searching for flaws.

By the time he reaches college, the BW student both resents and resists his vulnerability as a writer. He is aware that he leaves a trail of errors behind him when he writes. He can usually think of little else while he is writing. But he doesn't know what to do about it. Writing puts him on a line, and he does-n't want to be there. For every three hundred words he writes, he is likely to use from ten to thirty forms that the academic reader regards as serious errors. Some writers, inhibited by their fear of error, produce but a few lines an hour or keep trying to begin, crossing out one try after another until the sentence is hopelessly tangled. The following passage illustrates the disintegration of one such writer:[2]

Start 1
Seeing and hearing is something beautiful and strange to infant.
Start 2
To a infant seeing and hearing is something beautiful and strange to infl
Start 3
I agree that seeing and hearing is something beautiful and strange to a infants. A infants heres a strange sound such as work mother, he than acc
Start 4
I agree that child is more sensitive to beauty, because its all so new to him and he apprec
Start 5
The main point is that a child is more sensitive to beauty than there parents, because its the child a inftant can only express it feeling with reactions,
Start 6
I agree a child is more senstive to seeing and hearing than his parent, because its also new to him and more appreciate. His
Start 7
I agree that seeing and hearing have a different quality for infants than grownup, because when infants comes aware of a sound and can associate it with the object, he is indefeying and he parents acknowledge to to this
Start 8
I agree and disagree that seeing and hearing have a different quality for infants than for grownups, because to see and hear for infants its all so new and mor appreciate, but I also feel that a child parent appreciate the sharing
Start 9
I disagree I feel that it has the same quality to
Start 10
I disagree I fell that seeig and hearing has the same quality to both infants and parents. Hearing and seeing is such a great quality to infants and parents, and they both appreciate, just because there aren't that many panters or musicians around dosen't mean that infants are more sensitive to beautiful that there parents.

So absolute is the importance of error in the minds of many writers that "good writing" to them means "correct writing," nothing more. "As long as I can remember," writes a student, "I wanted to be an English teacher. I know it is hard, keeping verbs in their right place, s's when they should be, etc., but one day I will make them part of me."

Much about the "remedial" situation encourages this obsession with error. First, there is the reality of academia, the fact that most college teachers have little tolerance for the kinds of errors BW students make, that they perceive certain types of errors as indicators of ineducability, and that they have the power of the F. Second there is the urgency of the students to meet their teachers' criteria, even to request more of the prescriptive teaching they have had before in the hope that this time it might "take." Third, there is the awareness of the teacher and administrator that remedial programs are likely to be evaluated (and budgeted) according to the speed with which they produce correct writers, correctness being a highly measurable feature of acceptable writing.

Teachers respond differently to these realities. Some rebel against the idea of error itself. All linguistic forms, they argue, are finally arbitrary. The spelling of a word, the inflectional systems that carry or reinforce certain kinds of information in sentences—these are merely conventions that differ from language to language and from dialect to dialect. And because the forms of language are arbitrary, the reasoning goes, they are not obligatory, not, at least, in those situations where variant forms can be understood by a reader or where the imposition of new forms undermines the writer's pride or confidence in his native language or vernacular.

Such a view excludes many forms from the province of "error." Certainly it leaves no room for those refinements of usage that have come to be associated with writing handbooks—who-whom and that-which distinctions, the possessive form with the genitive, the split infinitive, etc. Beyond this, it would exclude variant grammatical forms and syntactical patterns that originate in varieties of English that have long been spoken but only recently written, and then only in folk and imaginative literature. These forms would include double negatives, regularized irregular verbs (grow, growed, growed), zero inflections in redundant situations (e.g., the omission of the plural s in *ten jobs* because plurality is already indicated by the number), and various orthographic accommodations to vernacular forms.

When one considers the damage that has been done to students in the name of correct writing, this effort to redefine error so as to exclude most of the forms that give students trouble in school and to assert the legitimacy of other kinds of English is understandable. Doubtless it is part of a much vaster thrust within this society not only to reduce the penalties for being culturally different but to be enriched by that diversity.

Nonetheless, the teacher who faces a class of writers who have acquired but a rudimentary control of the skill discovers that the issue of error is much more complex and troubling than it seems in theory. He finds, for example, that the errors his students make cannot be neatly traced to one particular source, namely, the habitual preference of a vernacular form over a standard form. Instead he finds evidence of a number of interacting influences: the generally humiliating encounter with school language, which produces ambivalent feelings about mastery, persuading the child on the one hand that he cannot learn to read and write and on the other that he has to; the pleasures of peer and neighborhood talk, where language flows most naturally; the contagion of the media, those hours of TV and radio and movies and ads where standard forms blend with all that is alluring in the society.

The writing that emerges from these experiences bears traces of the different pressures and codes and confusions that have gone to make up "English" for the BW student. At times variant and standard forms mix, as if students had half-learned two inflectional systems; hypercorrections that belong to no system jut out in unexpected places; idiosyncratic schemes of punctuation and spelling substitute for systems that were never learned and possibly never taught; evasive circumlocutions, syntactical derailments, timid script, and near-guesses fog the meaning, if any remains after the student has thus spent himself on the sheer mechanics of getting something down on paper. One senses the struggle to fashion out of the fragments of past instruction a system that will relieve the writer of the task of deciding what to do in each instance where alternative forms or conventions stick in the mind. But the task seems too demanding and the rewards too stingy for someone who can step out of a classroom and in a moment be in the thick of conversation with friends.

Confusion, rather than conflict, seems to paralyze the writer at this level. Language learners at any level appear to seek out, either consciously or unconsciously, the underlying patterns that govern the language they are learning. They are pressed by their language-learning faculties to increase the degree of predictability and efficiency in their use of language. This is less a choice they make than an urge they have to move across the territory of language as if they had a map and not as if they were being forced to make their way across a mine field. What has been so damaging about the experience of BW students with written English is that is has been so confusing, and worse, that they have become resigned to this confusion, to not knowing, to the substitution of protective tactics or private systems or makeshift strategies for genuine mastery of written English in any form. Most damaging of all, they have lost confidence in the very faculties that serve all language learners: their ability to distinguish between essential and redundant features of a language left them logical but wrong; their ability to draw analogies between what they knew of language when they began school and what they had to learn produced mistakes; and such was the quality of their instruction that no one saw the intelligence of their mistakes or thought to harness that intelligence in the service of learning.

There is no easy or quick way to undo this damage. The absence of errors, it is true, does not count much toward good writing, yet the pile-up of errors that characterizes BW papers reflects more difficulty with written

English than the term "error" is likely to imply. To try to persuade a student who makes these errors that the problems with his writing are all on the outside, or that he has no problems, may well be to perpetuate his confusion and deny him the ultimate freedom of deciding how and when and where he will use which language. For him, error is more than a mishap; it is a barrier that keeps him not only from writing something in formal English but from having something to write. In any event, students themselves are uneasy about encouragements to ignore the problem of error, often interpreting them as evasions of the hard work that lies before teachers and students if the craft of writing is ever to be mastered. Indeed, many students still insist, despite the miseries of their earlier encounters with grammar and despite the reluctance of teachers who have lost confidence in the power of grammatical study to affect writing, that they need more prescriptive grammar. Perhaps, as some would say, the propaganda of a long line of grammar teachers "took." But it may also be that grammar still symbolizes for some students one last chance to understand what is going on with written language so that they can control it rather than be controlled by it.

There is another reason why the phenomenon of error cannot be ignored at this level. It has to do with the writer's relationship to his audience, with what might be called the economics of energy in the writing situation. Although speakers and listeners, writers and readers, are in one sense engaged in a cooperative effort to understand one another, they are also in conflict over the amount of effort each will expend on the other. That is, the speaker or writer wants to say what he has to say with as little energy as possible and the listener or reader wants to understand with as little energy as possible. In a speech situation, the speaker has ways of encouraging or pressing for more energy than the listener might initially want to give. He can, for example, use attention-getting gestures or grimaces, or he can play upon the social responsiveness of his listener; the listener, in turn, can query or quiz or withhold his nods until he has received the "goods" he requires from the speaker.

Nothing like this open bargaining can go on in the writing situation, where the writer cannot keep an eye on his reader nor depend upon anything except words on a page to get him his due of attention. Thus anything that facilitates the transfer of his meaning is important in this tight economy of energy. Great writers, it is true, have drawn deeply upon the energies of readers, holding them through pages of exasperating density or withholding from them conventional word order or vocabulary or punctuation in order to refresh the language or create new perceptions; but even here the reader expects his investment to pay off in intellectual or emotional enrichment. He is, after all, a buyer in a buyer's market.

Errors, however, are unintentional and unprofitable intrusions upon the consciousness of the reader. They introduce in accidental ways alternative forms in spots where usage has stabilized a particular form (as is now true in spelling, for example, or in the familiar albeit "illogical" inflections). They demand energy without giving any return in meaning; they shift the reader's attention from where he is going (meaning) to how he is getting there (code). In a better world, it is true, readers might be more generous with their energies, pausing to divine the meaning of a writer or mentally to edit the errors out of his text without expecting to be rewarded for their efforts, but it would be fool-hardy to bank on that kind of persistence except perhaps in English teachers or good friends. (That errors carry messages which writers can't afford to send is demonstrated by the amount of energy and money individuals, business firms, publishing houses, etc., spend on error removal, whether by correcting fluids, erasers, scrapped paper, or proofreaders.)

All codes become codes by doing some things regularly and not others, and it is not so much the ultimate logic of these regularities that makes them obligatory but rather the fact that, logical or no, they have become habitual to those who communicate within that code. Thus the fact that in the general dialect the *-s* in *ten jobs* is a redundant form merely repeating what a numerical adjective has already established does not reduce the general reader's pause over *ten job*. The truth is that even slight departures from a code cost the writer something, in whatever system he happens to be communicating, and given the hard bargain he must drive with his reader, he usually cannot afford many of them.

This is not to say, of course, that the boundaries of error do not shift nor to suggest that certain battles along those boundaries are not worth waging. English has been robustly inventing itself for centuries—stretching and reshaping and enriching itself with every language and dialect it has encountered. Ironically, some of the very irregularities that students struggle with today are there because at some point along the way the English language yielded to another way of saying something.

But when we move out of the centuries and into Monday morning, into the life of the young man or woman sitting in a BW class, our linguistic contemplations are likely to hover over a more immediate reality—namely, the fact that a person who does not control the dominant code of literacy in a society that generates more writing than any society in history is likely to be pitched against more obstacles than are apparent to those who have already mastered that code. From such a vantage point, one feels the deep conserving pull of language, the force that has preserved variant dialects of English as well as the general dialect of literacy, and one knows that errors matter, knows further that a teacher who would work with BW students might well begin by trying to understand the logic of their mistakes in order to determine at what point or points along the developmental path error should or can become a subject for instruction. What I hope will emerge from this exploration into error is not a new way of sectioning off students' problems with writing but rather a readiness to look at these problems in a way that does not ignore the linguistic sophistication of the students nor yet underestimate the complexity of the task they face as they set about learning to write for college.

FOOTNOTES

[1]After having tried various ways of circumventing the use of the masculine pronoun in situations where women teachers and students might easily out-number men, I have settled for the convention, but I regret that the language resists my meaning in this important respect. When the reader sees *he*, I can only hope *she will* also be there.

[2]Unless otherwise indicated, the writers of sample passages are native to the United States, where they have had from twelve to thirteen years of public schooling, mostly in New York City. The topics of placement essays, from which many of the samples come, are given in the Appendix. In this essay, an initial class essay, the student was attempting to contrast the ways in which infants and adults see the world. Each of the "starts" in the present sample was crossed out in the original.

Who's Kicking Who?

RICHARD LANHAM

EDITOR'S NOTE: In Revising Prose, *Lanham explains and illustrates his eight-step "Paramedic Method" of editing for style. Steps one through five are described in this, the first chapter. The final three steps consist of marking off the rhythmic units of each sentence, reading it aloud, then marking off new sentence lengths based on the reading.*

No student these days feels comfortable writing simply "Jim kicks Bill." The system seems to require something like "One can easily see that a kicking situation is taking place between Bill and Jim." Or, "This is the kind of situation in which Jim is a kicker and Bill is a kickee." Jim cannot enjoy kicking Bill; no; for school use, it must be "Kicking Bill is an activity hugely enjoyed by Jim." Absurdly contrived examples? Here are some real ones:

> This sentence is in need of an active verb.

> Physical satisfaction is the most obvious of the consequences of premarital sex.

> In strict contrast to Watson's ability to control his mental stability through this type of internal gesture, is Rosalind Franklin's inability to even conceive of such "playing."

See what they have in common? They are like our Bill and Jim examples, assembled from strings of prepositional phrases glued together by that all-purpose epoxy "is." In each case the sentence's verbal force has been shunted into a noun and for a verb we make do with "is," the neutral copulative, the weakest verb in the language. Such sentences project no life, no vigor. They just "are." And the "is" generates those strings of prepositional phrases fore and aft. It's so easy to fix. Look for the real action. Ask yourself, who's kicking who? (Yes, I know, it should be *whom,* but doesn't it sound stilted?)

In "This sentence is in need of an active verb," the action obviously lies in "need." And so, "This sentence needs an active verb." The needless prepositional phrase "in need of," simply disappears once we see who's kicking who. The sentence, animated by a real verb, comes alive, and in six words instead of nine.

Where's the action in "Physical satisfaction is the most obvious of the consequences of premarital sex"? Buried down there in "satisfaction." But just asking the question reveals other problems. Satisfaction isn't really a *consequence* of premarital sex, in the same way that, say, pregnancy is. And, as generations of women will attest, sex, premarital or otherwise, does not always satisfy. Beyond all this, the contrast between the clinical phrasing of the sentence, with its lifeless "is" verb, and the lifegiving power of "lust in action" makes the sentence seem almost funny. Excavating the action from "satisfaction" yields "Premarital sex satisfies! Obviously!" This gives us a lard factor of 66% and a comedy factor even higher. (You find the lard factor by dividing the difference between the number of words in the original and the revision by the number of words in the original. In this case, $12-4=8$; $8 \div 12 = .66$. If you've not paid attention to your own writing before, think of a lard factor (LF) of one-third to one-half as normal and don't stop revising until you've removed it. The comedy factor in prose revision, though often equally great, does not lend itself to numerical calculation.) But how else do we revise here? "Premarital sex is fun, obviously" seems a little better, but we remain in thrall to "is." And the frequent falsity of the observation stands out yet more. Revision has exposed the empty thinking. The student makes it even worse by continuing: "Some degree of physical satisfaction is present in almost all coitus." Add it all together and we get something like, "People usually enjoy premarital sex" (LF, 79%). At its worst, academic prose makes us laugh by describing ordinary reality in extraordinary language.

The student writing about James Watson's *The Double Helix* stumbles on the standard form of absent-minded academic prose: a string of prepositional phrases and infinitives, then a lame "to be" verb, then more prepositional phrases and infinitives. Look at the structure:

> *In* strict contrast
> > *to* Watson's ability
> > *to* control his mental stability
> > *through* this type
> > *of* internal gesture,
> > *is* Rosalind Franklin's inability
> > *to* even conceive
> > *of* such "playing."

Notice how long this laundry list takes to get going? The root action skulks down there in "ability to control." So we revise: "Watson controls himself through these internal gestures; Rosalind Franklin does not even know such gestures exist." I've removed "in strict contrast" because the rephrasing clearly implies it. I've given the sentence two simple root verbs— "controls" and "knows." And I've used the same word—"gestures"—for the same concept in both phrases to make the contrast tighter and easier to see. We've reduced seven prepositional phrases and infinitives to one prepositional phrase, and thus banished that DA-da-da, DA-da-da monotony of the original. A lard factor of 41% but, more important, we've given the sentence shape; some life flows from its verbs.

The drill for this problem stands clear. Circle every form of "to be" ("is," "was," "will be," "seems to be") and every prepositional phrase. Then find out who's kicking who and start rebuilding the sentence with that action. Two prepositional phrases in a row turn on the warning light, three make a problem, and four invite disaster. With a little practice, sentences like "The mood Dickens paints is a bleak one" will turn into "Dickens paints a bleak mood" (LF 38%) almost before you've written them.

Prepositional phrase strings do not, of course, always come from undergraduates. Look at these "of" strings from a linguist, a literary critic, and a popular gourmet:

> It is the totality *of* the interrelation *of* the various components *of* language and the other communication systems which is the basis for referential memory.

> These examples *of* unusual appropriateness *of* the sense *of* adequacy to the situation suggest the primary signification *of* rhyme in the usual run *of* lyric poetry.

> Frozen breads and frozen pastry completed the process *of* depriving the American woman *of* the pleasure *of* boasting *of* her baking.

The "of" strings are the worst of all. They look like a child pulling a gob of bubble gum out into a long string. When you try to revise them, you can feel how fatally easy the "is and of" formulation can be for expository prose. And how fatally confusing, too, since to find an active, transitive verb for "is" means, often, adding a specificity the writer has not provided. So, in the first example, what does "is the basis for" really mean? And does the writer mean that language's components interact with "other communication systems," or is he talking about "components" of "other communication systems" as well? The "of" phrases refer back to those going before in so general a way that you can't keep straight what really modifies what. So revision here is partly a guess.

> Referential meaning emerges when the components of language interact with other communication systems.

Or the sentence might mean

> Referential meaning emerges when the components of language interact with the components of other communication systems.

Do you see the writer's problem? He has tried to be more specific than he needs to be, to build his sentence on a noun ("totality") that demands a string of "of's" to qualify it. Ask where the action is, build the sentence on a *verb*, and the "totality" follows as an implication. Noun-centeredness like this generates most of our present-day prose sludge.

The second example, out of context, doesn't make much sense. Perhaps "These examples, where adequacy to the situation seems unusually appropriate, suggest how rhyme usually works in lyric poetry." The third is easy to fix. Try it.

In asking who's kicking who, a couple of mechanical tricks come in handy. Besides getting rid of the "is's" and changing every passive voice ("is defended by") to an active voice ("defends"), you can squeeze the compound verbs hard, make every "are able to" into a "can," every "seems to succeed in creating" into "creates," every "cognize the fact that" (no, I didn't make it up) into "think," every "am hopeful that" into "hope," every "provides us with an example of" into "exemplifies," every "seeks to reveal" into "shows," and every "there is the inclusion of" into "includes."

And you can amputate those mindless introductory phrases, "The fact of the matter is that" and "The nature of the case is that." Start fast and then, as they say in the movies, "cut to the chase" as soon as you can. Instead of "the answer is in the negative," you'll find yourself saying "No."

We now have the beginnings of the Paramedic Method (PM):

1. Circle the prepositions.
2. Circle the "is" forms.
3. Ask "Who is kicking who?"
4. Put this "kicking" action in a simple (not compound) active verb.
5. Start fast—no mindless introductions.

Let's use the PM on a more complex instance of blurred action, the opening sentences of a psych paper:

> The history of Western psychological thought has long been dominated by philosophical considerations as to the nature of man. These notions have dictated corresponding considerations of the nature of the child within society, the practices by which children were to be raised, and the purposes of studying the child.

Two actions there—"dominate" and "dictate"—but neither has fully escaped from its native stone. The prepositional phrase and infinitive strings just drag them down.

The history
  of Western psychological thought
  by philosophical considerations
  as to the nature
  of man
  . . .
  of the nature
  of the child
  within society
  by which children
  to be raised
  of studying

We next notice, in asking "Who is kicking who?," all the *incipient* actions lurking in the nouns: *thinking* in "thought," *consider* in "considerations," more *thinking* somewhere in "notions." They hint at actions they don't supply and thus blur the actor-action relationship still further. We want, remember, a plain active verb, no prepositional phrase strings, and the natural actor firmly in charge. The actor must be "philosophical considerations as to the nature of man;" the verb "dominates;" the object of the action "the history of Western psychological thought." Now the real problems emerge. What does "philosophical considerations as to the nature of man" really mean? Buried down there is *a question:* "What is the nature of man?" The "philosophical considerations" just blur this question rather than narrow it. Likewise, the object of the action—"the history of Western psychological thought"—can be simply "Western psychological thought." Shall we put all this together in the passive form that the writer used? "Western psychological thought has been dominated by a single question: what is the nature of man?" Or, with an active verb, "A single question has dominated Western psychological thought: what is the nature of man?" Our formulaic concern with the stylistic surface—passives, prepositional phrases, kicker and kickee—has led here to a much more focused *thought.*

The first sentence passes its baton very awkwardly to the second. "Considerations," confusing enough as we have seen, become "these notions" at the beginning of the second sentence, and these "notions," synonymous with "considerations" in the second. We founder in these vague and vaguely synonymous abstractions. Our unforgiving eye for prepositional phrases then registers "*of* the nature *of* the child *within* society." We don't need "within society;" where else will psychology study children? And "the nature of the child" telescopes to "the child." We metamorphose "the practices by which children were to be raised" into "child-rearing," and "the purposes in study-ing the child" leads us back to "corresponding considerations of the nature of the child within society," which it seems partly to overlap. But we have now a definite actor, remember, in the first sentence—the "single question." So a ten-tative revision: "The same basic question has dictated three subsequent ones: What are children like? How are they to be raised? Why should we study them?" Other revisions suggest themselves. Work a couple out. In mine, I've used "question" as the baton passed between the two sentences because it clarifies the relationship between the two. And I've tried to expose what real, clear action lay hidden beneath the conceptual cotton-wool of "these notions have dictated corresponding considerations."

This two-sentence example of student academic prose rewards some reflection. First, the sentences *make no grammatical or syntactical mistakes.* Second, *they need not have come from a student.* Any issue of a psychology journal or text will net you a dozen from the same mold. Third, not one in a thousand TA's or professors reading this prose will think anything is wrong with it. Just the opposite. It reads just right; it sounds professional. The teacher's comment on this paper reads, in full: "An excellent paper—well con-ceived, well organized and well written—A+." Yet it makes clear neither its main actor nor action; its thought consistently blurs in vague general concepts like "considerations," "notions," and the like; and the cradle-rocking monot-ony of its rhythm puts us to sleep. It reveals a mind writing in formulae, out of focus, putting no pressure on itself. The student is not thinking so much as, on a scale slightly larger than normal, *filling in the blanks.* You can't build bridges thinking in this muddled way; they will fall down. If you bemuse yourself thus in a chemistry lab, you'll blow up the apparatus. And yet the student, obviously very bright, has been invited to write this way and is rewarded for it. He or she has been doing a stylistic imitation, and has brought it off successfully. Chances are great that the focused, plain-language version I've offered will get a much lower grade than the original. Revision is always perilous and paradoxical, but nowhere more so than in the academic world.

A Little Trip to the Writing Center
KATHLEEN P. HIGGINS

Oh, here we go again. We are taking a little trip. I've been tucked safely in her notebook, packed away in her backpack, slung over her shoulder, and carried away. I love these little trips that we take together. As long as we are not going to that dreadful writing center again. I hate it there. So far I have escaped its scrutiny, but I don't know how much longer I can hold my own.

You see, I am a sentence, an integral part of my family, the term paper. My father (the opening paragraph) and my mother (the closing paragraph) gave birth to me and my brothers and sisters. We, the children, are known as the body of the paper. As a family, we are content. We all have our own purpose, and we rather like our birth order.

Unfortunately, there is a greater force at work here. This force is the being that created my mom and dad, and in essence gave life to my whole family. I do not like this force, though. She is always trying to break my family apart and move us around. She has even done away with some of my siblings altogether. The loss is too great for me to talk of, but it gets worse. It appears She is not satisfied yet. We have arrived at the writing center. This is where most of the disruption occurs. She has brought me here twice before, and this, our third visit, is to be our last. The people here fill Her head with nonsense. They think they know so much about my family.

The process is always the same in the writing center. First he hands us over to a stranger who stares at us, one by one. Soon the two of them begin talking. The conversation is not about the weather, or their boyfriends, or even the great time they had last weekend; the conversation is about my family. How rude can you be? They talk about us like we are not even in the room. The writing center people tell our creator the good and bad points about us, and how to fix our bad qualities. Don't they realize that nobody is perfect? Comma splices, misspelled words, structural errors, break it up here, condense it there; I feel like I'm in counseling!

The two of them talk, and talk, and talk. Then they brandish their most destructive weapon, the pen. I cringe when I see this dangerous object, because I know the worst is yet to come. I'm telling you, no one is safe here. As I said before, I've managed to keep my original place and structure, but I live in fear. Am I next? Is my family going to be all right? Please don't hurt me! I can't bear to watch!

Two weeks later...

Well, the horror is over. I survived my trips to the writing center. I even triumphed over a much greater power than my creator: Her teacher. I have thought a great deal about the changes my family has been through. Now that it is all over, I realize that all the changes were for the best. Although I miss my discarded siblings, I realize that they were just bringing the family down. Others in my family have changed for the better, and we all get along much more smoothly as a result. To add to our newfound joy, my grandfather, A+, has decided to visit. He took his place at the end of the paper, next to Mom. I have a feeling he'll be around for a long time.

On Students' Rights to Their Own Texts: A Model of Teacher Response

Lil Brannon and C. H. Knoblauch

I.A. Richards has said that we begin reading any text with an implicit faith in its coherence, an assumption that its author intended to convey some meaning and made the choices most likely to convey the meaning effectively.[1] As readers, therefore, we tolerate the writer's manipulation of the way we see the subject that is being addressed. Our tolerance derives from a tacit acceptance of the writer's "authority" to make the statements we are reading.[2] When reading a textbook, for instance, we assume that its writer knows at least as much about the book's subject as we do, and ideally even more. When we read a newspaper article, we take for granted that the writer has collected all the relevant facts and presented them honestly. In either case, "authority" derives partly from what we know about the writer (for instance, professional credentials or public recognition) and partly from what we see in the writer's discourse (the probity of its reasoning, the skill of its construction, its use of references that we may recognize). The sources of writers' authority may be quite various. But whatever the reason for our granting authority, what we are conceding is the author's right to make statements in exactly the way they are made in order to say exactly what the writer wishes to say.

The more we know about a writer's skill, the more we have read of that individual's work or heard of his or her reputation, the greater the claim to authority. This claim can be so powerful that we will tolerate writing from that author which appears to be unusually difficult, even obscure or downright confusing. For instance, our having read Dylan Thomas' *Fern Hill* with pleasure may lead us to work harder at reading *Altarwise by Owlight*, although we may not understand it readily and may not derive the same pleasure from reading it. As readers, we see this harder material as a problem of interpretation, not a shortcoming of the composer. Writers may, of course, compromise their authority through evident or repeated lapses, but, in general, readers will assume that problematic texts demand greater effort from them, not rewriting from the author. Writers in fact depend on readers' willingness to stay with a text, even a difficult one, without judging it prematurely on the basis of its apparent violation of their own perspectives or impressions of some subject. The incentive to write derives from an assumption that people will listen respectfully and either assent to or earnestly consider the ideas expressed. And ordinarily readers will make an honest effort to understand a writer's text provided that its ideas matter to them and provided that the writer's authority is sufficient to compel their attention.[3]

When we consider how writing is taught, however, this normal and dynamic connection between a writer's authority and the quality of a reader's attention is altered because of the peculiar relationship between teacher and student. The teacher-reader assumes, often correctly, that student writers have not yet earned the authority that ordinarily compels readers to listen seriously to what writers have to say. Indeed, teachers view themselves as the authorities, intellectually maturer, rhetorically more experienced, technically more expert than their apprentice writers. Oddly, therefore, in classroom writing situations, the reader assumes primary control of the choices that writers make, feeling perfectly free to "correct" those choices any time an apprentice deviates from the teacher-reader's conception of what the developing text "ought" to look like or "ought" to be doing.[4] Hence, the teacher more often than the student determines what the writing will be about, the form it will take, and the criteria that will determine its success. Student writers, then, are put into the awkward position of having to accommodate, not only the personal intentions that guide their choice-making, but also the teacher-reader's expectations about how the assignment should be completed. The teacher's role, it is supposed, is to tell the writers how to do a better job than they could do alone, thereby in effect appropriating the writers' texts. In reading those texts and commenting on them, the teacher-evaluator "fixes" the writing in ways that appear to approximate the Platonic Discourse, the Ultimate Propriety, that any given student text may have suggested but not achieved. Of course, that Platonic Discourse exists only in the teacher's mind (where it often resides secretly as a guide to judging) and may have little to do with what individual writers initially tried to accomplish.

When teachers appropriate their students' texts, they do so with what appear to be the best of motives. By making elaborate corrections on student writing, teachers appear to be showing the discrepancy between what the writing has actually achieved and what ideal writing ought to look like, perhaps with the conviction that any student who perceives the difference can also narrow it. But this correcting also tends to show students that the teacher's agenda is more important than their own, that what they wanted to say is less relevant than the teacher's impression of what they should have said. The writer wants to talk about how she got her first job while the teacher wants an exercise in comparison and contrast. Once students perceive this shift of agenda, their motives for writing also shift: the task is now to match the writing to expectations that lie beyond their own sense of their intention and method. Therefore, far from controlling the responses of an intended reader, they are forced to concede the reader's authority and to make guesses about what they can and cannot say. Once consequence is often a diminishing of students' commitment to communicate ideas that they value and even a diminishing of the incentive to write.

We are not suggesting that students texts are, in fact, authoritative. But we do argue that incentive is vital to improvement and also that it is linked crucially to the belief that one's writing will be read earnestly. Since teachers do not grant students writers the authority that ordinarily justifies serious reading, they tend to undervalue student efforts to communicate what they have to say in the way they wish to say it. Yet it is precisely the chance to accomplish one's own purposes by controlling one's own choices that creates incentive to write. Denying students control of what they want to say must surely reduce incentive and also, presumably, the likelihood of improvement. Regardless of what we may know about students' authority, therefore, we lose more than we gain by preempting their control and allowing our own Ideal Texts to dictate choices that properly belong to the writers.

When we pay more attention to our Ideal Texts than to the writers' purposes and choices, we compromise both our ability to help students say effectively what they truly want to say and our ability to recognize legitimately diverse ways of saying it. Teaching from the vantage point of the Ideal Text is paternalistic: the teacher "knows best," knows what the writer should do and how it should be done, and feels protective because his or her competence is superior to that of the writer. This paternalism is sometimes liberal and sometimes conservative. The conservative teacher is prone to underestimate the writer's competence, using the Ideal Text to measure degrees of failure. Conversely, the liberal teacher is prone to exaggerate the writer's competence, assuming that, although the writer has not matched the Idea Text, some quality in the writing nonetheless excuses the lapse. For instance, a teacher might sympathize with a student's sincerity or effort despite misgivings about perceived errors. The trouble with both types of paternalism is the teachers' assumption that they always and necessarily know what writers mean to say and are therefore always reliable judges of how well writers actually say it. There is little suspicion that the Ideal Text may simply be irrelevant in terms of what a writer attempted to do. Hence, teachers are distracted from offering the best kind of assistance—that is, helping writers achieve their own purposes—while insisting on ideas, strategies, or formal constraints that are often not pertinent to a writer's own goals.

An example from our recent research demonstrates the extent to which adherence to an Ideal Text interferes with the ability to read student writing in ways that can best help writers to achieve their goals. We asked students to write an essay on the Lindbergh kidnapping trial, stating a purpose and an intended audience.[5] One student, John, decided to write out a version of the prosecution's closing oral argument. Here is an excerpt:

> Ladies and gentlemen of the jury, I whole-heartedly believe that the evidence which has been presented before you has clearly shown that the man who is on trial here today is beyond a doubt guilty of murder of the darling little, innocent Lindbergh baby.
>
> Sure, the defendant has stated his innocence. But who are we to believe? Do we believe the testimony of a man who has been previously convicted; in fact convicted to holding up innocent women wheeling baby carriages? Or do we believe the testimony of one of our nation's greatest heroes, Charles A. Lindbergh. Mr. Lindbergh believes the defendant is guilty. So do I.

> All I ask, ladies and gentlemen of the jury, is that you look at the evidence. First we have the evidence that the defendant suddenly became $44,486 richer since April 2. Is it only a coincidence that the ransom was paid the same night?
>
> Don't forget the testimony of Mr. Whited and Mr. Rossitor both of whom said they saw the accused on or around Feb. 27 in New Jersey even though the accused lives in the Bronx. The kidnapping occurred on March 1.

We asked forty teachers to assess the quality of this writing in light of what the writer was trying to do. They all responded in one of two ways, neither of which recognized the writer's control over choices. One group, the conservatives, felt that John was taking on the persona of the prosecuting attorney seriously addressing the jury at the time of the trial. However, this group concluded that John's argument was not convincing because of his blatant use of emotional appeal. These readers felt that no self-respecting member of the jury would be convinced by such sentimentalized language as "darling little, innocent Lindbergh baby." According to them, John tended to depend too much on emotions and too little on logic. The second group, the liberals, concluded, on the contrary, that John had adopted the persona of a "mock" attorney and that his writing was intentionally satirical. They too pointed to the use of emotional language but saw it as consistent with a satiric purpose. Each group, in other words, referred to exactly the same textual evidence to bolster its argument, even though the two arguments were diametrically opposed.

In both cases, the teachers were reading John's text from the perspective of their own shared Ideal Text, one in which staightforward logic, freed from patronizing emotional appeal, was sufficient for persuasion. The conservative group denied John the possibility that his writing could have been competent because they measured the limits of competence with reference to a model that ruled out John's overtly emotional appeal. The liberal teachers accepted precisely the same Ideal Text, but they credited John with more, rather than less, sophistication. They assumed that John must surely be writing satire because he could not possibly mean what he appeared to be saying on the page. Hence they granted him a competence that he may not have had while ignoring the competence that he actually manifested in his essay. Both groups were surprised when we showed them the actual transcript of the prosecution's summation in Hauptmann's trial. They discovered that its strategy and language were in fact very similar to those in John's essay:

> Why, men and women, if that little baby, if that little, curly-haired youngster were out in the grass in the jungle, breathing, just so long as it was breathing, any tiger, any lion, the most venomous snake would have passed that child without hurting a hair on its head.

The point is not that John's choice of language, or even the original prosecutor's choice, was "right" in some absolute sense. Rather, John's choice was simply not wrong; yet the teachers' Ideal Text interfered with their acceptance of John's perfectly plausible option.

What this example suggests is the value of consulting a student writer about what he or she wanted to say before suggesting how he or she ought to say it. In other words, it shows why we ought to relinquish our control of student writing and return it to the writers: doing so will not only improve student incentive to write, but will also make our responses to the writing more pertinent. But how and to what extent can we relinquish control? The question is attitudinal more than methodological. Teachers need to alter their traditional emphasis on a relationship between student texts and their own Ideal Text in favor of the relationship between what the writer meant to say and what the discourse actually manifests of that intention. This shift entails our recognizing that even inexperienced writers operate with a sense of logic and purpose that may not appear on the page but that nonetheless guides their choices.[6] We must replace our professional but still idiosyncratic models of how writing ought to appear, and put in their place a less authoritarian concern for how student texts make us respond as readers and whether those responses are congruent with the writers' intentions or not. The focus then will be, not on the distance between text and some teacher's personal notion of its most ideal version, but rather on the disparity between what the writer wanted to communicate and what the choices residing in the text actually cause readers to understand. Necessarily, the emphasis on form that mainly preoccupies us when we think in terms of an ideal model will change to an emphasis on the writer's ideas and communicative goals. And this changed emphasis will allow the writer to sense both a real control over the discourse and also the reader's real interest in what is being said. The consequence can be a reinforcement of the writer's incentive to keep writing and therefore an enriched environment in which to improve skills.

This change in teacher attitude and teacher-student relationship does, of course, demand some changes in pedagogy. Because students are largely unaccustomed to having their writing taken seriously, teachers may well have to dramatize the transfer of control they wish their students to perceive. Single-draft writing assignments, for instance, do not allow writers to assert control because they offer only one chance to write. Students, therefore, must accept a teacher's pronouncements without the opportunity to reassert their points of view or to explain what they were trying to do. Multiple-draft assignments, on the other hand, provide an opportunity for dialogue about how effectively the writer's choices have enabled the communication of intentions. Multiple-draft assignments also place emphasis on revision, on the progressively more complete achievement of communicative effect, so that what might be regarded as "errors" on a single-draft assignment may be seen as opportunities to clarify or refine relationships between intention and effect. By focusing on error, the teacher is the authority, a judge of the writing. But if revision is the focus, the writer retains control, assuming responsibility to create a discourse that conveys intended meanings in a way that enables a reader to perceive them.

It is not sufficient, however, simply to have students rewrite their statements. The way we talk to them about their successive drafts is just as important as offering them a chance to revise.[7] It would be easy to point out errors, just as on single-draft assignments, and to require copyediting on the next draft. But the concern is not merely to ask for editing in order to make discourse look superficially better; rather, it is to work with the writer in examining the effectiveness of some intended communication and to initiate improvement where possible. Nor is the concern merely to test the writer's ability to follow directions in order to approximate the teacher-evaluator's Ideal Text. Instead, it is to pursue writers' real intentions until they are satisfactorily conveyed. In other words, the teacher's proper role is not to tell the student explicitly what to do but rather to serve as a *sounding-board* enabling the writer to see confusions in the text and encouraging the writer to explore alternatives that he or she may not have considered. The teacher's role is to attract a writer's attention to the relationship between intention and effect, enabling a recognition of discrepancies between them, even suggesting ways to eliminate the discrepancies, but finally leaving decisions about alternative choices to the writer, not the teacher.

At the start, students and teachers need to share their different perceptions as makers and readers of a discourse. Writers know what they *intended* to communicate. Readers know what a text has *actually* said to them. If writers and readers can exchange information about intention and effect, they can negotiate ways to bring actual effect as closely in line with a desired intention as possible. Answering some general questions can help in the sharing of this information. If both teachers and students answer the questions separately, and then compare their answers, the differences in their answers can generate discussion and elicit other, more specific questions leading toward revision. The general questions include "What did the writer intend to do?" "What has the writing actually said?" and "How has the writing done what it is supposed to do?" The first one concerns the anticipated effect of a discourse; the second concerns its literal statements; and the third pertains to the writer's and reader's estimate of how or in what way the content, shape, and sequence of those statements achieve the desired effect. In the case of John's essay, a portion of which appeared earlier, an answer to the first question might be "the writing should show that the prosecution is convinced of Hauptmann's guilt." An answer to the second question might be, "the writing says that Hauptmann had a previous criminal record, etc." and an answer to the third question might be, "the use of sentimental language in describing the Lindbergh baby works on the jury's emotions and makes them unsympathetic to Hauptmann."

We can ask and answer the questions using several different teaching formats, including one-to-one conferences, peer-group collaborations, and even certain kinds of comments on student essays. Again, attitudes are more important than methods. The questions initiate a process of *negotiation,* where writer and peers or writer and teacher (or tutor) work together to consider, and if possible to enhance, the relationship between intention and effect. First, do the writer's and the teacher's responses agree or differ? If they differ, what evidence does each reader have to support the reading? Answering this question will lead both teacher and student into the text in order to discuss the reasons for variant perceptions. If the responses agree, does every part of the text contribute helpfully to sustaining the writer's intentions? And, finally, do the parts need clarifying or elaborating in order to improve their effectiveness? The teacher's principal concern in asking and cooperatively answering these questions is to make the writer think about what has been said, not to tell the writer what to do. The point is to return control of choice-making as soon as possible to the writer, while also creating a motive for making changes. Negotiation assumes, of course, that neither teacher nor writer stays relentlessly with an initial position. The teacher resists the temptation to say, "Do it this way," which reduces the writer's role to a trivial one of following directions. Meanwhile, the student, faced with the reality of a reader's misunderstanding, can no longer say, "But what I really meant was . . ." Of course, the process of negotiation does not move the writing toward the teacher's Ideal Text; in fact, it does not even guarantee a more successful next draft. But what it does is to force the writer to reassert control and thereby gain experience in revising. Since the impulse to revise arises out of a sense of not having fully communicated some intended message, the rewriting is not merely formulaic but is, in fact, inventive, a reconstituting of the meanings that the writer is concerned to convey.

Ideally, readers should respond to writers face to face. But to the extent that this is inconvenient, there is a way for teachers to simulate the conference model without having the student actually present. Students may compose drafts in which they also write out their intentions in a large column to the right of the text itself. After composing, the writers go back through their drafts and explain, paragraph by paragraph, what they were trying to say or do and how they expected the reader to react to it. Students will improve as estimators of their own intentions as they practice writing them out; but it is important to add that teachers remain free to raise questions about intentions that the writers may not have explained in the margin. Especially in the beginning, teachers may need to encourage their students to estimate intent at as many points in the draft as they can, sometimes even sentence by sentence, because, the more commentary the writers can provide, the more certain the teacher is about what the writers want to do and the more help the teacher can offer in doing it effectively.

Notice how John describes his intentions on the first draft of his simulated address to the jury:

Ladies and gentlemen of the jury, I whole-heartedly believe that the evidence which has been presented before you has clearly shown that the man who is on trial here today is beyond a doubt guilty of murder of the darling little, innocent Lindbergh baby.

Informal, putting the jury at ease.

Telling my (prosecution's) belief of guilt confidently.

Touching at human spirit.

Sure, the defendant has stated his innocence. But who are we to believe? Do we believe the testimony of a man who has been previously convicted; in fact convicted to holding up innocent women wheeling baby carriages? Or do we believe the testimony of one of our nation's greatest heroes, Charles A. Lindbergh. Mr. Lindbergh believes the defendant is guilty. So do I.

Showing the *negative* side of defendant and connecting his past with similarity of crime he is accused of now.

Showing the *integrity* of the father of the victim of the murder. Overall a very *biased* view.

All I ask, ladies and gentlemen of the jury is that you look at the evidence. First we have the evidence that the defendant suddenly became $44,486 richer since April 2. Is it only a coincidence that the ransom was paid the same night?

List of evidence, all against accused. Not too much detail is given, but if I leave the jury with a series of factual pieces of evidence against the defendant, the jury will say to themselves, "Wow, there is so much going against him, he's guilty."

Don't forget the testimony of Mr. Whited and Mr. Rossiter both of whom said they saw the accused on or around Feb. 27 in New Jersey even though the accused lives in the Bronx. The kidnapping occurred on Mar. 1.

Potentially, a comparison of John's stated intentions and the actual effects of the writing might give rise to various points of negotiation. Consider the third and fourth paragraphs. Although John has indicated what he wanted to accomplish ("List of evidence, all against accused. Not too much detail is given"), he may not yet have done what he thinks he has done ("if I leave the jury with a series of factual pieces of evidence against the defendant, the jury will say to themselves, 'Wow, there is so much going against him, he's guilty.'"). The teacher (or peer or tutor) might raise questions here ("Did the defense counter any of this testimony and thereby discredit it? If so, would the jury be convinced by John's listing of 'facts'?"). John's teacher did raise these questions, and John's response to them demonstrated his control of the writing. He agreed that his first idea, that all he needed to do was list the facts, would not create the effect that he desired. Later he extensively rewrote this portion of the text, noting the defense's inability to counter convincingly each piece of evidence submitted by the prosecution. The result of the dialogue between John and his teacher was to give John a chance to re-examine his initial choices and come up with a new strategy for creating the impact he wished to have on the jury. John remained in control of the choices, although it took the questions of a reader to help him see that he had not yet done what he thought he had done.

It may be that other teaching strategies beyond those suggested here work equally to promote the transfer of responsibility from teacher to student that we have been advocating. Our concern has been only secondarily to show how it can be done, and primarily to argue that it should be done. Although student texts are not, in fact, authoritative, we must nonetheless accept a student writer's authority to the extent that we grant the writer control over the process of making choices: that is, we tentatively acknowledge the composer's right to make statements in the way they are made in order to say what he or she intended to say. Often, to be sure, we will see deficiencies in the resulting discourse, but if we preempt the writer's control by ignoring intended meanings in favor of formal and technical flaws, we also remove the incentive to write and the motivation to improve skills. Conversely, granting students control of their own writing can create a rich ground for nurturing skills because the writer's motive for developing them lies in the realization that an intended reader is willing to take the writer's meaning seriously. If the writer is allowed to have something to say, then the saying of it is more likely to matter. The methods we have described allow the teacher to return control of a discourse to the writer as soon as possible by encouraging multiple drafts, each stimulated by the responses of a reader. Subsequent drafts are not always closer to a teacher's sense of formal, technical, or intellectual propriety, but they invariably show writers responding to the issues raised in their own texts, attempting to close perceived gaps between what was intended and what earlier drafts actually said. As these gaps are successfully narrowed, one draft at a time, the motive to solve technical problems is strengthened, in a context in which the writer's intentions matter more than teachers' Ideal Texts.

Eventually, of course, teachers judge student writing, and they invoke standards in the process. Preferably, in multiple-draft assignments, evaluation occurs only (1) after writers have had the opportunity to receive peer and teacher responses to their writing; (2) after they have had a chance to revise as they wish; and (3) after they have decided that their writing is finished and ready to be evaluated. And when evaluation is undertaken, as a last step in the process we propose, the standards invoked do not have to do with fixed preconceptions about form or content as stipulated by some Ideal Text. Instead, they relate to communicative effectiveness as an experienced reader assesses it in a particular writing situation. The standards of communicative effectiveness are how well the writer's choices achieves stated or implied purposes given the needs and expectations of an intended audience. If the evaluator finds the writer's choices to be *plausible* (as opposed to "correct") all of the time, the grade for that writing is higher than if the choices occasionally or frequently create uncertainties that cause failures in communication.

Evaluation, then, is the natural conclusion of the process of response and negotiation, carried through successive drafts. By responding, a teacher creates incentive in the writer to make meaningful changes. By negotiating those changes rather than dictating them, the teacher returns control of the writing to the student. And by evaluating, the teacher gives the student writer an estimate of how well the teacher thinks the student's revisions have brought actual effects into line with stated intentions. By looking first to those intentions, both in responding and in evaluating, we show students that we take their writing seriously and that we assume that they are responsible for communicating what they wish to say. The sense of genuine responsibility kindled in inexperienced writers can be a powerful first step in the development of mature competence.

FOOTNOTES

[1]See I. A. Richards, *Practical Criticism* (New York: Harcourt, Brace, 1929), especially Part III, passim.

[2]The concept of authority or *ethos* is, of course, an ancient one. For definition and elaboration see Aristotle, *Rhetoric* (1356a2).

[3]Reader-response criticism, as practiced by Wolfgang Iser, Norman Holland, Stanley Fish, Georges Poulet, and others, considers these issues in extensive scholarly detail. For a survey of this work, see *Reader-Response Criticism: From Formalism to Post-Structuralism.* Ed. Jane P. Tompkins (Baltimore: The Johns Hopkins University Press, 1980).

[4]For the prevalence of this style of commenting and some arguments about its insufficiency, see C. H. Knoblauch and Lil Brannon, "Teacher Commentary on Student Writing: The State of the Art," *Freshman English News,* 10 (Fall, 1981), 1-4. See also Dennis Searle and David Dillon, "The Message of Marking: Teacher Written Responses to Student Writing at Intermediate Grade Levels," *Research in the Teaching of English,* 14 (October, 1980), 233-42.

[5]We adapted this exercise from W. Edgar Moore, Instructor's Manual to *Creative and Critical Thinking* (Boston: Houghton Mifflin, 1967).

[6]For development of this assumption see David Bartholomae, "The Study of Error," *College Composition and Communication,* 31 (October, 1980), 253-69.

[7]Nancy Sommers has noted the radical unfamiliarity of unskilled writers with revision strategies that experienced writers take for granted. See Nancy Sommers, "Revision Strategies of Student Writers and Experienced Adult Writers," *College Composition and Communication,* 31 (December, 1980), 378-88.

In Defense of Thesis Statements
James E. Harrington

I was entering the second hour of my observation time. Today was the day I had moved back into my dorm after arthroscopic knee surgery. Therefore, I was preoccupied with the pain in my knee and the pain in my mind as I thought about all of the make-up work I had to do.

At six o'clock, Kristen came in to relieve Andre as the consultant on duty. Shortly after she arrived, one of my neighbors, Justin, came in with a paper. He came over to me and we talked for a minute while Kristen settled in. When he first came in, Justin had seemed a bit nervous. He was a freshman, so I assumed this was his first trip to the writing center. However, after he talked to me and found out about what I was doing there, he seemed to be a little more relaxed.

Kristen joined us at the table and we bagan to read Justin's essay. He had brought a draft which had already been passed in to the teacher. The teacher had responded with a number of comments about the essay. Justin's professor liked his thesis statement, but he did not think that Justin had developed it well enough in the paper.

As we read the paper, Kristen and I began to see what the teacher was talking about. Justin's essay was about people thinking and acting for themselves. His thesis was that people should try to be more independent and more concerned with themselves. Later in his essay, Justin used several stories from his life that he thought illustrated his point. The stories were interesting, but he did not connect them to the rest of his paper. Standing on their own, the stories didn't make much sense.

After we finished reading, we began to concentrate on the stories. As we talked with Justin about his paper, we discovered that he was having trouble with the thesis that he had written for this draft. Yet because his professor had said he liked the thesis, Justin was reluctant to change it. As we spoke to him, Justin realized that he would have to change the thesis in order to write the paper well. So before he left, Justin worked with us to revise his thesis and come up with one that was easier for him to understand.

I found this session interesting because it involved thesis statements. Throughout my education, teachers have always stressed the importance of having a thesis statement. However, because I have not had a problem with them, I never thought they were important. Exercises in high school classes where I had to pick out the thesis statement in my essay annoyed me. I thought they were useless.

The experience with Justin showed me otherwise. Seeing what a difficult thesis statement can do to a paper revealed the importance of this organizational tool to me. A thesis can give a paper focus when there is the potential to go off on a tangent. I still have some difficulty picking out thesis statements, but I am glad I now see the need for them.

"Look Back and Say 'So What'":
The Limitations of the Generalist Tutor

JEAN KIEDAISCH AND SUE DINITZ

Since 1983, when Tobey Fulwiler arrived at the University of Vermont and began promoting faculty interest in writing across the curriculum, our writing center has increasingly worked with students and recruited tutors from across the curriculum. Other writing centers have also moved in this direction. In the mid-1980's several articles appeared in the *Writing Lab Newsletter* and *The Writing Center Journal* encouraging writing centers to work with students and recruit tutors from across the disciplines (Haviland, Luce, Scanlon, Smith).

Initially, we were not very concerned about our tutors' ability to help students from various disciplines. We felt pretty confident that if we trained our tutors to be good facilitators, to use questioning to help students clarify their ideas, and to guide students through the writing process, they could help almost any student working on almost any paper. In an article in *The Writing Center Journal*, Susan Hubbuch goes so far as to suggest that the "ignorant" or generalist tutor can often be of more help than a tutor familiar with the discipline: "The ignorant tutor, by virtue of her ignorance, is just as likely— perhaps even more likely—than the expert to help the student recognize what must be stated in the text" (28).

But a few years ago our own experience teaching intermediate-level writing classes made us question this optimism. We had begun to encourage students to write the sorts of papers they might write within their disciplines. In working with these papers, we ourselves sometimes felt uncertain about what to say to students. For example, a business major wrote a market analysis divided into twenty subsections. When Sue said it seemed choppy and suggested transitions, the student responded that this is how market analyses are written. When Jean pointed out to an engineering student that she seemed to have similar information in her results, conclusions, and implications sections, the student responded that this is how lab reports are written. From our experience working with faculty and students in each of these disciplines, we suspected the business student was right and the engineering student was wrong. But how could we expect our peer tutors, less familiar with academic writing, to know when to accept the judgment of the "knowledgeable" student?

Wanting to look more closely at how a tutor's knowledge of the discipline affects a tutoring session, we videotaped twelve sessions over papers written in literature courses designed for majors, assuming that these papers would be expected to follow disciplinary conventions. At the end of each session, we had the tutor and student fill out a questionnaire so that we could determine whether they saw any connection between the quality of their session and the tutor's knowledge of the discipline. They did not. All of the students rated their session highly and credited their tutors with a good understanding of how to write literature papers. The tutors also rated their sessions highly, and none of them expressed concern over their level of knowledge of the discipline.

Thinking a teacher in the discipline might assess the help a student got differently from the student or the tutor, we asked three English teachers to view eight of the tapes and fill out a similar questionnaire. They did not find the sessions so uniformly good. All agreed that two of the sessions were excellent, two were good, and four were weak. And they did see a correlation between the tutor's knowledge of the discipline and the quality of the session: the disciplinary knowledge of the tutors in the excellent sessions was rated as high, while that of the tutors in the weak sessions was rated as low.

This preliminary work made us want to identify more precisely how the tutor's knowledge of the discipline affected each session. So we turned to analyzing the transcripts of the videotapes. What we saw led us to conclude that the "ignorant" or generalist tutor sometimes has limitations.

Anna, a senior English major, comes into the writing center with a paper for her Shakespeare course. The tutor on duty is David, a business major who had come to us highly recommended by two writing teachers. Anna's draft begins,

> Othello is a play that depicts the essense of deception. In the play, each character, except Iago, is deceived and in return they deceive. Iago is the master of deception and seeks out to deceive Othello who will in return eventually deceive his love, Desdemona. Iago is successful in his search for revenge upon Othello and he accomplishes his goal and that is to destroy the lives of the newly-married couple, Othello and Desdemona. Iago plants the seed of suspicion and then waits as Othello brings destruction to the life of Desdemona as well as himself.

The rest of the draft falls into three sections, each of which opens with a Roman numeral and heading:

    I. Why does Iago want to deceive Othello?
   II. How does Iago go about deceiving Othello?
  III. Othello deceives Desdemona

The last few sentences of the introduction and the outline both suggest that the draft moves quickly into a retelling of the plot. In a journal entry written for his tutor training class, David shows he recognizes that the paper needs to be more analytical: "She did a lot of plot summary, there is too much. It doesn't analyze the story."

To help Anna make the paper more analytical, David first tries to get her to narrow her focus:

David: What are three things you're trying to tell the reader?

Anna: Show how Iago is obsessed with deceiving Othello... To show why he deceives Othello. And how he does it. And then show how Othello is deceived. And how Othello in return deceives someone else.

David's journal entry shows he's satisfied with this list: "She needed to cut her focus down to smaller pieces. I got her to list three or four main points she wanted. They overlapped a bit, but at least I got her down to fewer points to be made." David doesn't seem to realize that the new list actually matches the Roman numeral headings that organize Anna's draft.

For the rest of the hour-long session, David and Anna read through the paper paragraph by paragraph. After each few paragraphs, David stops and asks her the point of that section, explaining:

> The best questions to try and answer I've always found are "so what" and "why." When you're trying to make a point after a few paragraphs, look back and say "so what." That will bring out of the summary your voice. That's what you definitely want, those two questions.

Does this general advice help Anna make the paper more analytical? Throughout the session, in response to David's questions, she re-describes that particular section of Othello, adding even more details about the plot and characters, as in the following example:

Anna: It's not really deception that he's doing at first.... He's getting ready to plant the seed of suspicion, so to get ready to do that you have to make sure that the person you're going to deceive... That they're going to trust you... And that they're going to be manipulated by this game.

David: OK, answer why.

Anna: Why? Because if Iago... doesn't have Othello's trust, it's not going to work, so he has to be sure he has Othello's trust.... One of the ways he knows he can do this is by saying that he's mad at Roderigo for doing this to Brabantio.... [She continues to explain how Iago gains Othello's trust.] He can't really go on with his plan till he knows for a fact that Othello's going to trust him.

David: [pause] Um, can you answer "so what" to that?

Anna: I guess I see it as really important because if I was in Iago's shoes, I would never go about a plan, until I knew I had that person's loyalty and trust... .

David: That's the kind of stuff you need in this as opposed to plot summary.

David doesn't seem to realize that in answering his questions Anna just keeps repeating her original point.

There's no evidence in the session that using the "so what" question helps Anna think more analytically. Even though they spend an hour going through the paper, the two never come up with any insights that will make the paper more analytical. Anna leaves the session saying, "So I just need to go through and after each paragraph add in a sentence saying why or so what." David responds, "Yeah, yeah."

This session made us question a generalist tutor's ability to help when a paper is discipline-specific. David seems unable to see that Anna's answers to his general questions about focus and the point of each section remain on the level of plot summary. Or perhaps he does see this but doesn't know what to do. Indeed, he seems uncomfortable during much of the session, stopping often to look at his watch, pausing often to think about what to do next, even asking, in seeming desperation, "Are you going to be seeing your professor before turning this in?" David doesn't seem to know what to do to move Anna beyond plot summary; he can't use her answers to generate even more questions and get a process going which will help Anna make her paper more analytical.

Cory, who is taking the sophomore-level introductory survey required of English majors, comes into the writing center with a paper that goes beyond plot summary to include several insights into Hawthorne's "The Birthmark." He is writing in response to the following assignment:

> Both the scientists in "The Birthmark" and "Rappaccini's Daughter" could be described as mad or fatally flawed. But critics have also associated these scientists with artists. What do Aylmer, Rappaccini and Baglioni have in common with artists? Could Hawthorne be expressing his anxiety about art as well as science? Discuss how Hawthorne connects art and science in one of these stories and what it means for him to do so.

This assignment asks the student to come up with two insights: one into how art and science are connected, and another into the meaning of this connection. Cory's paper begins,

> In Hawthorne's, "The Birthmark," Aylmer tries everything in his earthly power to improve upon a being that is as close to earthly perfection as possible. It is this relentless pursuit of perfection that ultimately leads to the destruction of Georgiana. The tension premising the story is the rivalry between Aylmer's two loves—the love he has for his wife, Georgiana, and the equal, if not superior love he has for science.

He goes on to offer several insights into the story, as is evident from the lead sentences to the six paragraphs that make up the body of the paper:

1. Like an artist has passion for his art, Aylmer has passionate [sic] for both his love of his wife and his love of science.
2. Nature is a reoccurring theme throughout the story. As an artist wishes to capture Nature, to mimic it, Aylmer wished to go a step further—to exercise "control over Nature."
3. As a poet is inspired by his muse, Aylmer is inspired by Georgiana.
4. Like an artist, Aylmer sought to create something that will live on eternally, something that would bare his mark, something that would prove that he had once inhabited this earth.
5. Perhaps Hawthorne was using science as a metaphor for art.
6. Perhaps, in some way, Aylmer was Hawthorne. Hawthorne may have been venting his frustrations at not being widely published.

These insights do go beyond plot summary. And they seem to match the two parts of the assignment: one through four are insights into how Hawthorne connects art and science and five and six are insights into what it means for him to do so. But there is no controlling insight. The ideas seem to be randomly ordered and taken together don't lead to an answer to the two main questions posed by the assignment.

But this does not seem to concern the tutor. Michelle, a political science major and one of our brightest and most sought-after tutors, comments, "I just think in each of these [paragraphs] it needs to be expanded a little bit." The two then go through the paper paragraph by paragraph discussing the points she thinks need to be expanded, such as what sort of passion Aylmer has for Georgiana, how an artist seeks to live on through his art, and whether Aylmer's failure results from his not being objective. In several paragraphs, she wants more detail about the artist in general, explaining, "I don't think we have a grip of what an artist is, in order to be able to compare a scientist to an artist." Even when Cory offers Michelle an opportunity to comment on more global concerns, she reassures him that he only needs to expand:

Cory: Take into account this is a first draft and all I did was write down ideas.

Michelle: It still is a good paper.... You're a good writer.... Your ideas, they flow and everything, they all make sense. I just think that they can be explained more.

Both David and Michelle failed to address global problems in their students' papers, but both were working with students who lacked knowledge of how to go about writing literature papers. Was a generalist tutor of more help to a knowledgeable student? Carl, another sophomore in the survey course for English majors, was writing in response to the following assignment: "Going beyond what was said in lecture, discuss androgyny in *The Sun Also Rises*". His paper begins,

The Hemingway man, on the whole, has a preoccupation with death. Once one is dead, one is dead. Therefore, the man must enjoy as many sensual pleasures as possible in his fleeting time on earth. It is this preoccupation that causes him to live life to the fullest. The Hemingway man is an avid lover, drinker, and eater. He enjoys and respects sport for the pure thrill, excitement, and for its intricacies; not necessarily because he is good at it. Where the typical Hemingway man is self-reliant and independent, the woman is passive and vulnerable—a pawn to be manipulated by her environment. She is the antithesis of the male. In The Sun Also Rises, Hemingway creates characters whose genders don't necessarily reflect their sex.

In TSAR the ideal man is Pedro Romero. Of all the characters, Romero exemplifies what Hemingway sees as the quintessential man—both inside the ring and out.

The paper goes on to discuss the male and female characteristics of all the main characters, beginning with Pedro Romero, the "quintessential man," followed by Brett and Jake, who exemplify both male and female characteristics, and ending with Robert Cohn, the "least masculine by Hemingway's standards."

Going beyond plot summary, Carl has classified the characters by the degree to which they're androgynous. He does have a controlling insight, which is supported in an organized and coherent essay. So this draft seems further along than Anna's or Cory's. What help can the generalist tutor provide here?

Jill, a psychology major, notices the lack of coherence between the last sentence of the first paragraph, which states that characters' genders don't reflect their sex, and the second paragraph, which discusses a character whose gender does reflect his sex. To solve this problem, Jill suggests reversing the order of the paragraphs so that Carl discusses the most feminine character (who happens to be a man) first. Carl suggests an even simpler solution: inserting the words "a spectrum" to alert the reader to how he's organized the paper. Carl changes the last sentence of the first paragraph to read: "In The Sun Also Rises Hemingway creates a spectrum of characters whose genders don't necessarily reflect their sex."

Jill and Carl continue to work on the paragraph and sentence levels, addressing such concerns as what aspects of Brett's nature are feminine, whether the paper "flows between characters well," what should be in the conclusion, whether more quotations are needed, and what "vague places" need work on the sentence level. But they ignore the possibility of making more global improvements. Carl's paper shows that there is androgyny in the novel, but this is stated in the assignment. We think most English teachers would expect students to go further, connecting descriptions of technique (the use of androgynous characters) to the meaning, effect, or context of the text. Again, a generalist tutor focused on local rather than global concerns.

Indeed the only tutors who worked successfully on the global level were knowledgeable tutors, as illustrated in the following session between Margaret, a sophomore working on the same Hawthorne assignment as Cory, and Tammi, a senior English major. Margaret's paper begins,

> During the period of american renassace [sic] the issue of science and art were a constant issue of ethics, still present today. It was a period of change and breaking from the norm. Today we try and use science as a way of altering or "fixing" nature, those who believe that medicine should prolong the lives of those incapable of sustaining their own lives. Hawthorne, as depicted in The Birthmark connects the meaning of art and science, and expresses his anxiety towards these new ideas and his conflict of whether in order for one to succeed the other must fail.

Rather than working with Margaret's draft, Tammi sets the paper aside after reading a few pages and talks with her about the assignment and the story. Over and over, Tammi brings Margaret back to the two key questions in the assignment, as in the following examples:

- So, if you're choosing "The Birthmark," how does he do it, connect issues of art and science, how does he do it?
- Ok, so the question here is "How does Hawthorne connect art and science in one of these stories?"
- Now if I ask you a question like "How does Hawthorne connect art and science in the story?" Ok, then, what does it mean for him to do it that way?
- So what does it mean then for him to have Aylmer as an artist and as a scientist?

In the following excerpt, Tammi uses questioning and repetition to help Margaret talk through her ideas to the point where she sees that one of her original answers can't be supported by the text:

Tammi: So what does it mean then for him to have Aylmer as an artist and as a scientist?

Margaret: That the two in his personality don't work together.

Tammi: How so?

Margaret: Because they conflict each other.

Tammi: How?

Margaret: Because in order for one to succeed.

Tammi: OK, for the scientist to succeed and to make.

Margaret: For him to be a good scientist.

Tammi: To be a good scientist, yes.

Margaret: The art part has to fail and to be bad.

Tammi: Why?

Margaret: Because, because what he created failed, it died.

Tammi: Oh, so for him to create the scientific purity, Georgiana without the birthmark.

Margaret: Right, he created her.

Tammi: He finishes his scientific project, he's made her.

Margaret: Perfect in his eyes.

Tammi: Perfect in his eyes.

Margaret: Then he ends up failing anyway because now he doesn't have her anymore.

Tammi: Ok so now we've discussed his role as scientist. How is that.

Margaret: I guess he doesn't fail as an artist.

By responding to Tammi's questions, Margaret ends up completely changing her answers to the assignment questions. Rather than saying Hawthorne connects art and science through nature, she concludes they're connected in the person of Aylmer. And rather than saying for one (art or science) to succeed, the other must fail, she concludes that Aylmer succeeds as both an artist and as a scientist, but at the cost of life itself.

Tammi, an English major, is able to assess how well Margaret's insights are supported, is confident enough to put Margaret's paper aside and turn to looking at the text with her, and knows what questions to ask to help Margaret reach new insights that can be supported using evidence from the text. Tammi knows not only what the disciplinary conventions are but also what process produces a paper that follows them. This is the process Margaret needs to learn to write other English papers. It makes sense for Tammi and Margaret to work on these higher-level thinking skills before turning to the other problems evident in her introduction, such as word choice and sentence structure.

We found, however, that the tutor's familiarity with the conventions of the discipline doesn't guarantee a good session. When Sandy, who is working on a Yeats paper for the survey class, meets with Joanne, an English major who has taken the same course with the same teachers, it leads to just what Susan Hubbuch is concerned about: the knowledgeable tutor taking an "authoritative stance" (26), thinking of "writing in terms of the final product" (29), and so, in Joanne's case, focusing on correcting the student's paper in order to help her get a better grade. Joanne begins by reading through the paper and making corrections. Within the first few minutes she adds some quotation marks, changes "onto" to "unto," underlines some repeated words, and corrects some spelling errors. She notes a sentence fragment and rewords to correct it. At one point Sandy asks the tutor to please use pencil rather than pen in case she decides not to make the changes.

In addition to editing the paper, Joanne insists on some specific changes in the ideas. As she reads along, she comes to the idea that "Yeats turns to religion and everlasting art." She stops and suggests a different relationship between the two ideas: "Or does he turn to everlasting art as a religion?" Sandy responds, "I thought that but then [I noticed] how he made the reference to God." Joanne continues to defend her interpretation concluding, "I think that the interconnection of art there with religion—sort of that God has to do with the creation of eternal art, that whole idea—I think you can safely connect those.... You can say he turns to everlasting art as a religion."

Is Joanne tempted to do too much because she knows so much? While making her corrections on Sandy's paper, Joanne explains, "I took this course, and I can't overemphasize the importance of a clean copy." We don't believe Joanne typically took an authoritative stance: there were no red flags in her journal, her lognotes, or her mock tutoring sessions to suggest she did.

We know we can't reach conclusions based on this small number of cases, but in the sessions we looked at, the tutor's knowledge of how to think and write in the discipline did seem important. Good tutoring strategies alone were not enough. All of these tutors were trained to address global before local concerns, to use questioning to draw out a student's ideas, to refrain from appropriating the student's paper. All of them had had numerous sessions with students in introductory writing courses in which they had successfully demonstrated these strategies. But David, Michelle, and Jill seem unable to apply them when working with students on assignments that require knowledge of a discipline other than their own. And Joanne, in her eagerness to use her knowledge, seems to forget her general tutoring strategies.

We began this project knowing that conventions differ from discipline to discipline and wondering whether tutors need to know these conventions to tutor effectively. Looking closely at these sessions suggested that tutors who don't know how to go through the process of writing a paper in a discipline may be limited in what they can accomplish, and that tutors who do know this process may be tempted to appropriate the student's paper. If more research supports these conclusions, what would be the implications for writing centers?

The most significant implication would be that students writing papers for upper-level courses would be best served by carefully trained tutors with knowledge of the discipline. If this is true, should writing centers try to provide such tutors? One method would be to match upper-level students with trained tutors from the discipline. But matching in a drop-in lab seems unwieldy, though it might be possible for special projects involving entire classes. Another method would be to turn our generalist tutors into knowledgeable tutors through a series of training sessions on writing across the curriculum, as suggested by Leone Scanlon. But would brief training sessions enable more sessions like Tammi's to occur? Tammi's work with Margaret makes us question this assumption. We could perhaps describe some of the disciplinary conventions in an hour or two but would this enable tutors to help students write papers that follow them? In the case of literature papers, wouldn't students outside the discipline need to go through the process themselves, need to learn how to ask questions, analyze, and interpret a text? Doing this for several disciplines would be impossible in a one-semester course. Still, it remains a possibility when a writing center knows a group of students will be coming from a certain discipline. For example, because we have so many students working on literature papers, we now not only have English professors come talk to the tutors about their expectations for such papers but also have all of the tutors write a critical analysis of a text, so that they go through the process of thinking in the discipline.

If we can't ensure that students writing for upper-level courses can meet with a knowledgeable tutor, should we be alarmed about relying on generalist tutors? We think not. First of all, in many of our sessions the tutors don't need to be more than generalists. About 70 percent of our sessions are over papers for composition classes, papers usually written to a general audience. And some upper-level students are sent to the writing center with papers written for a lay audience, such as an engineer's position paper on an environmental issue.

Second, it's hard to be alarmed when students leave pleased with their experience and enthusiastic about working further on their papers. All of the above students rated their session 5 on a scale of 1 to 5 (1=not successful, 5=very successful), all answered "very satisfied" to the question concerning the choices made about what to work on in the sessions, and all said they left with a clear idea of what to work on next. We feel that if students leave satisfied and motivated, they have benefitted. A session that is less than it could be is not by definition a bad session.

Third, it doesn't seem fair to place on our tutors' shoulders the responsibility for showing students how to think and write in the disciplines. It doesn't even seem fair to place learning this on the student writers' shoulders. Isn't this the responsibility of the departments? Indeed, when we see many students lacking knowledge of the process for writing within a discipline (though the students and tutors might not be aware of this lack), perhaps as directors we should go back to the department. In our case, we could share with our English faculty what we've learned about the difficulties some of their students are having, which might lead to a discussion of how writing in the discipline is being taught. Thus we have an opportunity to take up the charge given to writing centers by Nancy Grimm in her talk at the 1992 Conference on College Composition and Communication: to take what we have learned from working with students back to the academy.

WORKS CITED

Grimm, Nancy M. "Contesting 'The Idea of a Writing Center': The Politics of Writing Center Research." Conference on College Composition and Communication, Cincinnati, 21 March 1992.

Haviland, Carol Peterson. "Writing Centers and Writing-Across-the-Curriculum: An Important Connection." *The Writing Center Journal* 5.2 (1985): 25-30.

Hubbuch, Susan. "A Tutor Needs to Know the Subject Matter to Help a Student with a Paper: _Agree _Disagree _Not Sure." *The Writing Center Journal* 8.2 (1988): 23-30.

Luce, Henry. "On Selecting Peer Tutors: Let's Hear It For Heterogeneity." *Writing Lab Newsletter* May 1986: 3-5.

Scanlon, Leone. "Recruiting and Training Tutors for Cross-Disciplinary Writing Programs." *The Writing Center Journal* 6.2 (1986): 37-41.

Smith, Louise Z. "Independence and Collaboration: Why We Should Decentralize Writing Centers." *The Writing Center Journal* 7.1 (1986): 3-10.

Seeing the Light
Michael J. Pytlak

Although Crystal's session was not my first, or for that matter my last, it was by far my most memorable. Having already experienced a productive session, I was eager to observe and participate in another. I remember saying to myself, "Consulting is a breeze; come on, how hard can it get?" So when Melissa, the consultant on duty, informed me of a scheduled session, I was confident, perhaps too confident.

It was 4:15 and Crystal arrived looking somewhat frazzled. In fact, she looked as if she was ready to burst into tears. An uneasy feeling began to grab hold of me. Upon sitting down, Crystal informed us that her professor had accused her of plagiarism. Melissa and I exchanged panicked glances. In the holy domain of the writing center, plagiarism is a mortal sin. To make matters worse, Crystal confessed that this was her first research paper and she could not make heads or tails of the scientific terminology and theories involved in it. The beads of sweat began to build. We were writing consultants, not scientists.

Despite the technical barriers and our own nervousness, Melissa and I addressed the most problematic area of the paper, the appearance of plagiarism. I use the word "appearance" because after reviewing the paper, it became apparent that Crystal did not know how to cite other people's ideas. In sum, we did not put on imaginary lab coats, but instructed Crystal on the proper way to quote and paraphrase material. Having some doubts of her own, Melissa reached for the consultants' Bible, also known as the *Rinehart Handbook for Writers.*[1]

Flipping through this Holy Scripture, Melissa and I guided Crystal into the rites of quoting, paraphrasing, and citing authors and books. The three of us worked on the tedious technical aspects of the above, and then reflected on whether a quote or a paraphrase would contribute more to the strength of the paper. As with any conversion from dark to light, the journey was difficult. Slowly, Crystal began to incorporate the word of Rinehart into her paper; she was repenting her sin. After making sure Crystal had grasp of the rules for quoting and paraphrasing and had made the necessary corrections on her paper, we sent her on her way. She was a reborn writer.

In retrospect, I realize that consulting is definitely not a breeze; situations lie ahead which I will have a great deal of difficulty handling. The point is, though, that is all right. You do not have to be a walking *Rinehart Handbook;* you do not have to have all the answers; you do not have to be a writing god. Do not worry about catching all the mistakes. Just be confident in your writing ability. Confidence, the techniques you learn in class, and a little deep breathing will take you a long way.

Good luck!

FOOTNOTE

[1]Because *The Rinehart Handbook for Writers* was selected for across-the-curriculum use at Stonehill by an interdisciplinary panel of professors, consultants refer to it frequently in the writing center.—Editor.

Rethinking Writing Center Conferencing Strategies for the ESL Writer

Judith K. Powers

The University of Wyoming Writing Center has recently experienced a dramatic increase in ESL conferencing, brought about mainly by the establishment of a writing across the curriculum program on campus and by changes in the way we teach first-year composition courses for international students. In responding to the almost three-fold increase in numbers of ESL conferences over the past two years, our writing center faculty has begun to question whether traditional collaborative strategies are appropriate and effective for second-language writers.

Probably more than anything else, the past two years' influx of ESL writers has pointed up two significant—and interrelated—concerns to writing center faculty. The first is how firm our assumptions are about our job and the "right" way to accomplish it. The second is how little training we as a faculty have in the principles and techniques of effective ESL conferencing. On both counts, we probably do not differ greatly from writing center faculties across the country. This paper presents the problems we encountered in conferencing with ESL writers and discusses the processes that evolved as we sought solutions.[1]

Traditional Conferencing Strategies and the ESL Writer

Since our writing center faculty was largely untrained in teaching ESL writing and unaware of the many differences in acquiring first- and second-language writing skills, the increase in numbers of ESL conferences proved a mixed blessing. We were delighted, on the one hand, to be reaching a greater number of second-language writers on campus; on the other hand, we sometimes felt frustrated when these conferences did not work the way we expected. Unfortunately, many of the collaborative techniques that had been so successful with native-speaking writers appeared to fail (or work differently) when applied to ESL conferences.

When ESL writers came into the writing center, we tended to approach those conferences just as we would conferences with native-speaking writers, determining what assistance the writers needed through a series of questions about process and problems, purpose and audience. In both cases, our intention in adopting this strategy was to establish a Socratic rather than a didactic context, one which we hoped would allow us to lead writers to the solution of their own problems. Occasionally, conferences might involve the direct exchange of information (e.g., when numbers should be spelled out). More typically, though, we intended to lead writers to discover good solutions rather than answers, solutions that were theirs, not the tutor's. Unfortunately, this process, which has generally served native-speaking writers well (Harris, Leahy) and is justifiably a source of pride for those who can make it work, was often ineffective for our second-language writers, especially those confronting college-level writing in English for the first time.

Perhaps the major reason for this failure is the difference in what the two groups of writers bring to the writing center conference. Most native-speaking writers, for better or for worse, have come to us with comparatively broad and predictable experiences of writing and writing instruction in English. When they have problems with some concept or technique, it is therefore relatively easy for writing center faculty to intuit the source of their difficulty and adjust our questioning to help them discover new, more workable principles. A writer, for example, who is trying to force two points (or four points) into three paragraphs is likely to have been drilled in the five-paragraph essay format and can be guided fairly easily to discover that not all ideas break down into three parts. ESL writers, however, seldom come to the writing center conference with any substantial background in writing and writing instruction in English. Attempts, therefore, to play off such experience in devising collaborative strategies are likely to fail.

Furthermore, ESL writers typically come to the writing center conference with first-language rhetorics different from the rhetoric of academic English with which they are struggling (Grabe and Kaplan; Leki). Since what these writers already know about writing is based in those first-language rhetorics, it is likely that attempts to use common collaborative strategies will backfire and lead them away from, not toward, the solutions they seek. Consider, for example, the common and fairly simple problem of helping a writer understand that a conclusion should contain no new, unsupported ideas. While it is fairly easy to impress a native-speaking writer with the logic of this rule (because the term *conclusion* itself implies it), the rule is not at all logical to writers from cultures where effective conclusions do, in fact, include new ideas. In this, as in other conferencing situations, those attempting to assist second-language writers may be hampered not only by the writers' limited backgrounds in the rhetoric of written English but also by their learned patterns as educated writers of their own languages. As another example, bringing ESL writers to see the logic of placing important material at the beginnings of English paragraphs may, at times, involve overriding their longtime cultural assumptions that such material should appear at the end. Because collaborative techniques depend so heavily on shared basic assumptions or patterns, conferences that attempt merely to take the techniques we use with native-speaking writers and apply them to ESL writers may fail to assist the writers we intend to help.

The sense of audience that ESL writers bring to the writing center has also affected the success of our typical conferencing strategy. Experienced writing center faculty can lead native-speaking writers to a fuller awareness of certain writing principles through questions about their audience—what the members of their audience already know about a subject, what purpose a reader might have for reading their piece of writing, what kind of people make up their audience and what qualities will impress that group. Using this Socratic technique, in fact, helps us avoid the didactic role of identifying correct and incorrect approaches. However, second-language writers, already handicapped by an unfamiliar rhetoric, are likely to be writing to an unfamiliar audience as well. Part of what they need from us is knowledge of what that unknown audience will expect, need, and find convincing. Thus, ESL writers are asking us to become audiences for their work in a broader way than native speakers are; they view us as cultural informants about American academic expectations.

Predictably, as a result of these differences in the educational, rhetorical, and cultural contexts of ESL writers, our faculty found themselves increasingly in the role of informant rather than collaborator. We were becoming more direct, more didactic in our approach, teaching writing to ESL writers essentially as an academic subject.

Understanding the Need for Intervention

In this shifted role lay the crux of the difficulty we increasingly experienced with ESL conferencing. Because our whole writing center philosophy—our Socratic, nondirective approach—was (and is) geared away from the notion that we are teachers of an academic subject, it was not easy for us to see ourselves as cultural/rhetorical informants with valuable information to impart. One unfortunate result of this situation was that writing center faculty tended to define conferences where ESL writers got what they needed from us (i.e., direct help) as failures rather than successes.

This problem occurred in ESL conferences involving all aspects of writing. Writing center instructors found themselves, for example, telling writers what their audiences would expect rather than asking the writers to decide, answering questions about the sufficiency of the evidence provided in a particular context rather than leaving that decision to the writer, or showing writers how to say something rather than asking them what they wanted to say. When such exchanges occurred, we found it difficult to view them from the standpoint of the ESL writer for whom the conference might have been a success; rather, we measured them against our nondirective philosophy which we appeared to have betrayed.

The distance between the needs of the ESL writer and the assumptions of the system has perhaps been most apparent in conferences where ESL writers have come to us for help with editing and proofing. Like many writing centers, the University of Wyoming Writing Center handles the perennial problem of students wanting drafts edited with a policy statement: We will teach writers editing and proofing strategies but will not edit or proof for them. This distinction serves us reasonably well when dealing with native-speaking writers. It is less successful, however, in setting workable parameters for ESL conferences, partly because our ESL conferees have difficulty understanding the line it draws, but mostly because the techniques we use to teach editing/proofing strategies to native-speaking writers seldom work for ESL writers. These techniques, which largely involve reading aloud and learning to use the ear to edit, presume that the writer hears the language correctly and is more familiar and comfortable with the oral than the written word. Native-speaking writers reading aloud can typically locate problem passages, which we can then discuss with them, suggesting principles upon which they can base editing decisions. In this scenario, we hope writers learn to raise and answer their own questions.

Neither reading aloud nor editing by ear appears to work for the majority of ESL writers we see, however. Few beginning second-language writers "hear" the language "correctly," and many are more familiar with written than with spoken English. Since they have no inner editor prompting them to stop and raise questions, we are likely to adjust our technique to their needs and discover we are locating errors for ESL writers in a way that looks very much like editing. When we find ourselves backed into this situation, we immediately begin to raise questions about our appropriation of writers' texts, an anathema in writing center methodology not only for practical reasons inherent in working with classroom assignments but also because our aim is to demystify writing for conferees and increase their self-reliance and self-confidence. While the intervention that ESL writers appear to require of us in working with editing problems does not differ greatly from the intervention involved when we assist those same writers with rhetorical structure and audience, it strikes us more forcibly because it is familiar and easy to perceive. In fact, it looks very much like the "bad" kind of help native speakers sometimes want when they bring papers in to be "corrected."

The mixed feelings that the ESL editing issue engendered were not a new problem for the writing center. Throughout our history, we had faced and handled requests for assistance in editing ESL texts, responding to them more or less on a case-by-case basis, with varying levels of confidence in our decisions. Almost every semester, for example, the demand for editorial assistance with ESL theses and dissertations reaches the point at which writing center faculty begin to complain in frustration about ESL writers expecting them to correct and rewrite texts. Each year, the staff has vowed to establish a clearer policy that will prevent abuses of the system, discussed the subject vigorously, realized that doing so would limit the open-door policy we value so much, and consequently let the subject slide.

The primary difference between our past ESL conferencing experiences and our experiences of the last two years was our awareness of an emerging pattern in ESL conferencing that called into question some of our fundamental assumptions about what we do. Increased numbers of second-language conferences, as well as conferences involving a larger variety of writing tasks, highlighted difficulties in applying our traditional conferencing strategies to all aspects of second-language writing, not just editing. What had once appeared scattered instances of ineffectiveness in our typical approach became symptomatic of a broader inability to meet the needs of ESL writers with the same basic methods we use to assist native speakers. This realization led us to question whether our past reluctance to confront directly the issues involved in ESL conferencing was really the benign neglect we had assumed it to be or whether we were unintentionally undermining the principles we meant to protect and distancing ourselves from the needs of a large group of writers.

Adapting Conferencing Strategies to Assist ESL Writers

Once genuinely convinced that traditional collaborative strategies often do not work with ESL writers, our faculty realized that the key to more effective ESL conferencing was an attitude adjustment on our part. We had to accept that ESL writers bring different contexts to conferences than native speakers do, that they are, therefore, likely to need different kinds of assistance from us, and that successful assistance to ESL writers may involve more intervention in their writing processes than we consider appropriate with native-speaking writers.

For those of us whose experience has demonstrated the virtues of nondirective conferencing techniques, simple acceptance of the need to adopt more directive strategies was not always an easy first step. Part of the difficulty in taking this step stemmed from the fact that the differences between native-speaking and second-language writers are sometimes masked by a deceiving familiarity in what they say and do. When native-speaking writers come into the writing center expecting us to tell them what is *the answer* to a problem or the *right* way to express an idea, we may see them—often quite rightly—as either "timid" writers who need their self-confidence boosted, teacher-dependent writers who want an authority to appropriate their writing, or "lazy" writers who want someone else to do their work. In any of these cases, we see our job as getting the writer to assume responsibility for the writing. ESL writers who come to us expecting answers to questions about where their thesis statements should appear, how many developmental paragraphs they must have, how much and what kind of support a point requires, or how an idea should be phrased too often appear to fall into one of these categories: they appear to be insecure, to be abdicating responsibility for their texts for one of the above reasons.

Although the questions that ESL writers ask us are deceivingly similar to the questions native speakers sometimes raise, the contexts of the questions make them substantially different. What we discovered is that failure to recognize the essential difference in these seemingly similar questions severely undercuts our ability to assist second-language writers in acquiring the academic writing skills they need. If we assumed such writers were shy or dependent writers who merely needed encouragement to take charge of their texts, and if we adopted our usual collaborative approach to bring about that recognition of ownership, we were unlikely to achieve our accustomed results because we were applying an attitude solution to an information problem. If we assumed the worst—that the writers were lazy and were trying to get us to take over the writing—we might be travelling even further toward the wrong solution, based on the wrong evidence. We were, in fact, unlikely to provide useful help to ESL writers until we saw the questions they raised about basic form and usage not as evasions of responsibility but as the real questions of writers struggling with an unfamiliar culture, audience, and rhetoric.

To extend the benefits of conferencing and collaborative learning to ESL writers, writing center faculty must understand what these writers need from us and how their needs differ from those of native-speaking writers. The principal difference in the two conferencing situations appears to be the increased emphasis on our role as informant (rather than collaborator) in the second-language conference. Because we know little about ESL writers' rhetorics, backgrounds, and cultures, and because they know little about their current academic discourse community and the rhetoric of academic English, we can assist them only by becoming more direct in our approach, by teaching them writing as an academic subject. Doing so may, in fact, involve teaching them directly what their writing should look like by supplying them with formats for presenting written responses to various academic assignments and informing them of what their audiences will expect in terms of presentation, evidence, shape, etc.

Conclusion

Although collaborative learning is not a familiar process to most of the international students we see in the writing center, and some of the Socratic techniques we have developed as a result of this theory do not serve the ESL population particularly well, collaborative writing and conference teaching do work for these writers in some important ways. As with native-speaking writers, the process of verbalizing an idea often helps ESL writers discover a direction, and the act of sketching a structure (even with the help of a faculty member) clarifies the principles of that construct in a way merely reading about it cannot. ESL writers who describe their conferencing experiences mention a new awareness of audience, a clarification of the principles of organization, and the discovery of new vocabulary and sentence structures as benefits. In fact, just by acquiring a vocabulary to discuss their writing in English, second-language writers make a first step toward understanding and self-sufficiency.

But these benefits of collaboration accrue to ESL writers through *successful* writing center conferences. We can assist ESL writers to become more capable writers of English only if we understand what they bring to the writing center conference and allow that perspective to determine our conferencing strategies. Structuring successful ESL conferences probably requires that we reexamine our approach as outsiders might, making a real attempt to discard the rhetoric and patterns of thought that are so familiar to us as to seem inevitable. We might, for example, better assist our second-language writers by analyzing academic assignments from an outside perspective to see exactly what is expected in American academic prose, gathering information about audience expectations that recognize our culturally based assumptions, and learning to ask questions in conferences that will allow ESL writers to understand more about idea generation and presentation of evidence. Conferences based on this information and approach might appear different, on the surface, from conferences we conduct with native-speaking writers, but they bring us closer to accomplishing our writing center's goal of providing meaningful help to all campus writers with all kinds of writing questions.

When writing center faculty, with the best of intentions, apply collaborative techniques devised for native-speaking writers to ESL writers, the possibility of cultural miscommunication and failed conferences is inherent in the methodology itself. Since its inception, our writing center has struggled in concern and frustration over a frequent inability to make ESL conferences both successful for the participants and consistent with our conferencing philosophy. In retrospect, it appears that much of this struggle basically involved attempts to determine which of the conference participants was responsible for conferences that failed to meet one or both of these criteria. Sometimes we concluded that the writer was at fault for refusing to accept responsibility for the text and thereby undermining the collaborative process. More frequently, we blamed ourselves for failing to apply our conferencing principles and techniques appropriately or allowing ourselves to be drawn into directive conferencing by an unusually clever or forceful writer. Our experience of the past two years has convinced us that we will increase the effectiveness of ESL conferencing only when we understand, accept, and respond to the differences between the needs of ESL and native-speaking writers. Attempts to reform or reshape the participants in the conference are unlikely to prove effectual; we must reexamine and revise the method itself.

FOOTNOTE

[1]Our ESL population (currently 465 students) is almost exclusively international students who have studied English in their own countries before coming to the United States. The largest group of students come form China, India, Malaysia, Norway, and Taiwan; they have achieved a minimum TOEFL score of 525 and have been admitted to the university.

Works Cited

Grabe, William and Robert B. Kaplan. "Writing in a Second Language: Contrastive Rhetoric." *Richness in Writing: Empowering ESL Students*. Eds. Donna Johnson and Duane Roen. New York: Longman, 1989.

Harris, Muriel. "What's Up and What's In: Trends and Traditions in Writing Centers." *The Writing Center Journal* 11 (Fall/Winter 1990): 15-25.

Leahy, Richard. "What the College Writing Center Is—and Isn't." *College Teaching* 38 (Spring 1990): 43-48.

Leki, Ilona. "Twenty-five Years of Contrastive Rhetoric: Text Analysis and Writing Pedagogies." *TESOL Quarterly* 25 (1991):123-143.

Towards a Rhetoric of On-line Tutoring
DAVID COOGAN

In the spring of 1993 I got this great idea: why not turn a writing tutorial into an actual *writing* tutorial? So often writing center tutorials have nothing to do with the act of writing. Students read aloud, make conversation, do some editing or planning, but rarely compose or communicate in writing. And there is no guilt here: As Stephen North reminds us in "Training Tutors To Talk About Writing," the student's "text is essentially a medium" for conversation (439), a starting point, a place to *begin* the session, not end it. But what would happen to that conversation if I took away the paper, took away speech, and took away physical presence? What would happen to the idea of a writing tutorial if we decided to make the act of writing the main event?

To test this idea, I decided to conduct writing tutorials over electronic mail. I wanted to see how such interaction would work. My plan went like this: students would send me their texts and questions over e-mail during posted hours and I would respond right away. The motive was to exchange lots of e-mail—say, over the course of an hour. In a sense, I wanted to replicate the conditions of face-to-face tutoring: two people conversing about a text. What I learned, however (surprise, surprise), was that e-mail could not—and probably should not—replicate the conditions of face-to-face tutorials. Virtual appointments were hard to keep, and hardly anyone actually made contact with me during the posted hours (Sunday–Tuesday, 7:00 p.m.–12:00 a.m.).

It was just as well. The advantage of e-mail, I soon found out, was that you didn't *need* an appointment. You didn't even need regular hours for drop-in sessions. I began to advertise quick turn-around instead of appointments: "Send your text whenever you want. Get a response within six hours!" This became the drop-everything-and-tutor method. Instead of sitting in front of the monitor "doing time" waiting for someone to send me some e-mail, I'd log on every other hour: when there was e-mail, there was a session.

From these new working conditions, I began to figure out a methodology of e-mail tutoring. The main difference underlying all the issues I discuss below is that e-mail changes our sense of time, and in so doing, it changes the power dynamics of tutoring. After all, a face-to-face tutorial takes place in real time. It is bound by beginning, middle, and end. A session must have a point. And we often feel cheated if there is no point. (We're not comfortable with "dead air.") We even have to train ourselves to recognize different kinds of silence so that it doesn't *feel* like dead air. But e-mail tutorials have nothing but dead air. They are mute, silent—like any text. Often they take place over a few days. They are open-ended, sprawling, not bound by the hour or the actual writing center. E-mail tutorials could happen anywhere, anytime. However, access to the writing center doesn't necessarily get easier. In fact, it may get harder.

Many students don't know how to do e-mail, let alone upload files. (And it goes without saying that many students don't have PCs and modems in their rooms.) These sessions are also solitary. They take place at the scene of writing. Wherever the student and tutor may be—in a crowded user room or a room of one's own off campus—the student and tutor extend themselves into a social space, but only in their minds, only in writing. The tutor's job is to create a textual scene of learning. In this scene, the tutor and the student have time—perhaps too much time—to revise their thoughts and *construct* the tutorial. They became aware—even self conscious—of their emerging rhetorical identify: "tutor" and "student" become characters in a story, elements of an instructional "plot." Phatic cues no longer set the scene. All we have is text.

As we know from the writing center, presence is everything. A student wears his paper like clothing, often asking you right away, "how does this look to you? Is it ok?" The paper doesn't communicate by itself—the person communicates. But an electronic text *announces itself* as communication. It arrives in the mail without the benefit of speech to support its content, defend its appearance, or in other ways indicate who (or what) is inside. Thus in a face-to-face meeting, the student and tutor talk "over" a paper. The paper connects them. They see the same text. And the paper creates tension: who touches it? reads from it? marks it? The underlying question soon becomes, what will be DONE to the paper? As a methodology, then, the f2f tutorial is grounded by paper, and The Paper can limit tutor-student interaction.

In his experiment with an asynchronous, e-mail based writing class, Ted Jennings concludes the following:

> The crucial difference between the paper-bound and paperless environment lies in how a writer's texts are perceived. In the electronic medium they are harder to "own," harder to possess and defend, than are tangible pseudo-permanent sheaves of paper. Sharing an electronic text does not imply giving it away, and telling writers what you remember about their texts is not like defacing their intellectual property. (47)

The catch-all theory is that the paperbound environment creates vertical relationships while the paperless environment creates horizontal relationships, precisely because the student's "property" (in the paperless environment) is disembodied, less clearly marked. When students send me their electronic texts and we correspond, I'm asking them—implicitly or explicitly—to reenvision their writing: to use writing to improve their writing. I'm not asking them to focus on line five of paragraph six. The pedagogical idea is to encourage them to write by telling them how their words affected me while I read them; give them what Peter Elbow calls in *Writing Without Teachers,* a "movie of my mind"—a rendering of their text. In turn, the student stretches out to "me," the *idea* of a tutor, and in the process stretches her own thinking, her own writing. The net results is a bunch of e-mail stretched out on a clothes line.

Of course, movies of the mind are nothing new. Perhaps the only innovation here is that e-mail leaves a tangible trace—a transcript of the interaction.

Pedagogically, we could even say that *nothing* has changed. The spirit of tutoring—intervention in the composing process—remains intact along with the political issues defining that intervention. But the actual tutorial becomes something different. Classroom teachers who teach in a networked environment describe a similar change. Thomas Barker and Fred Kemp say that "using the computer as a communication medium 'purifies' informal exchanges in interesting and pedagogically advantageous ways" (21). They praise computer conferencing for its ability to cut to the chase, to foster a "pure," informal dialogue at the level of *ideas* instead of *personality*. Without the "distracting" elements of personality, computer-mediated discourse establishes a more egalitarian atmosphere. No one has to compete for the floor.

But without the classroom context, which Barker and Kemp rely on, how might on-line tutors gauge learning, or even communication, as discourse-specific? More to the point: as a cyborg tutor, am I an integral part of the writer's world or a ghost in the machine? Does my discourse construct a tutorial setting? Or does my discourse become something else? The fuel for somebody else's fire... .

E-mail tutoring, so it seems, puts us smack dab in the middle of the postmodern condition—the critique of presence in discourse. We hold onto this idea of "personality" in order to make tutoring work. But as Barker and Kemp show us, computer-mediated discourse reduces the guiding logic of personality. This makes it fascinating, but also confusing. I like the idea of intuiting a writer "in" the text. (I like to imagine I'm helping a real person.) But what I intuit ("who" I imagine) has nothing to do with the writer, per se. As Roland Barthes says, "I must seek out this reader (must 'cruise' him) without knowing where he is. A site of bliss is then created. It is not the reader's 'person' that is necessary to me, it is this site; the possibility of a dialectics of desire" (4).

This, of course, is tricky turf and I'm no postmodern theorist. In fact I'd rather keep this essay practical. But I bring up Roland Barthes to raise the specter of textual indeterminacy—our best laid plans to create a scene of learning slipping down a chain of signifiers. My instinct is to fight this. Let me put it to you this way. In face-to-face tutorials, half the job is reading the person, paying attention to silences, tone of voice, body language, and so on. On-line there is no difference between reading a person and reading a text. The threat seems to be that we could lose the tutorial by forgetting about these imaginary students we are helping. Another threat is more practical: e-mail tutoring lavishes a lot of time on the student's text—it takes a while to read and respond—and there is no guarantee that anything will happen. The student might not respond. (A challenge for the 21st century: how can we shape our e-mail instruction to elicit response and create a scene of learning?)

Michael Marx's study of e-mail exchanges between students in two composition courses at different colleges, explores the rhetoric of anonymous instruction. Students had to read essays by writers they had never met and write "critique letters," much like on-line tutors write feedback and questions to writers they have never met. The students' reactions to this experiment were complex. On the one hand, Marx indicates anonymous feedback was easy:

At the end of the semester one Skidmore student summarized her experience of writing for the network: 'When writing to someone in class, I can talk to them if they do not understand a point. When writing to Babson [College], I found that I was concentrating on giving a complete critique. I also found new freedom because I did not have to worry about the Babson student getting upset with me.' (31)

But on the other hand, e-mail critiques were demanding—more focused and intense. Another student comments, "I wanted to make sure that I made useful suggestions because they couldn't get in touch with me; so my critique needed to be self explanatory" (34). Marx concludes that e-mail "creates a distance between student critics and student authors which, ironically, brings students closer together in analyzing and discussing written texts" (36). The pressure to communicate fights the pressure of ambiguity.

But even that's not enough. As Andrew Feenberg summarizes, "communicating online involves a minor but real personal risk, and a response—any response—is generally interpreted as a success while silence means failure" (24). If Feenberg is right, and I think he is, then the goal of an on-line tutorial must never be to fix meaning on the "page" but to engage meaning in a dialectic. We need ambiguity. We need open texts. Ironically, ambiguity works *for* us and *against* us. In a different context, Stephen North describes this dialectic between readers as acts of "textual good faith." Specifically, he describes his written correspondence with David Bartholomae, and more generally, the impulse to find 'common sense' in composition studies, as "negotiating (establishing, maintaining) good faith agreements about the conditions that will make it possible for us to communicate. Or, to put it another way, negotiating (establishing, maintaining) good faith agreements about which of the conditions that make communication impossible we will set aside so that we can communicate" ("Personal Writing" 117). When e-mail tutorials work, so it seems, they work by engaging this dialectic. They work when we somehow negotiate a scene of learning.

One graduate student sends me a long philosophy paper and asks if his main idea is coming across. He wants to send the paper out for publication. I read the text, comment extensively in six separate messages (snapshots of my mind), and we correspond for about a week. The ideas percolate. A relationship forms. Eventually we meet in the writing center to talk about the paperbound issues: sentence level stuff, the actual length of the manuscript, bibliography, and so on. We are both encouraged and amazed at the novelty of this arrangement. Where else in the university can two people correspond about a work-in-progress? As a partner to the face-to-face tutorial, or even a solo act, e-mail could help us sustain long-term instructional relationships, much like Internet discussion groups such as Wcenter or MBU help us sustain our own professional relationships.

This of course represents the ideal. I *dream a network nation where we all exchange out texts*. But there is no network nation, at least not the kind I imagine. The technology, itself, is not the problem. The Internet is certainly growing. The Conference on College Composition and Communication will be on-line in 1995. But who in the university values the lateral exchange of texts, the "pure" exchange of ideas unfastened from the classrooms? Let me be specific here. For students to even *use* the on-line tutorial service at SUNY-Albany, they need to know how to use a word processor, save an ASCII (text-only) file, upload it to the VAX mainframe, and send it to the virtual writing center as an e-mail message. That's asking a lot—especially on a campus where most computer labs are NOT linked to the mainframe, and posters for the service have to compete with commercial advertisements for proofreading services. Advertisements on the mainframe, though successful, tend to lure students more interested in computing than in writing (an unfortunate division of talent). The vast majority of paper-writers (students in the humanities and social sciences) don't know about the e-mail tutorial service. How could they?

I guess what I'm concluding is that the idea of e-mail tutoring cannot change these institutional politics. I can dream a network nation if I want. But the reality is something else. Again, this is not a technical problem. We just don't know what we want technology to do. The university and the larger society still value paper, intellectual property, and authorship (all deregulated on the net), and the writing center—for good reason—still values face-to-face interaction over a text. But while we continue to work face-to-face, new technologies such as e-mail will continue to grow. If we don't decide what to do with them, somebody else will. As the writing center moves into the 21st century, I'd urge us to grab the bull by the horns: we should have a say. That's our responsibility. This essay is just one attempt to imagine the future. But what the on-line tutorial will *actually* become is something we are just beginning to understand.

Works Cited

Barker, Thomas, and Fred Kemp. "Network Theory: A Postmodern Pedagogy for the Writing Classroom." In *Computers and Community*. Ed. Carolyn Handa. Portsmouth, NH: Boynton/Cook, 1990. 1-27.

Barthes, Roland. The *Pleasure of the Text*. New York: Hill and Wang, 1973.

Elbow, Peter. *Writing Without Teachers*. New York: Oxford UP, 1973.

Feenberg, Andrew. "The Written World: On the Theory and Practice of Computer Conferencing," *Mindweave*. Ed. Robin Mason and Anthony Kaye. New York: Pergamon Press, 1989, 22-39.

Jennings, Edward M. "Paperless Writing Revisited." *Computers and the Humanities*. 24 (1990): 43-48.

Marx, Michael Steven. "Distant Writers, Distant Critics, and Close Readings." *Computers and Composition*. 8.1 (1991): 23-39.

North, Stephen. "Training Tutors to Talk About Writing." *College Composition and Communication* 33 (1982): 434-441.

—. "Personal Writing, Professional Ethos, and the Voice of Common Sense." *PRE/TEXT* 11.1-2 (1990): 105-119.

The Processing Process
RUSSELL BAKER

For a long time after going into the writing business, I wrote. It was hard to do. That was before the word processor was invented. Whenever all the writers got together, it was whine, whine, whine. How hard writing was. How they wished they had gone into dry cleaning, stonecutting, anything less toilsome than writing.

Then the word processor was invented, and a few pioneers switched from writing to processing words. They came back from the electronic frontier with glowing reports: "Have seen the future and it works." That sort of thing.

I lack the pioneer's courage. It does not run in my family, a family that arrived on the Atlantic beach 300 years ago, moved 50 yards inland for security against high tides, and has scarcely moved since, except to go to the drugstore. Timid genes have made me. I had no stomach for the word processor.

Still, one cannot hold off forever. My family had given up saddle and stirrups for the automobile, hadn't it? Had given up the candle for the kerosene lamp. I, in fact, used the light bulb without the slightest sense of betraying the solid old American values.

And yet...My trade was writing, not processing words. I feared or detested almost all things that had "processing," "process" or "processed" attached to them. Announcements by airplane personnel that I was in a machine engaged in "final landing process" made my blood run cold. Processed words, I feared, would be as bland as processed cheese.

So I resisted, continued to write, played the old fuddy-duddy progress hater when urged to take the easy way and switch to processing words.

When former writers who had turned to processing words spoke of their marvelous new lives, it was the ease they always emphasized.

So easy—the processing process made life so easy (this was what they always said)—so infinitely easier than writing. Only an idiot—and here I caught glances fraught with meaning—only an idiot would continue to suffer the toil of writing when the ease of processing words was available to be wallowed in.

To shorten a tedious story, I capitulated. Of course I had doubts. For all those years I had worked at writing only because it felt so good when you stopped. If processing words was so easy, would there be any incentive left to write?

Why are we moved to act against our best judgment? Because we fear public abuse and ridicule. Thus the once happy cigarette addict is bullied out of his habit by abuse from health fanatics, and the author scratching away happily with his goose quill puts it aside for a typewriter because he fears the contempt of the young phalanxes crying, "Progress!"

My hesitation about processing words was being noticed by aggressive young persons who had processed words from their cradles and thought the spectacle of someone writing was as quaint as a four-child family. I hated being quaint. I switched to processing words, and - man alive! Talk about easy!

It is so easy, not to mention so much fun—listen, folks, I have just switched right here at the start of this very paragraph you are reading—right there I switched from the old typewriter (talk about goose-quill pen days!) to my word processor, which is now clicking away so quietly and causing me so little effort that I don't think I'll ever want to stop this sentence because— well, why should you want to stop a sentence when you're really well launched into the thing—the sentence, I mean—and it's so easy just to keep her rolling right along and never stop since, anyhow, once you do stop, you are going to have to start another sentence, right?—which means coming up with another idea.

What the great thing—really great thing—really and truly great thing is about processing words like this, which I am now doing, is that at the end, when you are finally finished, with the piece terminated and concluded, not to say ended, done and thoroughly completed to your own personal, idiosyncratic, individual, one-of-a-kind, distinctive taste which is unique to you as a human person, male or female, adult or child, regardless of race, creed or color—at the end which I am now approaching on account of exhausting available paper space the processing has been so easy that I am not feeling the least, slightest, smallest or even somewhat minuscule sensation of tired fatigue exhaustion, as was always felt in the old days of writing when the mechanical machines, not to mention goose-quill pens, were so cumbersomely difficult and hard to work that people were constantly forever easing off on them, thus being trapped into the time-wasting thinking process, which just about does it this week, spacewise, folks.

ACKNOWLEDGEMENTS

Baker, Russell. Originally appeared in *The New York Times* (Feb. 10, 1985). Copyright © 1985 by The New York Times Company. Reprinted by permission.

Brannon, Lil, and C.H. Knoblauch. "On Students' Rights to Their Own Texts: A Mode of Teacher Response." Originally appeared in *College Composition and Communication* 33 (1982). Copyright © 1982 by the National Council of Teachers of English. Reprinted with permission.

Brice, Jennifer. "Northern Realities, Northern Literacies: The Writing Center in the 'Contact Zone." Originally appeared in *The Writing Lab Newsletter* 20.8 (1996). Reprinted with permission. All Rights and Title reserved unless permission is granted by Purdue University. Material will not be reproduced in any form without express written permission.

Broadwell, Jeannine A. "Rehabilitating the Writing Center Junkie." Originally appeared in *The Writing Lab Newsletter* 20.5 (1995). Reprinted with permission. All Rights and Title reserved unless permission is granted by Purdue University. Material will not reproduced in any form without express written permission.

Bruffee, Kenneth A. "Peer Tutoring and the Conversation of Mankind." Originally appeared in *Writing Centers; Theory and Administration*. Ed. Gary A. Olson. Evanston, IL: NCTE, 1984. Copyright © 1984 by the National Council of Teachers of English. Reprinted with permission. See also Kenneth Bruffee. *Collaborative Learning: Higher Education, Interdependence, and the Authority of Knowledge.* Baltimore, MD: Johns Hopkins University Press, l993.

Coogan, David. "Towards a Rhetoric of On-line Tutoring." Originally appeared in *The Writing Lab Newsletter* 19.1 (1994). Reprinted with permission. All Rights and Title reserved unless permission is granted by Purdue University. Material will not be reproduced in any form without express written permission.

Elbow, Peter. "The Voyage Out." From *Writing with Power: Techniques for Mastering the Writing Process* by Peter Elbow. Copyright © 1981 by Peter Elbow. Used by permission of Oxford University Press, Inc.

Farmer, Joy A. "The Twenty-Minute Solution: Mapping in the Writing Center." Originally appeared in *The Writing Lab Newsletter* 20.7 (1996). Reprinted with permission. All Rights and Title reserved unless permission is granted by Purdue University. Material will not be reproduced in any form without express written permission.

Flower, Linda, and John R. Hayes. "The Cognition of Discovery: Defining a Rhetorical Problem." Originally appeared in *College Composition and Communication*. 31 (1980). Copyright © 1980 by the National Council of Teachers of English. Reprinted with permission.

Foote, Elizabeth. "An Experience to Remember." Printed with the author's permission.

Gajtka, Lynette. "I Am Eager to Begin." Printed with the author's permission.

Higgins, Kathleen. "A Little Trip to the Writing Center." Printed with the author's permission.

Kiedaisch, Jean, and Sue Dinitz. "Look Back and Say 'So What?': The Limitations of the Generalist Tutor." Originally appeared in *The Writing Center Journal 14.1* (1993). Copyright © National Writing Centers Association 1993. Reprinted with permission.

Lanham, Richard. "Who's Kicking Who?" Originally appeared in *Revising Prose.* Copyright © 1987. All rights reserved. Reprinted by permission of Allyn & Bacon.

Maloney, Jennifer. "Progression." Printed with the author's permission.

Powers, Judith K. "Rethinking Writing Center Conferencing Strategies for the ESL Writer." Originally appeared in *The Writing Center Journal* 17.2 (1997). Copyright © National Writing Centers Association 1997. Reprinted with permission.

Pytlak, Michael. "Seeing the Light." Printed with the author's permission.

Shaughnessy, Mina. Introduction. From *Errors and Expectations: A Guide for the Teacher of Basic Writing* by Mina P. Shaughnessy. Copyright © 1979 Mina Shaughnessy. Used by permission of Oxford University Press, Inc.

Sommers, Nancy. "Revision Strategies of Student Writers and Experienced Adult Writers." Originally appeared in *College Composition and Communication* 33 (1982) Copyright © by the National Council of Teachers of English 1982. Reprinted with permission.

Tilt, James. "The Session That Wasn't Quite a Session." Printed with the author's permission.

Trimbur, John. "'Peer Tutoring': A Contradiction in Terms?" Originally appeared in *The Writing Center Journal* 7.2 (1987). Copyright © National Writing Centers Association 1987. Reprinted with permission.